BEHAVIOR SCIENCE BIBLIOGRAPHIES

ANNOTATED BIBLIOGRAPHY OF AFGHANISTAN

by

Donald N. Wilber

3rd Edition

HUMAN RELATIONS AREA FILES PRESS

New Haven

1968

BEHAVIOR SCIENCE BIBLIOGRAPHY

ANNOTATED BIBLIOGRAPHY OF AFGHANISTAN

by

Donald N. Wilber

3rd Edition

HUMAN RELATIONS AREA FILES PRESS
New Haven
1968

Library of Congress Catalog Card Number: 68-22209

© Copyright 1968
Human Relations Area Files, Incorporated
New Haven, Connecticut

Manufactured in the United States of America

PREFACE TO THE FIRST EDITION

Principal features: Just as Afghanistan has long remained isolated and outside the realm of international interest and concern, so too has it failed to attract scholarly research until recent years. Now, however, the Afghans themselves are opening up subjects and areas which will be pursued by scholars of other countries. In the field of bibliography, the Russians made an impressive be-ginning for the general area in the nineteenth century, but up until this time only one important work devoted to Afghanistan has been published. This is the Bibliographie Analytique de l'Afghanistan (No. 11) by Mohammed Akram, which was published in 1947. Only the first volume, dealing with works pub-lished outside of Afghanistan, was issued and the present writer has been in-formed that no other volumes are forthcoming. The present publication aug-ments and extends the work of Akram, since it takes in a wider range of mate-rial in respect to time, places, and tongues, including--in addition to material in the usual European languages--works in Russian, Arabic, Persian, and Pushtu, published both within and outside of Afghanistan.

The bibliography is annotated and indexed, with the items numbered con-secutively and arranged alphabetically under subject headings. Within each subject heading the most valuable items are marked by asterisks.

Afghanistan defined: For the purposes of this bibliography, Afghanistan is de-fined as the country within its existing frontiers. The delimitation of the coun-try may be said to date from the middle of the eighteenth century and the con-quests of Ahmad Shah Durrani, since in earlier times no extensive, cohesive country known as Afghanistan existed. Instead, at many different times rulers of Iran controlled regions north and south of the Amu Darya River, while less frequently local rulers in the area south of the Hindu Kush widened their con-trol or moved on to take over parts of the Indian subcontinent.

With this limitation to present-day Afghanistan, it is necessary to exclude material on the once-vast areas of Transoxiana and Khorasan, areas which took in regions north and south of the Amu Darya. In the same way, such key cen-ters for the old history and culture of Afghanistan as Bokhara and Samarqand, both now within the U.S.S.R., fall beyond this scope. However, in these par-ticular examples and in other cases where the area under Afghan rulers once covered a larger amount of territory than today, a limited number of primary sources and general surveys have been included.

The former North West Frontier Province, just to the east of the Afghan frontier, also falls outside of the geographical limits of this bibliography, al-though in cases where the residents of this area have blood relatives within Af-ghanistan or have mutually inclusive codes of behavior, some items have been included. The skeletal material presented on this region--now within Pakistan--may be greatly augmented from Pakistan: A Select Bibliography (No. 59), by A. R. Ghani, published in 1951.

Coverage described: This bibliography is designed to be comprehensive but not exhaustive. It is selective inasmuch as an effort has been made to leave out repetitious, diffusive, inapplicable, and uncritical material. A few examples of the type of coverage given to various subjects may be of interest.

Much of the published material on Afghanistan was the direct result of the conflict of the Russian and the British empires in the nineteenth century. The efforts of the British to anticipate and to meet the threatening Russian advance toward India resulted in their occupation of the eastern border regions of the Afghans and led to the First and Second Anglo-Afghan Wars. Scores of military men wrote of their years of duty, exploration, and warfare, and since Afghanistan was otherwise sealed off from the outer world, the country was known primarily through the eyes of these somewhat biased participants. About a fourth of all the titles in Akram's Bibliographie Analytique de l'Afghanistan are by these officers or by their contemporaries in India and England. These titles have been reviewed and a great many eliminated.

Some bibliographies dealing with Moslem countries contain a chapter or heading on Islam, under which may be found a great many titles dealing with the religion itself, and its various sects, manifestations, customs, and practices. Such items appear here under the most appropriate heading, but all material not directly applicable to the country has been eliminated. Afghanistan is avowedly and ardently Moslem, but there has been very little written by local writers in the way of applicable commentaries on Islam or descriptions of the sects, shrines, practices, and present status of the faith within the country.

Only in a very few technical or specialized subjects has the coverage been so extensive that a process of selection was possible. In the field of geology, however, a considerable number of rather ephemeral and dated articles have been left out, as well as some sketchy notes on flora and fauna.

In view of the fact that contemporary coverage in European languages is limited, consideration was given to the inclusion of all known books and articles. However, examination of the material itself led to the exclusion of articles which reworked secondary sources and made no original contribution. In the same way, numerous topographical notes with attractive and provocative titles proved to be valueless and were discarded.

While the coverage in European languages is less exhaustive in the publication than in the research stage, the coverage in the local languages of Afghanistan is adequate only within the limits of material available in this country. Comments will be made on the subject of items in Persian and Pushtu in other paragraphs; here it is necessary to say only a few words on the availability of such material. No organ nor institution within Afghanistan publishes lists of books published within the country, nor is there an index of articles in local periodicals. Such periodicals may notice new books, but these descriptions do not conform to bibliographical standards. While the Afghan government promised assistance in the compilation of published material presented in a standardized format, such aid did not materialize in time for inclusion in this text.

An effort was made, however, to examine every item in these languages available in major collections, and to this end the author had direct access to the Afghan material at the Library of Congress, at Harvard University, and at Princeton University.

<u>Annotation:</u> The majority of the items in the bibliography are annotated, the intention being to describe the contents of the item, to identify the author if possible, to evaluate the items, and to point out any special features. Certain items in European languages are not annotated, either because the books are not to be found in this country or because they are not in collections available to the researchers of this bibliography. Certain articles are not annotated because of the fact that they were published in inaccessible periodicals. In the case of books printed in Persian or in Pushtu, all items were inspected and recorded, but since it was not possible to read and summarize every book, not every such item is annotated. Manuscripts are not annotated in any detail, since adequate descriptions are included in the catalogues of the collections in which the manuscripts are to be found.

<u>Asterisks:</u> The items marked with asterisks represent those sources considered to be essential in gaining an over-all understanding of the topic represented.

<u>Transliteration and translation:</u> Although the bibliographical cards from which this text was made up supply the full paraphernalia of macrons, overlines, underlines, and other signs and symbols used to indicate characters of the Cyrillic and Arabic alphabets, as well as those Persian and Pushtu characters supplementary to the Arabic alphabet, requirements of reproduction necessitated the omission of such markings. The Arabic characters ayn and hamzah are indicated, without distinction, as apostrophes.

The transliteration of the Arabic characters and of the languages other than Arabic which employ these characters is certain to draw the critical comments of linguists, each scholar favoring his personal modification of one of the more usual systems. In this case, the source has been the publication entitled: The Transliteration of Arabic and Persian. Special Publication No. 78. Department of the Interior. U.S. Board on Geographical Names. Washington, D.C. November, 1946. Unfortunately lacunae become apparent when this system is applied. For this bibliography, the author was fortunate in securing the services of Dr. Rudolph Mach, Arabic and Persian cataloguer for the Princeton University Library, to handle the material in these languages. Dr. Mach was able to extend the system referred to above and to achieve internal consistency.

The translation and transliteration of titles in Pushtu presented a special problem. For such translation, the author secured the assistance of Muhammad Bashir Ludin of Washington, D.C. The transliteration was complicated by the fact that Pushtu includes the Arabic characters employed in both Arabic and Persian and, in addition, some eight special Arabic symbols that are not found in any other orthography. It may be that grammarians have underdeveloped aesthetic sensibilities; at any rate they must enjoy producing words which look as if they would not be pleasant to pronounce. Applied to Pushtu, the tendency has been to indicate the special Arabic symbols as doubled consonants and the long vowels as doubled vowels, producing such results as zzbaarre, raddioo (radio) and even afghaanistaan. Since pedagogical exactitude with respect to phonology is not the primary objective of this bibliography, in most cases the special Arabic characters in Pushtu have been transliterated in terms of their closest normal Arabic or Persian symbols. In this way the users of the bibliography should have all the information required to identify each work.

Another problem stems from the way in which the names of authors writing in Persian, Arabic, and Pushtu should be presented. An approach which has been used in catalogues of manuscripts has been to list the name of each author in the order in which the name is spoken, with the first word of the name supplying the index letter for the entire name. This manner of dealing with Arab-type names is no longer satisfactory, however, since the Moslem world is actively adopting family names of the type common in Europe. Family names were brought into being by law in both Turkey and Iran more than a score of years ago. Within Afghanistan, the swing to family names is just gathering momentum. Some government officials have taken such names and some have not, but in order to be listed in the Kabul telephone directory a family name is mandatory. All individuals who are engaged in historical writing, research into linguistics and cultural background, journalism, and the editing of Persian and Pushtu manuscripts have taken such names and would object to being listed under the additive form. Given the fact that the names of the present-day Afghan writers are to be indexed exactly as those of European authors, the current problem concerns the manner of indexing earlier Eastern authors. A decision was made to extract the core of the additive name wherever possible, and in cases where this method was impractical, to employ the form as found in catalogues of manuscripts. While this approach has not resulted in complete consistency, it is hoped that it has made the bibliography convenient and easy to use.

Acknowledgments: It is a pleasure to record the invaluable support and assistance received from a number of scholars and researchers. At the Library of Congress, Dr. Robert F. Ogden, Head, Near East Section of Orientalia, and Dr. Benjamin Schwartz of the same section gave the author every facility for inspecting nearly 2,000 volumes in Persian and Pushtu and contributed freely of their time. At Harvard, D. W. Lockard, Executive Secretary, Center for Middle Eastern Studies, and Professor Richard N. Frye arranged for the author to enjoy access to the collections of the Harvard University Library. Professor Frye also checked the titles of Russian items and made additions, while Dr. Charles A. Ferguson of Harvard reviewed the linguistic items of the bibliography and made valuable comments. Dr. Peter G. Franck, of Washington, D.C., undertook the task of investigating and reporting on unpublished studies and documents relating to the economic structure and situation of Afghanistan.

At Princeton, Dr. Rudolph Mach of the Princeton University Library staff translated and transliterated the items in Arabic and Persian. Anne Lucie McCabe worked as a researcher for the author for a period of months and with that background took over the responsibility for typing the manuscript.

February 1956   Donald N. Wilber

PREFACE TO THE SECOND EDITION

This second edition includes a Supplement covering articles and books which have appeared between 1956 and June 1962. It also includes a number of items published prior to 1956 which were not noted in the first edition.

As in the first edition, the aim has been to produce a bibliography which is comprehensive, but selective rather than exhaustive. A serious effort was made to record the growing volume of material printed in Persian and Pushtu at Kabul. Although no single source keeps track of new publications, the writer acknowledges the assistance of the Press Department of the government of Afghanistan in assembling the necessary information. Since the quarterly Afghanistan appears to reach a very limited audience, the listing of all its articles, begun in the first edition, was not continued. Many of the titles of items in Russian have been selected from the publications of the Central Asian Research Centre in London. For a more exhaustive coverage of works in Russian, the reader should consult these publications and the extensive bibliographies of recent Soviet works on Afghanistan.

Scholarly users of the first edition found that the systems used for transliterating Persian and Pushtu were not identical with their favorite systems, and-- to cite a single illustration--Pashto is preferred to Pushtu by this community. However, scholars able to read Persian and Pushtu can certainly recreate the original titles of the works they wish to consult. Valuable help in the translation of Pushtu titles and in their annotation was given by M. H. Maiwandwal, Ambassador of Afghanistan in Washington; while Professor Martin B. Dickson of Princeton University undertook the transliteration and translation of titles in Russian.

July 1962   Donald N. Wilber

PREFACE TO THE THIRD EDITION

This third edition has been extensively revised and re-edited. Rather than presenting new material in a Supplement, as was the case for the second edition, all the titles have been integrated into a consecutive numerical sequence.

The last several years have witnessed a rising tide of books and articles on Afghanistan. As a result, it has not been possible to annotate all the more recent items, especially those in Russian and in the languages of Afghanistan.

Attention is directed to two very important recent bibliographies of Afghanistan. One is item No. 61, the first bibliography of its kind to be published in Afghanistan. It is indexed under the name of its compiler, Ghulam Riza Mayel Heravi, with the title translated as "List of Books Printed in Afghanistan from the year 1951 to 1965 (15 years)." The second (No. 28) is indexed under Bibliografiya Afganistana, with the full title translated as "A Bibliography of Afghanistan: Literature in Russian." It lists some 5,680 items.

In 1964, Afghanistan adopted a new constitution, one of the articles of which names the national languages of the country as Dari and Pushtu. Dari is the name now officially given to the form of the Persian (farsi) language used in Afghanistan, sometimes known as farsi-Kabuli. Recent works in Persian have, therefore, been described as published in Dari.

Very valuable assistance in the transliteration and translation of Pushtu and Dari titles was given by Peter B. Edmonds, while Mary E. Armstrong undertook the transliteration and translation of titles in Russian. Arthur Paul generously placed his uniquely extensive library of books on Afghanistan at the disposal of the writer.

1967   Donald N. Wilber

CONTENTS

CONTENTS

I. GENERAL SOURCES OF INFORMATION
AND REFERENCE WORKS

Bibliographies; encyclopedias;
catalogues; histories and
surveys; periodicals

The titles listed within this chapter are somewhat less than adequate for the presentation of a comprehensive and currently accurate account of the country. Within the category of bibliographies, particular care was devoted to publications covering the languages common to Afghanistan. However, there are so many catalogues covering so many collections of manuscripts in Persian, Pushtu, Arabic, Urdu, etc., that it was necessary to restrict the number of manuscripts cited; the general rule has been to list only those manuscripts which have not been edited in printed or lithographed versions. Also, since this work is concerned with the present area of Afghanistan and not with this region as part of a much greater area, many comprehensive histories have been eliminated.

Few periodicals are included, again with the aim of avoiding unwieldy diversity. Given the existence of specialized guides to periodical literature, the reader may go directly from these sources to the article rather than to the file of periodicals.

1 *Afghanistan. Quarterly publication first appearing in 1946 at Kabul.
   Early years offered separate editions in French and English; later on a single edition, each issue with some articles in French and some in English. Articles by local scholars, public officials and informed foreigners on history, archaeology, social institutions, foreign relations, topography, etc.

2. Afghanistan: Development in Brief. London: Information Bureau, Royal Afghan Embassy, n.d. (1958). Pp. 120.
   A well-illustrated review of recent developments, followed by a brief review of the geography, history, culture, and people of the country.

3. Afgánistán: Zeměpisný, hospodářský, politický a kulturní přehled [Afghanistan: Geographical, Economic, Political and Cultural Survey]. Prague: Orbis, 1952.

4 Afghanistan at a Glance. Kabul: Government Printing House, 1957. Pp. 170 and 28.
   A general description of the country.

I. GENERAL SOURCES

5 Afghanistan dar hal-i pishraft va taraqi [Afghanistan in a State of Advance and Progress]. [Kabul]: no publisher, n.d. Not paged.
An illustrated brochure sponsored by the United States A.I.D. mission.

6 Afghanistan Present and Past. Kabul: Government Printing House, 1958. Pp. 86.
A general survey published by the Board of Afghan Publicity, Cultural Relations Office, Department of Press and Information.

7 Ahlan bikum fi Afghanistan [Welcome to Afghanistan]. Cairo: al-Maktab al-thaqafi wa-al-sihafi, 1965. Pp. 132.

8 Ahmad, Fazl (Zurmati). Rahnuma-yi Afghanistan [Guide to Afghanistan]. Kabul: Matba'eh-yi 'umumi, 1327 [1948]. Pp. 382; map.
Material collected by the Department of Press presented in Persian by a member of that department. Chapters deal with subjects such as agriculture, trade, finances, government, education, etc., and a long section describes the routes through the countries and the important towns along these routes.

9 *Ahmad, Jamal-ud-din and Muhammad Abdul Aziz. Afghanistan: A Brief Survey. London and New York: Longmans, Green and Co., 1936. Pp. xx, 160; bibliography; appendices.
A concise summary of information on Afghanistan, divided into sections on geography, history, and government. The section on history gives a brief account of the successive conquerors and their dynasties, with a note on the cultural influence of each. That on government gives biographies of the Kings Nadir Shah and Zahir Shah, and of the leading members of the royal family; an outline of national, local and tribal administration, and short paragraphs on many such subjects as prisons, finance, roads, industry, etc.

10 Akhramovich, R. T. and L. A. Erovchenkov, trans. Afganistan [Afghanistan]. Moscow: Gosudarstvennoe izdatel'stvo geographicheskoy literaturi, 1957. Pp. 141; map.
An abridged translation of the New Guide to Afghanistan of Mohammad Ali, see item 15.

11 *Akram, Mohammed. Bibliographie Analytique de l'Afghanistan. I. Ouvrages parus hors de l'Afghanistan [Analytical Bibliography of Afghanistan. I. Works Issued outside of Afghanistan]. Paris: Centre de Documentation Universitaire, 1947. Pp. 504.

I. GENERAL SOURCES

Annotated list of nearly 2,000 titles, grouped under subject headings. Comprehensive but not exhaustive, and not as strong in Arabic, Persian, and Pushtu references as for European languages.

12 Aleksandrov, I. and R. Akhramovich. Gosudarstvennǐỹ stroy Afganistana [The Governing Class of Afghanistan]. Moscow: Gosudarstvennoe izdatel'stvo yuridicheskoy literaturǐ, 1956. Pp. 62.
A pamphlet in the semi-popular series, The Governing Class of the Countries of the World. Includes chapters on the constitution, the powers of the ruler, government administration, history, and the economic situation.

13 Ali, Mohammad. Progressive Afghanistan. Lahore: Punjab Educational Electric Press, 1933. Pp. xiv, 232.
By the rather prolific Professor of History at Habibiya College, Kabul. The title may be somewhat misleading in that the book deals with the overthrow of Amanullah, the short domination of Bacha Saqqa, and the restoration of authority by Nadir Khan. The closing pages deal with the inauguration of Nadir Shah and with his plans for the future.

14 Ali, Mohammad. Guide To Afghanistan. Kabul, 1938. Pp. 181; appendices.
Part I includes a general survey of the geography, the people and their mode of life, while Part II is on government. Part III presents a tourists' guide to Afghanistan. With bibliographies of books in Russian on Afghanistan, books in oriental languages and a list of periodicals.

15 Ali, Mohammed. A New Guide to Afghanistan. Lahore: Northern Pakistan Printing and Publishing Co., 1959. Pp. 131; appendices; bibliography; map.
A revised third edition of no. 14.

16 Ali, Mohammed. The Afghans. Lahore: Punjab Educational Press, 1965. Pp. 161.
A popular work which repeats material published elsewhere by the same author, notably that on Afghan manners and customs.

17 Aperçu Général sur l'Afghanistan [General Survey of Afghanistan]. Paris: Mazarine, 1958. Pp. 31.
Includes brief description of areas attractive to tourists.

I. GENERAL SOURCES

18 Arberry, A. J. Catalogue of the Library of the India Office. Vol. 2,
Part IV: Persian Books. London, 1937. Pp. 571.
The books are listed by title and by author, with annotations under the
title entries.

19 Arunova, Marianna R., ed. Afganistan: spravochnik [Afghanistan: A hand-
book]. Moscow: "Nauka," 1964. Pp. 276; index.

20 Aryana [Aryana]. A monthly periodical which began publication in Kabul
in 1942.
Printed in Persian, it is the organ of the Anjuman-i Tarikh [Historical
Society] of the Afghan Academy.

21 Aryana da'iratu'l-ma'arif [Aryana Encyclopedia]. Shu'a', mir 'Ali Asghar,
ed. Kabul: Matba'eh-yi 'umumi, 1328 - [1949 -].
This comprehensive work began to come off the press in a Persian edition in 1949, with separate fascicules appearing in rapid order. Most
of the articles are by Afghan scholars and officials, although some were
taken from a comparable work put out at Tehran by Dehkhoda. In 1951
a Pushtu edition of the work began to come off the press.

22 Atlantic Report. Atlantic 210, no. 4, pp. 26, 28, 34, 36, October 1962.
A useful, well-written general survey.

23 Bartholomew, John George. A Literary and Historical Atlas of Asia. New
York: E. P. Dutton and Co. (Everyman's Library), n.d. Pp. xi, 226;
maps; plates.
Maps showing the great empires, the routes of the explorers, tempera-
ture, rainfall, vegetation, etc., many of which include Afghanistan.
There is a brief chapter on the coinages of Asia and a "Gazetteer of
Towns and Places in Asia," with short historical notes on each.

24 Basic Facts on Afghanistan. Washington, D.C.: Department of Research,
American Friends of the Middle East, Inc., 1961. Pp. 20.
A brief, useful, and generally reliable summary of the topography,
history, and modern developments.

25 Becka, Jiri. Afghanistan. Prague: Nakladatelstvi politicke literatury,
1965. Pp. 143; bibliography.
A pocket-size, reliable general survey with emphasis on the present.
Includes a chapter on Czech-Afghan relations.

26 Beeston, Alfred F. L. Catalogue of the Persian, Turkish, Hindustani and
   Pushtu Manuscripts in the Bodleian Library. Part III: Additional Persian
   Manuscripts. Oxford: Clarendon Press, 1954. Pp. viii, 177.

27 Bibliografiı̂a Avganistana [Bibliography of Afghanistan]. S. D. Maslovskii,
   ed. Obshchestre vostokovedeniı̂a. Sbornik sredne-aziatskogo otdela.
   Part 2. St. Petersburg, 1908.

28 *Bibliografiya Afganistana: literatura na russkom yazyka [A bibliography
   of Afghanistan: Literature in Russian]. Tatiyana I. Kukhtina, comp.;
   Yuriy V. Gankovskiy, ed. Moscow: "Nauka," 1965. Pp. 271.
   Lists 5680 items.

29 Bibliographie géographique internationale [International Geographic Bib-
   liography]. Paris: Libraire Armand Colin.
   An annual publication first issued about 1890 under the title of Bibliographie géographique and taking its present title in 1931.

30 Bibliography of Asian Studies. Journal of Asian Studies.
   Annual publication.

31 *Bibliography of Recent Soviet Source Material on Soviet Central Asia and
   the Borderlands. London: Central Asian Research Centre.
   A biannual which began publication in 1957, listing books and articles
   in some 51 periodicals and newspapers. Russian titles are given in
   transliteration, but are not translated into English although each item
   is annotated.

32 *Bibliography of Russian Works on Afghanistan. London: Central Asian Research Centre, 1956. Pp. 12.
   Some 160 titles of books and articles, most listed with transliteration
   and translation of the Russian.

33 Bisnek, A. G. and K. I. Shafrovskii. Bibliografiı̂a bibliografii Srednei
   Azii [Bibliography of the Bibliographies of Central Asia]. Bibliografiı̂a
   Vostoka. Parts 8 and 9. Leningrad, 1935.
   Not as valuable a work as is suggested by the impressive title: it does
   list rare items not noticed elsewhere.

34 Blümhardt, James Fuller. Catalogues of the Hindi, Penjabi, and Pushtu
   Printed Books. London: British Museum, 1893.

35 Bolshaia sovetskaia entsiklopedia [The Great Soviet Encyclopedia].
   5 vols. Moscow: 1949-1950.
   Afghanistan is covered on page 492 f. of Volume Three.

36 Burke, J. Fight for the Land of Hindu Kush. Life 55, August 9, 1963.
   Pp. 18-27.

37 Caspani, E. and E. Cagnacci. Afghanistan Crocevia dell'Asia [Afghani-
   stan, Crossroads of Asia]. 2d ed. Milan: Antonio Vallardi, 1951.
   Pp. xv, 282.
   An informed, up-to-date compendium on history, customs and habits,
   and modern life by two Italians who resided in Afghanistan for more
   than a decade. Includes itineraries for the main motor routes and
   descriptions of monuments and points of interest.

38 Catalogue of the Marathi, Gujarati, Bengali, Assamese, Oriya, Pushtu,
   and Sindhi Manuscripts in the Library of the British Museum. London:
   British Museum, 1905.

39 *Central Asian Review. London: Central Asian Research Centre.
   A quarterly which began publication in 1953. Issues since 1956 con-
   tain reviews of Soviet writing on Afghanistan under the heading,
   Borderlands of Soviet Central Asia.

40 *Current Problems in Afghanistan. Princeton: Princeton University Conference, 1961. Pp. 150.
   Articles presented at the thirteenth Near East Conference at Princeton
   University by twelve authors concerned with history, contemporary
   politics, natural resources, foreign relations, education, foreign private
   enterprise, education, the Durand Line of 1893, Soviet aid, American
   aid, and problems of social development.

41 Dagher, Joseph A. L'Orient dans la litterature française d'après guerre
   1919-1933 [The Orient in Post-War French Literature, 1919-1933].
   Beirut: Edouard Angelil, 1937.
   Of interest primarily for references to articles in French periodicals on
   specialized subjects.

42 Deutsche im Hindukusch; Bericht der deutschen Hindukusch-expedition
   1935 der deutschen Forschungsgemeinschaft [Germans in the Hindu Kush.
   Report of the German Hindu Kush Expedition of 1935 of the German Exploration Society]. Berlin: Karl Siegismund, 1937. Pp. viii, 351; maps.

Contains some ten valuable articles, such as a study on the speech and people of Nuristan, by W. Lentz, and others on topography and entomology.

43 Dollot, René. L'Afghanistan [Afghanistan]. Paris: Payot, 1937. Pp. 318.
A traveler's survey--not burdened by profundity--of the history, physical features, folklore, customs, and archaeology of the country, by a former French Ambassador at Kabul. Special emphasis is placed upon the impact of French culture on Afghanistan and French sponsored activities within the country.

44 Dupree, Ann, Louis Dupree, and A. A. Motamedi. A Guide to the Kabul Museum. The National Museum of Afghanistan. Kabul: Education Press, 1964. Pp. 157; illus.

45 *Dupree, Louis. American Universities Field Staff Reports. South Asia Series (Afghanistan). 1959- .
Occasional reports, on a variety of subjects, by an unusually well-informed observer.

46 *Dvoryankov, N. A., ed. Sovremennïy Afganistan [Contemporary Afghanistan]. Moscow: Izdatel'stvo vostochnoy literaturi, 1960. Pp. 502; maps; charts; tables; bibliography; indices.
Some 26 writers contributed to this handbook which covers every aspect of modern Afghanistan. Statistical and other detailed material takes up the final 115 pages. The fifteen-page bibliography lists sources in the language of origin, each in its own script. Many of the Russian titles have not been included in this publication and the specialist should consult the Soviet handbook.

47 Edwards, Edward. A Catalogue of the Persian Printed Books in the British Museum. London, 1922. Pp. viii, 484.
The books are listed and annotated under the author's name, with an index of titles and a subject index.

48 *Elphinstone, Mountstuart. An Account of the Kingdom of Caubul, and its Dependencies in Persia, Tartary and India: Comprising a View of the Afghaun Nation, and a History of the Dooraunee Monarchy. London: Longman, Hurst, and John Murray, 1815. Pp. xxi, 675; map; appendices.
The first detailed account of Afghanistan from a Western observer,

compiled by an envoy from the East India Company to the court at Kabul in 1809. A number of members of the envoy's mission collected information on such subjects as geography, government, languages, manners and customs, education, religion, and tribes. Its popularity resulted in French editions in 1817 and 1842 and an expanded English edition in 1842.

49 *Engert, Cornelius van H. A Report on Afghanistan. U. S. Department of State, Division of Publications. Series C. No. 53. Afghanistan No. 1. Washington, 1924. Pp. iv, 225; extensive bibliography; appendices; map.

In response to Afghan overtures towards formalizing relations with the United States, a young diplomatic officer was sent to Kabul to study the situation. His report, covering the history and background, as well as contemporary events, is of great value. Trends and developments which he saw taking shape are now in full swing.

50 Ethe, Hermann. Catalogue of the Persian Manuscripts in the Library of the India Office. Vol. 1. Oxford: Horace Hart, 1903. Pp. xxiii, columns 1631.

Histories of the Afghans, columns 230-238.

51 Ethe, Hermann. Catalogue of the Persian, Turkish, Hindustani and Pushtu Manuscripts in the Bodleian Library. Part II: Turkish, Hindustani, Pushtu and Additional Persian Manuscripts. Oxford: Clarendon Press, 1930. Columns 1159-1766.

52 Ethe, Hermann and Edward Edwards. Catalogue of the Persian Manuscripts in the Library of the India Office. Vol. 2: Containing Additional Descriptions and Indices. Oxford: Clarendon Press, 1937. Pp. vi, columns 1374.

53 Evans, Hubert. Recent Soviet Writing on South and Central Asia. Royal Central Asian Journal 51, no. 2 (1964): 149-158; 51, no. 3/4 (1964): 306-314; 52, no. 2 (1965): 146-154; 53 (1966): 50-58.

54 Farid, Ahmad. Bibliyugrafi [Bibliography]. Kabul: Puhani matba'eh, 1344 [1965]. Pp. 27.

Two hundred and fifty-six titles of books published in Afghanistan in Dari, Pushtu, and English are grouped under the headings of sponsoring organizations such as ministries, faculties of Kabul University, and learned societies. Within these headings, the arrangement is not

alphabetical, and there is no index. The majority of the books listed
were published within the last decade.

55 Farrukh, Mahdi. Tarikh-i mukhtasar-i Afghanistan [A Brief History of
Afghanistan]. Tabriz: no publisher, 1316 [1937]. Pp. 78.

56 Field, Henry. Bibliographies on Southwestern Asia: I-VII. Coral Gables:
University of Miami Press, 1953-1962. Pp. 1,834; subject indexes
(1959-64) 429 pp.
Includes some 50,000 titles from 6,000 journals in 43 languages and
covers the subjects of anthropology, natural history, zoology, and
botany. More than 90 titles dealing with Afghanistan, mostly from
elusive periodicals, are included.

57 *Fraser-Tytler, Sir W. Kerr. Afghanistan. A Study of Political Developments in Central Asia. London: Oxford University Press. (1st ed.)
1950; (2d ed.) 1953. Pp. xiii, 330; maps; selected bibliography;
genealogical table.
Decades of service in India, the North West Frontier Province, and
Afghanistan where he held diplomatic posts at Kabul including that of
British Minister created a knowledgeable background for the author's
study of the "Great Game" in Central Asia--the rivalry of the Russian
and British empires for control of Afghanistan. Rounded out with historical material and descriptions of the various ethnic groups. The
second edition contains an added chapter of 18 pages on events in Afghanistan from 1947 through 1951.

58 *Furon, Raymond. L'Iran: Perse et Afghanistan [Iran: Persia and Afghani-
stan]. Paris: Payot, 1951. Pp. 336; bibliography; maps.
Represents the reworking of two books published in 1926 and in 1938.
The author, a French geologist with years of residence and travel in
Iran and Afghanistan, has much of value to convey but many of the
pages are sketchy and impressionist rather than factual.

59 Ghani, A. R. Pakistan: A Select Bibliography. Lahore: Ripon Printing
Press, 1951. Pp. xxii, 330.
Titles relating to ethnic groups within Afghanistan may be found on
pages 41-45 dealing with the North West Frontier Province and on pages
86-91 dealing with the peoples of Pakistan.

60 Henning, W. B. Bibliography of Important Studies on Old Iranian Subjects.
Tehran: Ketab-Khaneh Danesh, 1950. Pp. 53.

I. GENERAL SOURCES

This work, by the then professor at the School of Oriental and African Studies, London, contains a short introduction in Persian by a faculty member of the Tehran University. Items relating to Afghan languages and dialects are found on pages 38-44.

61 *Heravi (Ghulam Riza) Mayel. Fehrest-i kotob matbu' Afghanistan az sal 1330 ila 1344. 15 sal [List of Books Printed in Afghanistan from the year 1951 to 1965. (15 years)]. Kabul: Doulati matba'eh, 1344 [1965]. Pp. 77.
   Lists 450 titles in Dari and Pushtu alphabetically under the first letter of the titles. An index identifies authors and translators. Regrettably, the quality of the printing is poor.

62 Heravi (Ghulam Riza) Mayel. Mo'arefi ruznameh-ha, jaraid, majallat Afghanistan [Introduction to the Newspapers, Journals, and Magazines of Afghanistan]. Kabul: Parwan doulati matba'eh, 1341 [1962]. Pp. 144.
   One hundred and eight items are described, with the descriptions varying in length from a brief paragraph to several pages.

63 Houtsma, Martyn Theodor. The Encyclopedia of Islam: A Dictionary of the Geography, Ethnography, and Biography of the Muhammadan Peoples, Prepared by a Number of Leading Orientalists. Leyden and London, 1913-1916.
   Excellent articles may be found under such subject headings as Afghanistan, Durrani, Ghaznavids, Ghor, Hazara, etc. A new edition, which began to appear in 1955, included a revised article on Afghanistan.

64 Imperial Gazetteer of India. New Edition Published under the Authority of His Majesty's Secretary of State for India in Council. Oxford: Clarendon Press, 1907-1908. Afghanistan, vol. 5, 26-65; map. Afghan-Turkistan, vol. 5, 65-69.
   This is the third edition of an extremely valuable work of reference. The article on Afghanistan represents a condensed survey of topography, climate, history, population, resources, administration, etc. The heading Afghan-Turkistan is typical of many other entries relating to places, peoples, etc. of Afghanistan.

65 Indiya i Afganistana: ocherki istorii i ekonomiki [India and Afghanistan: Essays on history and economics]. Moscow: Izdatel'stvo Vostochnoy Literatury, 1958. Pp. 290.

I. GENERAL SOURCES

66 Jawhar, Hasan Muhammad and 'Abd al-Hamid Baywami. Afghanistan.
   Cairo: Dar al-ma'ref, 1961. Pp. 117.

67 Kabul [Kabul] . Founded in 1931 at Kabul.
   An illustrated monthly in Pushtu, published by the Pushtu Tulaneh section of the Afghan Academy. The intervals of publication have varied
   from year to year.

68 *Da Kabul Kalani [The Annual of Kabul] . Kabul: Matba'eh-yi 'umumi.
   Publication of this annual, sponsored by the Afghan government, began
   in 1311 [1933] under the title of Sal-nameh-yi Kabul [The Kabul An-
   nual] . Each issue of several hundred pages contained articles in Persian and Pushtu, and some issues contained a few pages in French. In
   1319 [1940] the name of the publication was changed to Da Kabul
   Kalani and more articles in Pushtu feature the succeeding issues. Some
   contained short summaries in English. In 1331 [1952] the publication
   appeared under the name of Da Afghanistan Kalani. Each issue has
   been extensively illustrated and over the years the editors have included
   such scholarly writers as Na'imi, Binava, Rishtiya, and Taraki.

69 Kessel, Joseph. Afghanistan. London: Thames and Hudson, 1959. Pp. 45;
   201 plates.
   Striking illustrations in black and white and in color, accompanied by
   a description of the plates, a record of the author's travels, and a very
   brief account of the country and the people.

70 Kratkaya Bibliografiya knig i statey po Afganistanu, Iranu i Turtsii,
   vyshedshikh v 1963 g. (Na Russk. yaz) [A short bibliography of books and
   articles about Afghanistan, Iran and Turkey which have appeared in Russia during the year 1963 (in Russian)] . Tat'yana Kukhtina and A. K.
   Sverchevskaya, comps. Moscow, Institut Narodov Azii, Kratkiye
   Soobshcheniya 77 (1964): 130-137.

71 Lentz, Wolfgang. Sammlungen zur afghanischen Literatur-und Zeitge-
   schichte [Collections in Afghan Literature and Contemporary History] .
   Zeitschrift der deutschen morgenländischen Gesellschaft 91 (1937); 711-
   732.
   Cursive treatise on a number of headings illustrative of Afghan bibliography. Includes material published in Afghanistan, such as newspapers, government publications and Pushtu literature, with titles transliterated.

72 Lival, Rahmatullah. Rahnuma-yi tajer [Commercial Guide]. Kabul: Matba'eh-yi 'umumi, 1326 [1947]. Pp. 150.

73 *Massignon, Louis, ed. Annuaire du Monde Musulman. Statistique, historique, social et économique [Yearbook of the Musulman World. Statistical, Historic, Social and Economic]. Paris: Presses Universitaires de France, 1955. Pp. xvi, 428.
  Afghanistan is dealt with on pages 157-162 under such headings as population, government, administration, labor, and production.

74 The Middle East (year); A Survey and Directory of the Countries of the Middle East, Compiled by the Publishers in Collaboration with the Intelligence Unit of The Economist. London: Europa Publications, Ltd.
  This volume has appeared annually since 1950, with each issue giving the year as part of the title. Encyclopedic type of information on each country, including Afghanistan.

75 Middle East Journal. Washington, D.C.: The Middle East Institute.
  A valuable quarterly, which began publication in 1947. Each issue contains a Bibliography of Periodical Literature, in which some 150 periodicals are reviewed, including all those which would carry material on Afghanistan except for those published within the country.

76 Military Report, Afghanistan. History, Geography, Resources, Armed Forces, Forts and Fortified Posts, Administration and Communications. Calcutta: General Staff, India, 1925.

77 Nusraty, Mohammad Yonus, ed. Afghanistan, Land of Culture. Washington: International Student Press, 1963. Pp. 53.
  Contains 28 short articles written by Afghan students on various aspects of Afghan life.

78 *Pazhwak, Abdur Rahman. Aryana (Ancient Afghanistan). Hove, England: Key Press, Ltd., n.d. (1954?). Pp. 144.
  An expanded reissue of an earlier undated and anonymous booklet of the same title and from the same press. A popular, well-written, general account of the ancient and modern history of the country and of many aspects of local life. The author has been attached to the Afghan Information Bureau in London.

79 Pearson, J. D., comp. Index Islamicus. Cambridge: W. Heffer & Sons, Ltd.

I. GENERAL SOURCES

A catalogue of articles on Islamic subjects in periodicals and other collective publications. The volume covering the years 1906-1955 appeared in 1958, that for 1956-1960 in 1962.

80 Pikulin, M. G. Afghanistan: Ekonomicheskiy ocherk [Afghanistan: An Economic Survey]. Tashkent: Akademiya Nauk Uzbek SSR, 1956. Pp. 301; bibliography.
A general account of the country with emphasis upon economic data through 1953.

81 Pocket Guide to Afghanistan. Washington: U. S. Department of State, U. S. Government Printing Office, n. d. (1946). Pp. 51; map.
Small format and too brief to be of real value. Provided with a small-scale, useful, folding map.

82 Point Four: Near East and Africa. A Selected Bibliography of Studies on Economically Underdeveloped Countries. Washington: U. S. Department of State, Division of Library and Reference Services, 1951.

83 Rasmi Jarideh [Official Journal].
A bimonthly publication of the Ministry of Justice. First issue, March 1964. Contains Pushtu and Persian (Dari) texts of new laws, royal decrees, cabinet decisions, treaty documents, and all information having legal status.

84 Redard, Georges, ed. Indo-Iranica, mélanges présente à Georg Morgenstierne à l'occasion de son soixante-dixième anniversaire [Indo-Iranica, miscellanea offered to Georg Morgenstierne on the occasion of his seventieth anniversary]. Wiesbaden: Otto Harrassowitz, 1964. Pp. viii, 195.
Articles relating to the interest of this preeminent scholar of Iranian languages.

85 Reisner, Igor Mikhailovich and R. T. Akhramovich. Nash sosed Afganistan [Our Neighbor Afghanistan]. Moscow: "Znaniye," 1956. Pp. 48.

86 Rieu, Charles. Catalogue of the Persian Manuscripts in the British Museum. 3 vols. London, 1879, 1881, 1883. Pp. (1) 1-432; (2) vii, 433-877; (3) xxviii, 881-1229.
The manuscripts are catalogued under subject headings, with a note under each on the writer, the manuscript and its contents. In the

I. GENERAL SOURCES

Classed Index (vol. 3, page 1192) are listed the eleven manuscripts which concern the Afghans.

87 Rieu, Charles. Supplement to the Catalogue of the Persian Manuscripts in the British Museum. London: Gilbert and Rivington, Ltd., 1895. Pp. ix, 308.

88 Sachau, Edward and Hermann Ethe. Catalogue of the Persian, Turkish, Hindustani, and Pushtu Manuscripts in the Bodleian Library. Part I. The Persian Manuscripts. Oxford: Clarendon Press, 1889. Pp. xii, columns 1150.

89 Sal-nameh-yi Kabul [The Kabul Annual]. (See no. 68.)

90 Schlag nach über Iran, Afghanistan, Arabien und Indien; wissenwerte Tatsachen, Übersichten und Tabellen nebst einer mehrfarbigen Übersichtskarte [Research on Iran, Afghanistan, Arabia and India; Valuable Facts, Surveys and Tables with a Colored Survey Map]. Leipzig: Fachschriftleitungen des Bibliographischen Instituts, 1942. Pp. 32; maps.

91 A Select Bibliography: Asia, Africa, Eastern Europe and Latin America. New York: American Universities Field Staff, 1960. Pp. 534.
Contains some 6,000 titles, more than a third of which are annotated. Supplements were issued in 1961, 1963, and 1965.

92 Selected Bibliography of Published Material on the Area Where Pushtu Is Spoken: Afghanistan, Baluchistan and the North-West Frontier Province. U.S. Department of State, Division of Library and Reference Service, Bibliography No. 60, October 30, 1951. Pp. 11.
Neither exhaustive nor selective, with emphasis upon articles in periodicals of recent date.

93 *Shalizi, Abdussattar. Afghanistan. Ancient Land with Modern Ways. No place (Washington, D.C.): no publisher, no date (1961). Pp. 199; 247 unnumbered illustrations.
Excellent illustrations in black and white and in color, accompanied by pages of matching text in English and in Pushtu.

94 Shalizi, Prita K. Here and There in Afghanistan. Kabul: Education Press, 1966.
A collection of articles originally printed in Afghan newspapers and periodicals. Subjects include travel sketches, women in society, and the Afghan cuisine.

I. GENERAL SOURCES

95   Sharqawi, Muhammad 'Abd al-Mun'im al-, et al. Afghanistan. Cairo:
     Matbu'at ma'had al-darasat al-Islamiyah, 1961. Pp. 135.
     A survey, in Arabic, by several authors.

96   Sovetskoye Afganovedeniye za 40 let. Tekst na yaz. farsi-kabul [Soviet
     Afghan studies over 40 years. Text in Farsi-Kabuli]. Moscow:
     Izdatel'stvo Vostochnoy Literatury, 1960. Pp. 95.

97   Sovetskoye Afganovedeniye za 40 let. Tekst na yaz. pushtu [Forty Years
     of Afghan Studies in the USSR. Text in Pushtu]. Moscow: Izdatel'stvo
     Vostochnoy Literatury, 1961. Pp. 128.

98   Storey, Charles A. Persian Literature. A Bio-Bibliographical Survey.
     Vol. 1. London: Luzac and Co., 1927, 1935, 1936, 1939, 1953.
     Pp. 1443.
     The sections of Volume 1, Qur'anic Literature; History and Biography,
     were published at intervals and paged consecutively. An index of titles
     and an index of authors, subjects, etc. closes the volume.

99   *Sykes, Sir Percy M. A History of Afghanistan. 2 vols. London: Mac-
     millan and Co., 1940. Pp. (1) xiii, 411; (2) ix, 414; maps; appen-
     dices; list of authorities.
     A painstakingly constructed compilation of material on the region and
     on the country of Afghanistan. Invaluable as a reference book. The
     closing chapters contain reliable material on trends of the 1930s.

100 Taillardat, C. F. Études sur l'Afghanistan [Studies on Afghanistan].
     L'Asie Française, 1928. Pp. 266-278.

101 Trudy Sessii po voprosam istorii i ekonomiki Afganistana, Irana, Turtsii
     [Reports of the Session on the History and the Economy of Afghanistan,
     Iran and Turkey]. Moscow, Institut Narodov Azii, Kratkiye Soobscheniya
     73 (1963): 252.

102 Valiyan, 'Abd al-'Azim. Kolliyat az: awza'-i siyasi u iqtisadi u ijtima'i-
     yi Afghanistan [Collection concerning the Political, Economic and Social
     Situations of Afghanistan]. Tehran: Zavvar, 1340 [1961]. Pp. 170;
     maps.
     A work in Persian.

103 Vaneček, Petr. Afghanistan. Prague: Mladá fronta, 1952.

I. GENERAL SOURCES

104 Voelkerkundliche Bibliographie. Asien. Allgemeine Voelkerkunde ab 1928 [Ethnological Bibliography. Asia. General Ethnology from the Year 1928]. Stuttgart: E. Schweizerbart, 1937.

105 Von Hentig, Werner Otto. Mein Leben, eine Dienstreise [My Life, A Journey of Service]. Göttingen: Vandenhoeck & Ruprecht, 1962. Pp. 497.
> The story of a German diplomat whose posts included Kabul in 1915.

106 Waleh, Abdul H. Afghanistan Today. Washington: Royal Afghan Embassy, 1963. Not paged.
> An attractive, illustrated survey for the general reader.

107 Watkins, Mary Bradley. Afghanistan. Land in Transition. Princeton: D. Van Nostrand, 1963. Pp. 262; bibliography; index.
> A general survey, with emphasis on contemporary society and progress.

108 *Wilber, Donald N., ed. Afghanistan. New Haven: Human Relations Area Files, 1956. Pp. 501; charts; tables; maps; bibliography; index.
> A volume in the publisher's Country Survey Series. A comprehensive study of the history, ethnology, sociology, government, politics, and economic structure by five contributors.

109 *Wilber, Donald N., ed. Afghanistan its people its society its culture. New Haven: Human Relations Area Files Press, 1962. Pp. 320; maps; charts; tables; illustrations; bibliography; index.
> An extensively revised and rewritten edition of item 108, with contributions by six specialists.

110 Yusufi, Muhammad Akbar. Tatbiq-i sanavat [Comparative Years]. Kabul: Doulati matba'eh, 1342 [1963]. Pp. 86.
> Tables for conversion of the dates of the Muslim lunar calendar to Christian solar years.

111 Zambaur, Eduard Karl Marx von. Manuel de généalogie et de chronologie pour l'histoire de l'Islam, avec 20 tableaux généalogiques hors texte et 5 cartes [Manual of Genealogy and Chronology for the History of Islam, with 20 Genealogical Tables Separate from the Text and 5 Maps]. Hanover: H. Lafaire, 1927. Pp. xii, 388; a supplementary volume includes the tables and maps.
> The standard work on this subject; a monument of devotion to accuracy and detail.

II. GEOGRAPHY

Geology; topography; exploration;
travel and description; natural
history; atlases and maps

Much of the earlier work on the topography of the country was concentrated on descriptions of the country between India and Kabul and Qandahar.
This period was followed by one in which the General Staff, India, made detailed studies of the routes within the country and compiled military reports,
which included exhaustive accounts of the topography and resources of the country: these publications remain unavailable or very hard to obtain.

Recent material in this general category fails to reflect present oppor
tunities for travel and exploration. Such writing is largely concerned with those
towns, sites and developments along the so-called "great circle route"--the
roads that encircle the country, beginning at Kabul and running north to Mazar-i
Sharif, then west to Herat, then south and east to Qandahar and, finally, north
through Ghazni to Kabul. Articles in periodicals bear titles of promise with
reference to the more remote regions, but most of them add relatively little information. The vast central area of Afghanistan remains unknown, as does the
southeastern region--the homeland of the Pushtu-speaking groups. Afghan
writers have begun to take cognizance of the gaps in knowledge and to publish
accounts of their journeys in local periodicals, but until some systematic survey
is undertaken by the Afghan government these various contributions will be scattered and sketchy.

Afghanistan is inadequately mapped. It has not been considered necessary to include older, superseded maps in the bibliography, and those of recent
date are few in number and continue to reflect the basic lack of knowledge.

112 Aitchison, James Edward T. On the Flora of the Kuram Valley in Afghanistan. Journal of the Linnean Society (London), Botany 18 (1881): 1-
113; 19 (1882): 139-200; folding map; plates.
An account of the summer of 1879, spent with the British forces in the
Kuram Valley. A description of the country, plants and agriculture
gives an intimate picture of the rural life of the inhabitants. There
are lists of specimens, plates, and a folding map.

113 Aitchison, James Edward T. The Botany of the Afghan Delimitation Commission. The Transactions of the Linnean Society. Botany, 2d ser., 3,
1-139; maps; plates. London, 1888.
A readable description of the plants found in Northern Baluchistan, Afghanistan and Persia. There are lists of the specimens and incidental
notes on the country and the people. The author was Secretary to the

Surgeon-General of Her Majesty's Forces in Bengal, and attached as naturalist to the Afghan Delimitation Commission.

114 Akram, Mohammad. La géomorphogénie de l'Ouest [The Geomorphogeny of the West]. Afghanistan 3, no. 2, 67-71; no. 3, 5-12. 1948.
A fairly detailed description of the valley of the Hari Rud River and an account of the lower Helmand case; short bibliography.

115 Akram, Mohammad. Les grandes voies de passage à travers l'Afghanistan [The Great Travel Routes across Afghanistan]. Afghanistan 4, no. 4, 27-35; map. 1949.
Of only moderate interest, this sketch emphasizes the antiquity of certain of the routes.

116 Akram, Mohammad. L'Ouest afghan (étude physique) [The Afghan West (A Physical Study)]. Afghanistan 6, no. 2, 57-62. 1951.
A geological description of the mountain ranges and basins of West Afghanistan.

117 Akram, Mohammad. Ouvrage nouveau sur l'Afghanistan [A New Work on Afghanistan]. Afghanistan 6, no. 3, 56-57. 1951.
A review of the revised edition of Raymond Furon's Iran: Perse et Afghanistan (see no. 58).

118 Alexander, Michael. Offbeat in Asia. London: Weidenfeld and Nicholson, 1960. Pp. 180.
Inconsequential travel, livened by the companionship of a "beautiful model girl."

119 Ali, Mohammed. Afghanistan's Mountains. Afghanistan 3, no. 1, 40-52. 1953.
The location of Afghanistan's mountains, their appearance, vegetation, and the routes of the mountain passes.

120 Aristov, N. A. Ob Avganistane i ego naselenii [About Afghanistan and its Population]. Zhiraia Starina, 8. St. Petersburg, 1896.
Characteristic work by a leading Tsarist authority on Afghanistan; an ethnologist by training. This article, and others listed under other headings are now outmoded as well as containing speculative material which has not stood the test of time.

121 Balsan, Francois. Inquisitions de Kaboul au Golfe Persique [Research from
Kabul to the Persian Gulf]. Paris: J. Peyronnet et Cie., 1949.
Pp. 285; maps.
Somewhat limited observations of a French business man who traveled
through Southern Afghanistan in 1937.

122 Bayderin, Viktor A. Za Gindukushem; putevyye zametki [Across the
Hindu Kush; Notes of a Journey]. Stalinabad: Tadzhikgosizdat, 1961.
Pp. 128.

123 Bellew, Henry Walter. From the Indus to the Tigris; A Narrative of a
Journey through the Countries of Balochistan, Afghanistan, Khorassan
and Iran, in 1872. London: Trubner and Co., 1874. Pp. vii, 496.

124 Beneva, Abdul Raouf. "Punjwai." Afghanistan 8, no. 3, 23-26. 1953.
A rambling account of Punjwai's caves, the moat surrounding the
ruined city, and the graves of three local poets.

125 Beneva, Abdul Raouf. Dawar ou Zamine Dawar [Dawar or Zamine Dawar].
Afghanistan 9, no. 4, 26-30. 1954.
On the region along the Helmand River called Zamine Dawar--its
ancient cities, its agriculture, and its people.

126 Binkowski, Andrzej. Von Taschkent nach Kabul [From Tashkent to Kabul].
Leipzig, 1962. Pp. 238.
A translation into German from a travel account in Polish.

127 Bochkarev, P. Afganistan [Afghanistan]. Moscow: Gosudarstvennoe
izdatel'stvo geograficheskoi literatury, 1953. Pp. 66; map.
A brief, unimportant survey by a student of Reisner.

128 Boernstein-Bosta, F. Mandana Baschi. Reisen und Erlebnisse eines deutschen Arztes in Afghanistan [Mandana Baschi. Travels and Experiences
of a German Doctor in Afghanistan]. Berlin: Reimar Hobbing, n.d.
(1925). Pp. 176; map.
The travels of the German doctor took him from Europe into Afghanistan by way of Herat, thence to Kabul--to which town he devoted
most of his observations--and then on to India.

129 Bouvat, Lucien. Un voyage en Afghanistan [Travel in Afghanistan]. Revue du Monde Musulman 9, 289-291. 1912.

II. GEOGRAPHY

An abridged version of the account of the travels of Muhammad Reza Shirazi in Afghanistan.

130 Bruckl, Karl. Über die Geologie von Badakhschan und Kataghan [The Geology of Badakhshan and Qataghan]. Neues Jahrbuch für Mineralogie, Abt. B, 74, 360-401. 1935.

131 Butcher, George. Unbelievable Valley--Bamiyan. Middle East Forum, no. 2, pp. 12-16. 1955.
Enthusiastic account of a visit to the site in 1954.

132 Caspani, P. E. Picnic Grounds and Archaeology. Afghanistan 2, no. 2, 42-46. 1947.
Lists excursions and walks in the vicinity of Paghman, west of Kabul, each featured by the presence of Moslem shrines or modern royal villas.

133 Cizancourt, H. de. Remarque sur la structure de l'Hindou-Kouch [Note on the Structure of the Hindu Kush]. Bulletin de la Société Géologique de France, sér. 5, 7, 377-400; bibliography. 1938.
Reliable technical description from personal observations by the author and his associates. Not, however, a definitive statement on this subject.

134 Codrington, K. de B. A Geographical Introduction to the History of Central Asia. Geographical Journal 104, nos. 1/2, 27-40; nos. 3/4, 73-91; map. 1944.
Part I is a verbose paper on the influence of geography on history-- through trade, art and nomadic movements. There is more of history than geography. Part II is again more historical than geographical-- particularly there is an account of the Greek Kings of Bactria and their successors.

135 *Conolly, Arthur. Journey to the North of India, Overland from England through Russia, Persia, and Afghanistan. London, 1838. Pp. 834.
This is the second edition of a useful work which contains itineraries and descriptions of the routes followed over hundreds of miles.

136 *Cressey, George B. Crossroads: Land and Life in Southwest Asia. Chicago: J. B. Lippincott Company, 1960. Pp. 593; bibliographies; glossary; index; many unnumbered illustrations; tables; charts.

II. GEOGRAPHY

Chapter 17, pages 545 through 582 deal with the transport system, water resources, and human environment of Afghanistan, and pages 136 through 139 with the Helmand River.

137 Curzon, George Nathaniel. A Recent Journey in Afghanistan. London: W. Clowes and Sons, Ltd., 1895. Pp. 12.
Permanent record of a lecture by the noted scholar and diplomat.

138 De Baer, Oliver R. The Cambridge Expedition to Afghanistan, 1955. Royal Central Asian Journal 43, 121-125. 1956.
Summary account of the travels of a group of students in the province of Badakhshan. See item 139.

139 De Baer, Oliver R. Afghan Interlude. London: Chatto & Windus, 1957. Pp. 223.
The light-hearted account of a tour by automobile from England to Afghanistan, including the "great circle" route, by four Cambridge undergraduates. See also item 242.

140 De Croze, J. Berjane. Images de route vers Mazar-i-Charif [Pictures of the Road to Mazar-i Sharif]. Afghanistan 1, no. 4, 22-29. 1946.
Transitory and precious impressions of landscapes by night and day.

141 De Croze, J. Berjane. Dreaming of Kabul. Afghanistan 2, no. 3, 12-16. 1947.
Fugitive memories of Kabul as it is and as the author would like to see it.

142 Delapraz, Alan and Micheline Delapraz. Afghanistan. Neuchâtel: Avanti Club, 1964. Pp. 127.
An historical sketch, followed by an account of travels, beautifully illustrated with color photographs and drawings. Also, separate editions in French and German.

143 Diver, Katherine Helen Maud. Kabul to Kandahar. London: P. Davies, 1935. Pp. 191.

144 Douglas, William O. Beyond the High Himalayas. New York: Doubleday & Co., 1952. Pp. 352.
Includes accounts of two visits to Afghanistan, the longer one across the country by automobile.

II. GEOGRAPHY

145 Dunin, M. S. Iz Kabula v Szhelalabad [From Kabul to Jalalabad].
Vokrug Sveta, no. 12, 39-43. Moscow, 1952.

146 Dunin, M. S. Po Afganistanu, Pakistanu, Indii [To Afghanistan, Pakistan, and India]. Moscow: Gosudarstvennoe izdatel'stvo geograficheskoi literatury, 1952. Pp. 382; maps.
A second edition was published in 1954.

147 Dunsheath, J. and E. Baillie. Afghan Quest. London: George G. Harrup
& Co. Ltd., 1961. Pp. 236.
Two intrepid British women climb mountains and collect botanical
specimens to the astonishment of the rural Afghans.

148 Eiselin, Max. Wilder Hindukusch, Erlebnisse in Afghanistan [The Wild
Hindu Kush, Experiences in Afghanistan]. Zurich: Orell Füssli, 1963.
Pp. 185; 2 maps; illus. and plates.

149 Emmanuel, W. V. Some Impressions of Swat and Afghanistan. Journal
of the Royal Central Asian Society 26, pt. II, 195-213; maps. 1939.
Descriptive mainly of Northern India and Afghanistan, with some
references to the people and the political and economic situation.
The material on Afghanistan begins on page 202.

150 *Ferrier, J. P. Caravan Journeys and Wanderings in Persia, Afghanistan,
Turkistan, and Beloochistan; With Historical Notices of the Countries
Lying Between Russia and India. Translated by Captain William Jesse.
London: John Murray, 1857. Pp. xxii, 534; map.
The French officer, General Ferrier, came out to this part of the world
to be Adjutant-General to the Persian Army. Traveling extensively
from Iran across Afghanistan and Central Asia into India he developed
a masterly knowledge of the history, geography, and languages of the
area. The present work is valuable for its description of remote regions of Afghanistan, such as the Hazara and Ghur areas and the
Helmand Valley.

151 Forbes, Rosita. Forbidden Journey. Kabul to Samarqand. London:
Cornell and Co., 1937. Pp. xii, 290; map.
Title is misleading. Lively, rather shallow account of a trip by truck
from Peshawar to Kabul and then with a British Legation escort across
the Hindu Kush.

152 *Forrest, George W. , ed. Selections from the Travels and Journals Pre-
served in the Bombay Secretariat. Bombay: Government Central Press,
1906. Pp. xxviii, 304.
Of the thirteen documents printed in this volume, eight are directly
concerned with Afghanistan and with the period between 1830 and 1850.

153 *Fox, Ernest F. Travels in Afghanistan, 1937-1938. New York: The
Macmillan Company, 1943. Pp. xxiv, 285; map.
Travels of an American geologist, searching for mineral deposits, into
remote northeastern and south central Afghanistan. Fine account of
rugged travel and primitive accommodations at a time when fanati-
cism was losing its traditional force.

154 Fox, John, as told to Roland Goodchild. Afghan Adventure. London:
Robert Hale Ltd. , 1958. Pp. 190.
A tale of high adventure in the year 1945. A special force, traveling
by caravan, tracks down smugglers of war material in western Pakistan
and at Kabul.

155 *Fraser-Tytler, Sir W. Kerr. Afghanistan: A Brief Description. Journal
of the Royal Central Asian Society 29, 165-175. 1942.
By a former British officer and diplomat who spent thirty years in the
general area and left Kabul in 1941, vacating his post as British Minister. The article is a succinct account of the topography, principal
routes and population elements of Afghanistan--with the people grouped
into dwellers in Afghan Turkistan, within the Hindu Kush, or in Southern and Eastern Afghanistan.

156 *Fraser-Tytler, Sir W. Kerr. A Great North Road. Journal of the Royal
Central Asian Society 29, Pt. II, 129-135; sketch map. 1942.
Details the historical routes across the Hindu Kush, lists efforts to
create roads in modern times and describes the building of the motor
road across the Shibar Pass.

157 *Furon, Raymond. L'Hindou-Kouch et la Kaboulistan. Contribution a
l'étude géologique et géomorphogénique de l'Afghanistan [The Hindu
Kush and Kabulistan. A Contribution to the Geological and Geomor-
phogenical Study of Afghanistan] . Paris: Albert Blanchard, 1927.
Pp. 169; maps.
The reflection of research in the field, made in the vicinity of Kabul--
here called Kabulistan--and in one section of the Hindu Kush.

158 *Furon, Raymond. Géologie du Plateau Iranien (Perse-Afghanistan-
Baloutchistan) [Geology of the Iranian Plateau (Persia-Afghanistan-
Baluchistan)]. Mémoires du Muséum National d'Histoire Naturelle,
n.s. 7, pt. 2, 177-414; geological map; bibliography. Paris, 1941.
This lengthy article is based upon nearly a score of years of field
work and study on the subject. Certainly the most important work in
the field and accompanied by a list of over 400 titles in the field as
well as the first geological map of the country. Unfortunately in a
publication difficult to find.

159 Furon, Raymond and Louis-Felicien Rosset. Contribution a l'étude de
trias en Afghanistan [Contribution to the Study of the Triassic in Af-
ghanistan]. Afghanistan 7, no. 2, 19-28. 1952.
Descriptions of triassic specimens.

160 Furon, Raymond and Louis-Felicien Rosset. L'Afghanistan et les milieux
paléontologiques mondiaux [Afghanistan and the World Paleontological
Contexts]. Afghanistan 9, no. 4, 48-50. 1954.
A summary of the completed stratigraphic series in Northern Afghanistan.

161 Gabriel, Alfons. Aus den Einsamkeiten Irans; Dritte Forschungsfahrt durch
die Wüste Lut und Persisch-Balocistan mit einer Reise durch Süd-
Afghanistan [From the Solitudes of Iran; Third Expedition through the
Lut Desert and Persian Baluchistan, with a Journey through Southern Af-
ghanistan]. Stuttgart: Strecker und Schroder, 1939. Pp. xv, 186.
The author's journey through southern Afghanistan, with observations
on the land, the people and the climate (pages 153-168). Information
is rather heavily interlarded with poetic flights.

162 Galkin, M. Po dorogam Afganistana [Along the Roads of Afghanistan].
Vokrug Sveta, no. 5, pp. 24-28; no. 6, pp. 34-37. Moscow, 1954.

163 Gerber, Alfred. Afghanische Mosaiken, Erlebnisse im verschlossenen
Land [Afghan Mosaics, Experiences in a Locked Land]. Braunschweig:
G. Wenzel, 1942. Pp. 150; map.

164 Grodekov, N. I. (Grodekoff, N.). Itinéraire dans le Turkestan afghan
[Itinerary in Afghan Turkistan]. Bulletin de la Société de Géographie,
sér. 6, 20, 124-141. Paris, 1880.
A version, freely rendered into French from a Russian account, of the
difficulties of this Russian General Staff Officer in attempting to

overcome local resistance to travel in the area in question. Includes
an account of strategic considerations of the region. See also no. 235.

165 Gurevich, Aleksandr Mikhailovich. Afganistan [Afghanistan]. Moscow:
Izdatel'stvo TSK MOPR SSSR, 1929. Pp. 60; map; bibliography.

166 Hackin, Joseph. In Persia and Afghanistan with the Citroen Trans-Asiatic
Expedition. Geographical Journal 83, 353-363; map. 1934.
A running account of a trip to Herat and return via the great circle
route through Afghanistan with knowledgeable comments on such sites
as Bamiyan.

167 *Haekel, Ingeborg, ed. Botanische Ergebnisse der deutschen Hindukusch-
expedition 1935 [Botanical Results of the German Expedition of 1935 to
the Hindu Kush]. Dahlem bei Berlin: Verlag des Repertoriums, 1938.
Pp. v; plates; bibliographies.

168 Hahn, Helmut. Die stadt Kabul (Afghanistan) und ihr Umland. I. Ge-
staltwandel einer orientalischen Stadt [The City of Kabul (Afghanistan)
and its Vicinity. I. The Changing Form of an Oriental City]. Bonn:
Ferd.Dümmlers Verlag, 1964. Pp. 88; bibliography; 3 city plans.

169 *Hamilton, Angus. Afghanistan. London: William Heinemann, 1906.
Pp. xxi, 562; map; appendices.
Much of the material within the volume falls outside the scope of the
title for several chapters deal with Russian Turkistan and another
with Sistan, which the author saw while a member of the survey mission of Sir Henry MacMahon. However, the work contains descriptions
of the Murghab Valley, Herat, Qandahar and Kabul, and reflects a
tremendous energy in the avid collection of material on the government, army, trade, and foreign relations--much of it presented in appendices.

170 Hanstein, Otfried von. Im Wilden Afghanistan, ein Land der Zukunst,
Reisen, Abenteuer und Forschungen [In Wild Afghanistan, a Land of the
Future, Travel, Adventure and Research]. Leipzig: Deutsche Buch-
werkstatten, 1928. Pp. 176; map.

171 Hashmat, A. Notes of a Journey. Afghanistan 3, no. 4, 30-43. 1948.
An account, in diary form, by the Afghan who accompanied a Danish
expedition into Nuristan and north to Fayzabad. Scattered material on
the Nuri tribes.

II. GEOGRAPHY

172 Havelka, Jan. Afghanistan tajuplnosti zbaveny [Mysterious, Entertaining Afghanistan]. Prague: Lidova demokracie, 1961.

173 Hay, William R. Demarcation of the Indo-Afghan Boundary in the Vicinity of Aramdu. Geographical Journal 82, 351-354; maps. 1933.
The paper describes briefly the work of a Commission to settle the Afghan-Indian dispute over the boundary to Dokalim. Major Hay was the British member of the Commission. A technical note by Captain D. R. Crone, of the Royal Engineers, follows the article proper.

174 *Hay, William R. Band-i-Amir. Geographical Journal 87, 348-350. 1936
Popular description of the five, sparkling blue lakes, together with local legends regarding their formation. The lakes are precisely located by latitude and longitude.

175 Hayden, H. H. The Geology of Northern Afghanistan. Memoirs of the Geological Survey of India 39, 1-96. Calcutta, 1911.
Deals with the region in which the Hindu Kush and the Kuh-i Baba ranges come together. Drawings, photographs and a colored geological map at the scale of 1: 2,027,520.

176 Herbordt, O. Die Erzlagerstatten Afghanistan [Afghanistan as a Mining Country]. Internationale Bergwirtschaft vol. 2. Leipzig, August-September, 1926.

177 *Holdich, Thomas Hungerford. Afghan Boundary Commission; Geographical Notes. Proceedings of the Royal Geographical Society, n.s. 7, 39-44, 160-166, 273-292, map. 1885.
Parts I and II are a description of the country from Quetta to Herat, with special attention to the water supply. Part III is preceded by some historical remarks on the Commission by General J. T. Walker, and contains a description of a Sarik Turkoman camp. A discussion of the paper, giving some information on the politico-geographical situation, begins on page 284.

178 Holdich, Thomas Hungerford. An Orographic Map of Afghanistan and Baluchistan. Geographical Journal 16, 527-531; folding map, scale 1" - 96 miles, opposite p. 596. 1900.
The brief article is a technical description of the principal physical features of the area.

179 Holdich, Thomas Hungerford. The Gates of India, Being an Historical
     Narrative. With Maps. London: Macmillan and Co., 1910. Pp. xvi,
     555; maps.
        Chapters 3 through 17 contain an extended history of the explorations
     of Afghanistan.

180 Howland, Felix. Afghanistan Has No Frontiers. Asia 40, 633-636. 1940.

181 Howland, Felix. Crossing the Hindu Kush. Geographical Review 30,
     272-278; 2 small maps. 1940.
        Describes the roads and trails which traverse the Hindu Kush, with
     particular attention to the motor road, ordered by Nadir Shah and
     completed in 1933. The pass on this road is variously referred to as
     Shibar or Ghilan and is at 9, 800 feet.

182 Humlum, Johannes. Pirzada; Rejser i Indien og Afghanistan [Pirzada;
     Journey to India and Afghanistan]. Copenhagen: Gyldendalske
     boghandel, Nordisk forlag, 1950. Pp. 211; maps.

183 *Humlum, Johannes. La géographie de l'Afghanistan [The Geography of
     Afghanistan]. Copenhagen: Gyldenal, 1959. Pp. 421; 349 illustra-
     tions; tables; maps; bibliography; index.
        An extremely valuable and reliable work which ranges far beyond its
     title, including material on farming practices, ethnic groups, politi-
     cal structure, and numerous other subjects.

184 Hunter, Edward. The Past Present. London: Hodder and Stoughton, 1959.
     Pp. 352.
        The record of a year in Afghanistan with travel notes and critical judg-
     ments on "an inflammable area. "

185 Huntington, Ellsworth. The Afghan Borderland: Part I, The Russian Front-
     ier. Part II, The Persian Frontier. National Geographical Magazine
     20, 788-799; 866-876. 1909.
        Relation of a journey by the author in 1903 and 1904 along the north-
     western and western frontiers of Afghanistan. The first section deals
     with the Russian boundary and the second part with the frontier with
     Persia. Fairly specific material on geographical and strategic aspects.

186 Hussein, Mia. Merve Rud. Afghanistan 9, no. 3, 8-17; no. 4, 19-25.
     1954.
        Description of the city and its ruins, and of the cities which once

surrounded it, with a list of their famous scholars and poets.

187 Iavorskii, I. L. Puteshestvie russkogo posol'stva po Avganistanau i
Bukharskomu Khanstvo v 1878-1879 [Travels of a Russian Embassy in
Afghanistan and the Khanate of the Bokhara People in 1878-1879].
2 vols. St. Petersburg, 1882-1883.
An interesting document which, in spite of its comprehensive title,
is primarily concerned with Afghanistan.

188 Iran, Afganistan i Sin'tszian (Zap-Kitai) (Politiko-ekonomicheskie
ocherki) pod redaktsiei V. Petrina (Iran) Prof. I. M. Reisnera (Afgan-
istan) i Prof. P. M. Fesenko (Sin'tszian) S prilozheniem dvukh kart
[Tran. Afghanistan and Sinkiang (Western China) (Politico-Economic
Outlines) Edited by V. Petrin (Iran) Prof. I. M. Reisner (Afghanistan)
and Prof. P. M. Fesenko (Sinkiang). With Two Maps]. Moscow:
Gosudarstvennoe Sotsial'no-ekonomicheskoe izdatel'stvo, 1936.
Pp. 400; two folding maps; bibliographies.

189 *Iven, H. E. Das Klima von Kabul [The Climate of Kabul]. Breslau:
F. Hirt, 1933. Pp. 74.
Invaluable study based on precise observations taken at Kabul from
1924 until 1932 and dealing with rainfall, humidity, temperatures,
winds, overcasts, etc. Seventeen tables and comparison with climatic
conditions in neighboring areas.

190 *Iven, Walther. Vom Pandshir zum Pandsch. Bericht über eine Forschung-
reise im Hindukusch und in Nordost-Afghanistan [From Pandshir to
Pandsh. Report of a Voyage of Discovery in the Hindu Kush and in
Northeastern Afghanistan]. Petermanns Geographische Mitteilungen
81, 113-117, 157-161; map. 1935.
In 1932 the German author and two companions set out from Kabul to
follow up the valley of the Panjshir River. Crossing the Hindu Kush
they went into Badakhshan and then returned to Kabul by a different
pass across the Hindu Kush. Acute observations on geography, geology and social life and the 1: 500,000 map contains corrections of
earlier ones.

191 James, Ben. The Secret Kingdom: An Afghan Journey. New York:
Reynal and Hitchcock, 1934. Pp. 295.
A young American writer and adventurer pridefully penetrated a re-
mote land and emerges with general observations, primarily relating

to the political scene and atmosphere. A London edition of a year
later is entitled Afghan Journey.

192 Jones, Paul S. Afghanistan Venture. San Antonio: The Naylor Company,
1956. Pp. 454; index.
Sub-titled, "Discovering the Afghan people--the life, contacts and
adventures of an American Civil Engineer during his two year sojourn
in the Kingdom of Afghanistan." The author was engaged in the construction of dams on the Helmand river.

193 Kasim, Jan Mohd. Aryans in the East. Boston: Meador Publishing Co.,
1935. Pp. 91; map.
Discusses the historical, geographical, social and political events of
the past and present Aryan land of Asia--Afghanistan.

194 Katrak, Sorab K. H. Through Amanullah's Afghanistan. A Book of Travel.
Karachi: D. N. Patel, 1929. Pp. xxxiv, 145; bibliography.
An Indian commercial traveler puts together an account of progress un-
der King Amanullah and of the inconveniences and trials of travel.
Includes a limited bibliography and the full text of the Afghan-British
Treaty of November 22, 1921.

195 Kessel, Joseph, Karl Flinker, and Max Klimburg. Legende Afghanistan
[Legendary Afghanistan]. Köln: M. DuMont Schauberg, 1959. Pp. 55;
163 illus.; map.
Another edition of item 69.

196 Khalil, Muhammad Ibrahim. Mazarat-i shahr Kabul [Tombs of the city
of Kabul]. Kabul: Doulati matba'eh, 1339 [1960]. Pp. 268.

197 *Khalili, Afghan. Asar-i Harat [Monuments of Herat]. 3 vols. Herat:
Matba'eh-yi fakhriyeh-yi saljuqi, 1309-1310 [1930-1931]. Pp. (1)
196; (2) 197-510; (3) 281.
An exhaustive account in Persian of the major mosques and shrines of
Herat, of its minor tombs, and of the pious and learned men resident
in this ancient town.

198 Khanikoff, Nicolas de. Mémoire sur la partie méridionale de l'Asie centrale. (Khorassan, Afghanistan, Seistan, midi de la Perse) [Memoir on
the Southern Part of Central Asia. (Khorasan, Afghanistan, Sistan and
Central Persia)]. Recueil de voyages et de mémoires publiés par la
Société de Géographie 7, 239-451. Paris, 1861.

199 Khoroshkhin, A. Sbornik statei, Kasaiushchikhsia do turkestanskogo
     Kraia [Collected Articles Dealing with the Turkistan Region]. St.
     Petersburg, 1876.

200 King, Peter. Afghanistan: Cockpit in High Asia. London: Geoffrey
     Bles, 1966.
     Experiences while searching for medicinal plants.

201 Klass, Rosanne. Afghanistan Land of the High Flags. New York: Random
     House, 1964. Pp. 319.
     A travel memoir of an American who taught in Kabul from 1951 to
     1954.

202 Kohzad, Ahmad Ali. The Panjsher. Afghanistan 3, no. 4, 17-29. 1948.
     A topographical description of this attractive valley, some 80 kilo-
     meters north of Kabul, is followed by a list of villages and some com-
     ments on community life.

203 Kohzad, Ahmad Ali. Afghanistan Coeur de l'Asie [Afghanistan, Heart of
     Asia]. Afghanistan 5, no. 1, 25-28. 1950.
     General description and praise of Afghanistan.

204 Kohzad, Ahmad Ali. Along the Koh-i-Baba and the Hari-Rud. Afghan-
     istan 6, no. 1, 1-16; no. 2, 1-21; 7, no. 1, 50-55; 8, no. 4, 54-
     65; 9, no. 1, 20-43; no. 2, 1-21. 1951, 1952, 1953, 1954.
     Lengthy description of a journey.

205 K[ohzad], A[hmad Ali]. Les sommets des montagnes du monde [The
     Summits of the Mountains of the World]. Afghanistan 9, no. 3, 22-
     35. 1954.
     The identification of the five mountains of Ghur, described by a
     medieval historian, Quazi Menhadje Seradje, as the mountain tops of
     the world, with five not-so-high mountains of modern Ghur, which
     are now known by other names.

206 Kohzad, Mohammad Nabi. Notes de voyage [Travel Notes]. Afghani-
     stan 3, no. 3, 47-53; no. 4, 8-13. 1948.
     An account, in diary form, of two trips on which the Afghan author
     accompanied a foreign scholar.

207 Kohzad, Mohammad Nabi. Un coup d'oeil sur la Vallée de Nedjrau [A
     Glance at the Valley of Nedjrau]. Afghanistan 9, no. 2, 60-62. 1954.

A description of the fertile valley and of its crops, with a note on the four languages, especially Paratchi, spoken there.

208 Kohzad, Mohammad Nabi. Les Sites Touristiques de l'Afghanistan [Tourist Sites in Afghanistan] . Kabul: Government Printing House, n. d. Pp. 20.

209 Koie, M. and K. H. Reichinger. Symbolae Afghanicae [Afghan Contributions] . Konglige Danske Videnskabernes Selskab, Biologiske Skrifter 8, no. 1, 1-80. Copenhagen, 1955.

210 Koie, M. and K. H. Reichinger. Symbolae Afghanicae. Copenhagen: Ejnar Munksgaard, 1956. Pp. 215.
These works (nos. 209 and 210), in Danish, enumerate and describe the plants collected by the Third Danish Expedition to Central Asia. A third volume was by Reichinger and was published in Copenhagen in 1959. It was entitled Leguminosae, and dealt with the subject in 208 pages.

211 Krause, Walter W. Wenn es zwolf schlagt in Kabul [When it Strikes Twelve in Kabul] . Munich, 1957. Pp. 291.
An account of travel.

212 Kreyberg, Leiv. Afghanistan; en norsk leges reise i Hindu-Kusj-landet [Afghanistan: A Norwegian Physician's Journey into the Hindu Kush Country] . Oslo: J. W. Cappelen, 1951. Pp. 164.

213 Kuhi, Muhammad Nasir. Armaghan-i Maymaneh [Souvenir of Maymaneh] . Maymaneh: Matba'eh-yi storai, 1328 [1949] . Pp. (unnumbered) 266.
A compilation of material about this town of Northern Afghanistan, its shrines and monuments, its residents, and about the surrounding area.

214 Kuhn, Delia and Ferdinand Kuhn. Borderlands. New York: Alfred Knopf, 1962. Pp. 335.
A perceptive account of travels, which includes a section on Afghan Turkestan.

215 Kushkaki, Burkhan al-Din Khan. Kattagan i Badakhshan. Dannye po geografii strany, estestvenno-istoricheskim usloviiam naseleniiu, ekonomike i putiam soobshcheniia. S 34 Kartami. Perevod s persidskogo P. P. Vvedenskogo, B. I. Dolgopolova i E. V. Levkievskogo

pod redaktsiei, s predisloviem i primechaniiami prof. A. A. Semenova [Qataghan and Badakhshan. Information about the Geography of the Country, the Natural-Historical Conditions, the Economy, and the Means of Communication. With 34 Maps. Translated from the Persian by P. P. Vvedenskii, B. I. Dolgopolov, and E. V. Levkievskii, under the Editorship and with a Preface and Remarks by Professor A. A. Semenov]. Tashkent, 1926. Pp. xiii, 248; maps.

A translation from the Persian. The notes of Semenov, a retired professor of Arabic at the Central Asian University, are especially valuable. The book is very complete, but has many inaccuracies.

216 *Lal, Mohan. Journal of a Tour through the Panjab, Afghanistan, Turkistan, Khorasan, and a Part of Persia, in Company with Lieut. Burnes and Dr. Gerard. Calcutta: Baptist Mission Press, 1834. Pp. xx, 340. First edition of a work published in London in 1835 and again in somewhat different form at London in 1846. The author was an Indian clerk thoroughly familiar with Persian and avid at collecting information.

217 Leech, R., trans. Journal of a Tour through Parts of the Panjab and Afghanistan in the Year 1837, by Agha Abbas of Shiraz, Arranged and Translated by Major R. Leech. Journal of the Asiatic Society of Bengal 12, 564-621. 1843.

Disguised as a fakir, Agha Abbas, a soldier of fortune, traveled in India and Afghanistan, making notes on the villages, population and fighting strength for Major Leech. To preserve his disguise, he unblushingly distributed charms, discovered thieves and cured the sick, usually with the aid of detonating powder.

218 Le Fevre, Georges. Expédition Citroen Centre-Asie. La Croisière Jaune. Troisième mission Haardt-Audouin-Dubreuil [The Citroen Expedition to Central Asia. The Yellow Cruiser. Third Haardt-Audouin-Dubreuil Mission]. Paris: Plon, 1933. Pp. xlvi, 368; maps.

Chapter III, pages 33-53, deals with the arduous motor crossing of Afghanistan in 1931. Well illustrated. An English translation appeared in 1935 under the title of An Eastern Odyssey.

219 Le Roy, Marie. Étude préliminaire sur le facies lagunaire: Bajocien-Bathonien de Karkar [Preliminary Study of the Lagoon Facies: Bajocian-Bathonian of Karkar]. Afghanistan 8, no. 2, 33-39. 1953.

A discussion of some fossils found at Karkar and of the indications that a great lagoon, part of the Jurassic Sea, covered that part, at least, of Afghanistan.

220 Le Roy, Marie. La mer triasique à Douab [The Triassic Sea at Douab] .
   Afghanistan 8, no. 3, 18-22. 1953.
   A description of fossils which indicate the existence of a triassic
   sea in Northern Afghanistan.

221 *Le Strange, Guy. The Lands of the Eastern Caliphate. Mesopotamia,
   Persia and Central Asia, from the Muslim Conquest to the Time of
   Timur. Cambridge University Press, 1930. Pp. xx, 536; maps.
   Reprint of a work of great value for indicating reliable source mate-
   rial which first appeared in 1905. Several chapters are directly con-
   cerned with the area covered by present-day Afghanistan.

222 Linchevskii, I. A. and A. V. Prozorovskii. K pozhaniiu rastitel'nosti Afganistana [On the knowledge of the vegetation of Afghanistan] .
   Botanicheskii Zhurnal 29, no. 4, 114-23. Moscow, 1944.

223 Linchevskii, I. A. and A. V. Prozorovskii. Osnovnye zakonomernosti
   raspredeleniia rastitel'nosti Afganistana [The Principal regularities in
   Vegetation Distribution in Afghanistan] . Sbornik Nauchnykh Rabot
   Botanicheskii Instituta imena V. L. Komarova, 1946, 183-218.
   Leningrad, 1946.

224 Linchevsky, I. A. and A. V. Prozorovsky. Basic Principles of the Distribution of the Vegetation of Afghanistan. Kew Bulletin 2, 179-214;
   map. London, 1949.

225 Lindberg, K. Observations au sujet de quelques grottes asiatiques: Afghanistan [Observations on Some Asiatic Caves: Afghanistan] . Afghanistan 4, no. 3, 39-44. 1949.
   Notes by a Swedish doctor and speleologist on how to hunt caves in
   Afghanistan and what he found.

226 Mackenzie, Franklin. Brief Glimpses of Afghanistan. Afghanistan 4,
   no. 3, 49-59. 1949.
   Impressions of a trip by motor bus from Peshawar to Kabul, another
   bus trip north to Mazar-i Sharif, a third to Ghazni, and a fourth to
   Bamiyán. By an American teacher employed in a Kabul technical
   school.

227 MacMahon, A. H. The Southern Borderlands of Afghanistan. Geographical Journal 9, 392-415. 1897.

Following the agreement on the Durand Line in 1893 Captain MacMahon was charged to establish the precise boundary between Afghanistan and Baluchistan: work carried on in 1894 through 1896 is described.

228 Maillart, Ella K. The Cruel Way. London: William Heinemann Ltd., 1947. Pp. 217.
    One of several books about travel in Asia by this Swiss journalist. The second hundred pages deal with Afghanistan, describing the wearing journey in the author's tortured car from Herat along the northern route through Mazar-i Sharif and back across the Hindu Kush to Kabul. Burdened by exaggerated sensibilities and problems of personal relationships An edition in French was published at Geneva in 1952.

229 Map. Afghanistan. Scale, 1: 2,000,000. New York, United Nations Map. No. 279, rev. 2, provisional edition January, 1954.
    Topographic sheet with approximate contours, figures indicating height of passes and peaks, routes of motorable roads, outline of provincial boundaries, etc. The circulation of this map is restricted by the United Nations.

230 Map. Persia and Afghanistan. Scale, 1: 4,550,050, or one inch equals 64 miles. Directorate of the Military Survey, Geographic Section, General Staff,Great Britain 2149, 1912, 3d edition revised for railroads and boundaries in 1950.
    Physical features map with reliable material and the local transportation systems.

231 Map of Kabul. Kabul: Matba'eh-yi doulati, n.d. Single folding sheet.
    Useful map of the capital with English text issued by the Afghan Tourist Organization.

232 *Maps. Afghanistan. Quarter-inch Series. Scale 1: 253,440. Survey of India, Dehra-Dun; numerous sheets revised cr reprinted by the Directorate of Military Survey as Geographic Section, General Staff, Great Britain 3919, 1941 --
    Covers the country in large 1 degree x 1 degree topographical sheets. On a number of sheets contouring is missing in parts and unreliable in others. Many place-names are incorrect or garbled and the entire series would benefit by a reworking on the ground.

233 *Maps of Afghanistan. International Series, Scale 1: 1,000,000. Latest edition. Sheets NG41, NH41, NH42, NI41, NI42, NI43, NJ41, NJ42.

I. GEOGRAPHY

234 *Markoroski, Bruno. Die materielle Kultur des Kabulgebietes [The Material Culture of the Kabul Region]. Leipzig: Asia Major, 1932. Pp. vii, 154; bibliography.
Reflections of a residence of three years at Kabul expressed in a systematic study of the environment and patterns of living of the Afghans.

235 Marvin, Charles, trans. Colonel Grodekoff's Ride from Samarqand to Herat, through Afghan Turkestan. London, 1880. Pp. 244.
Translated into English and published the same year that the original Russian edition appeared in St. Petersburg. Covers areas not included in his account of Turkestan (see no. 164).

236 Marvin, Charles. Reconnoitering Central Asia: Pioneering Adventures in the Region Lying between Russia and India. London: S. Swan Sonneinschein and Co., 1884. Pp. xviii, 418.
A British journalist, specialist on the subject of Russia in Asia and author of several books on that subject, collects a number of contemporary accounts of travel and exploration in the region of Russia and Afghan Turkistan.

237 Masal'skii, F. I. Turkestanskii Krai [The Turkistan Region]. Rossiia . . . vol. 19. St. Petersburg, 1913.

238 *Masson, Charles. Narrative of Various Journeys in Belochistan, Afghanistan, and the Panjab; Including a Residence in those Countries from 1826 to 1836. 3 vols. London: Richard Bentley, 1842. Pp. (1) xxvii, 471; (2) xvi, 464; (3) xvi, 496.
In spite of the rather general title of the work these volumes by a British traveler are devoted almost entirely to Afghanistan. Displaying a keenist observation and a devotion to detail they were long consulted as a major work of reference. Volume 3 includes an account of the commercial mission of Burnes to Kabul in 1836-37.

239 Mazhar, 'Ali. Afghanistan [Afghanistan]. Cairo: Matba'ah al-sanah al-muhammadiah, 1369 [1950]. Pp. 141; list of sources.

240 Mele, Pietro F. Afghanistan. Milan: Amilcare Pizzi, 1965.
Some 56 photographs, with a sketchy introduction and unsatisfactory captions.

241 Michel, Aloys A. On Writing the Geography of Strange Lands and Faraway Places Afghanistan, for example. Economic Geography 36, no. 4,

355-368. 1960.

A review article inspired by the publication of La Géographie de l'Afghanistan by J. Humlum, see no. 183.

242 Michel, Janine, trans. Intermede afghan [Afghan Interlude]. Paris: Julliard, 1958. Pp. 287.

A translation of no. 139.

243 Michener, James A. Afghanistan, Domain of the Fierce and the Free. Reader's Digest 67, no. 403, 161-172. November, 1955.

A rather romanticized description, emphasizing the beauty and contrast of the country; ending with the reassurance that Afghanistan is turning to the United States rather than to Russia.

244 Minaev, I. Svedenia o stranach po verkhov'iam Amu-Dar'i [Information about the Countries on the Upper Amu Darya]. St. Petersburg, 1879.

245 Mohn, Paul. Resa till Afghanistan [Travel in Afghanistan]. Stockholm: F. A. Norstedt, Soners Forlag, 1930. Pp. 364; map.

Several principal subjects are treated in this Swedish account: a general historical survey; an account of the provinces of Kabul and Badakhshan; and the period of transition between Amanullah and Nadir Shah.

246 Monakhov, F. I. Kharakteristika afganskikh glubokofokusnykh zemletriasneii [Characteristics of Afghan Deep-Focus Earthquakes]. Akademiia Nauk S. S. S. R., Geofizicheskii Institut, Trudy, No. 14 (1952): 3-12. Moscow.

247 Moorcroft, William and George Trebeck. Travels in the Himalayan Provinces of Hindustan and the Panjab; in Ladakh and Kashmir; in Peshawar, Kabul, Kunduz, and Bokhara; from 1819 to 1825. 2 vols. London: John Murray, 1838. Pp. (1) lvi, 459; (2) viii, 508.

In the second volume the authors, British army officers, recount a ride from Peshawar to Bokhara by way of Kabul, Bamiyan, Qunduz and Mazar-i Sharif. The emphasis is upon description of the route and the delays and difficulties caused by local authorities.

248 Morgan, Delmar E. The Pamir: A Geographical and Political Sketch. The Scottish Geographical Magazine 8, 15-23. 1892.

Informative description of some of the six divisions that make up the valleys of the Pamir.

249 Muhammad 'Ali Khan. Afghanistan. Lahore: Mufid-i 'amm, 1306
    [1927]. Pp. 163; map.
    An account in Persian of the geography and topography of Afghanistan.

250 Muhammad Husayn Khan. Jughrafiya-yi Afghanistan [Geography of Af-
    ghanistan]. Lahore: Mufid-i 'amm, 1306 [1927]. Pp. 71.
    A summary account of the subject in Persian.

251 Nalivkin, I. D. Obzor geologii Pamira i Badakchana [The Geological
    Survey of the Pamirs and Badakhshan]. Moscow-Leningrad: Transac-
    tions of the United Geological and Prospecting Service of the U. S. S. R.,
    1932. Pp. 104; geological map.
    The essential conclusions of this Soviet study are summarized in Eng-
    lish on pages 73-101.

252 Nariman, G. K. Afghanistan Today. Islamic Culture 1, 252-258.
    Hyderabad, 1927.
    Account of a visit to Afghanistan by an Indian subject in response to
    an invitation from Amir Amanullah. A stay of two months is reflected
    in a multitude of scattered observations on the people and the rapid
    surge of modernization: the author did regret that his modest supply
    of whiskey was confiscated when he entered the country.

253 Nesterovich, S. Russkiye puteshestvenniki v Afganistane [Russian Trav-
    elers in Afghanistan]. Zvezda Vostoka, no. 3, pp. 158-160. 1958.
    An account of the favorable reception accorded to Soviet visitors to
    Afghanistan.

254 Newby, Eric. A Short Walk. New York: Doubleday and Co., 1959.
    Pp. 240.
    A literate, informative, and entertaining account of travel in the
    Hindu Kush and in Nuristan.

255 *Niedermayer, Oskar von. Afghanistan [Afghanistan]. Leipzig: K. W.
    Hiersemann, 1924. Pp. xv, 70; 246 illustrations.
    The head of the secret German expedition to Afghanistan in 1914-1917
    (see no. 555) put together a short but interesting text dealing with
    economic and social conditions and the problems of the tribes as a
    framework for an abundance of marvelous photographs of landscape,
    people, and ancient and modern sites.

II. GEOGRAPHY

256 Niedermayer, Oskar von. Persien und Afghanistan.(Handbuch der geo-
graphischen Wissenschaft: Vorder- und Südasien) [Persia and Afghanistan. (Handbook of Geographical Science: Near and South Asia)].
Potsdam, 1937.
Listed for its potential value, considering the background and experience of the author: there appears to be no copy in this country.

257 Obruchev, Vladimir A. Iskopayemyye bogatstva Afganistana [Mineral
Wealth of Afghanistan]. Novyy Vostok, no. 16-17 (1927): 226-231.
Moscow.

258 Pernot, Maurice. L'inquiétude de l'Orient. En Asie Musulmane [The
Uneasiness of the Orient. In Moslem Asia]. Paris: Hachette, 1927.
Pp. viii, 244.
Some 40 of the opening pages are devoted to personal impressions of
Afghanistan by a writer commissioned to travel from the Mediterra-
nean to India.

259 Peter of Greece (and Denmark), Prince. A Trip to the Oxus. Journal of
the Royal Central Asian Society 34, 51-55. 1947.
An account of what the author claimed to be the first motor trip from
Mazar-i Sharif to the Oxus (Amu Darya) River.

260 Proudlock, R. V. The Miranzai Valley. Journal of the Royal Central Asian
Society 36, 307-308. 1949.
Brief note on this valley astride the Afghan-Pakistan frontier by a mili-
tary observer of raids and tribal migrations through the valley.

261 Pulyarkin, Valery A. Afganistan; ekonomicheskaya geografiya [Afghan-
istan; Economic Geography]. Moscow: Mysl', 1964. Pp. 253; maps.

262 Qamus-i a'lam-i jughrafiya'i-yi Afghanistan [Dictionary of Geographical
Names of Afghanistan]. Kabul: Matba'eh-yi 'umumi, 1327 [1948].
Pp. 168.
A valuable work in Persian, issued by the Da'iratu'l-ma'arif [Encyclo-
pedia] board.

263 *Rahnuma-yi Qattaghan va Badakhshan ya'ni mulakhkhas-i safar-nameh-
yi 1301 sipahsalar-i sardar-i Muhammad Nadir Khan vazir-i harbiyeh
murattabeh-yi janab Mawlawi Burhan al-Din Khan Kushkaki [Guide to
Qattaghan and Badakhshan, that is, Selections from the Travel Diary of

1301 of General Muhammad Nadir Khan, Minister of War, Arranged
by His Excellency Mawlawi Burhan al-Din Khan Kushkaki]. Kabul,
1304 [1925].

A valuable account of a trip made through two northern provinces in
1923 and containing material on geography, resources, history and
population groups. (For a translation into Russian, see no. 215.)

264 Rathjens, Carl. Kabul, Die Hauptstadt Afghanistans [Kabul, The Capital
of Afghanistan]. Leben und Umwelt 13, 73-82. 1957.

265 Rattray, James. The Costumes of the Various Tribes, Portraits of Ladies
of Rank, Celebrated Princes and Chiefs, Views of the Principal Fortresses
and Cities, and Interior of the Cities and Temples of Afghaunistaun.
London: Hering and Remington, 1848. Pp. 34; plates.

266 Raverty, Henry George. An Account of Upper Kash-Kar and Chitral or
Lower Kash-Kar, together with the Independent Afghan State of Panj-
Korah, including Talash. Journal of the Asiatic Society of Bengal 33,
125-151. 1864.

267 *Reinaud, M. Mémoire géographique, historique et scientifique sur l'Inde
antérieurement au milieu du XIème siècle de l'ère christienne, d'après
les écrivans arabes persans et chinois [Geographical, Historical and Scientific Memoirs on India prior to the Middle of the Eleventh Christian
Century, Taken from Arab, Persian and Chinese Writers]. Paris: Imprimerie nationale, 1849. Pp. ii, 400; map.

Includes very useful material on the area now covered by Eastern Afghanistan.

268 Reisner, Igor Mikhailovich. Nesavisimy Afganistan [Independent Afghan-
istan]. Moscow: Trudy Moskovskogo Instituta Vostokoredenia N. N.
Narimanova, 1929. Pp. 221.

Reisner has long been known as the leading professor of Colonial History at Moscow and the greatest Soviet specialist on Afghanistan. This
useful text faithfully reflects Marxist doctrines.

269 *Reisner, Igor Mikhailovich. Afganistan. S Kartami i skhemami [Afghan-
istan. With Maps and Charts]. 2d ed. Moscow: Kommunisticheskaia
Akademiia. Institut Mirovogo Khoziaistva i Mirovoi Politiki. Kolonial'naia Seriia, 1939. Pp. viii, 267.

A later and more comprehensive reworking of the same author's Independent Afghanistan, including certain ideological revisions.

270 Rishtin, Sadiqullah. Da Hind safar [The Hind Voyage]. Kabul, 1334
    [1955]. Pp. 172.
    An account in Pushtu of a visit to India.

271 Rishtiya, Sayed Qasim. The Rivers of Afghanistan. Afghanistan 2, no. 2,
    8-14. 1947.
    A general introduction is followed by accounts of the courses of the
    Kabul and the Amu Darya Rivers.

272 Ross, Frank E., ed. Central Asia. Personal Narrative of General Josiah
    Harlan, 1823-1841. London: Luzac and Co., 1939. Pp. 155; fold-
    ing map.
    In 1826 Harlan attached himself to an ex-king of Kabul in exile in
    India and soon went into Afghanistan in disguise and as a secret agent:
    probably the first American to visit the country. Later he took service
    under Amir Dost Muhammad. His story stresses two subjects, an ac-
    count of the province of Balkh and its inhabitants and a military to-
    pography of Northern Afghanistan.

273 Rosset, Louis-Felicien. Les pierres précieuses en Afghanistan [Precious
    Stones in Afghanistan]. Afghanistan 2, no. 1, 23-44; no. 2, 21-41.
    1947.
    Deals with the incidence and types of diamonds in Afghanistan and
    their current local prices. A number of pages describe Kabul River
    Valley sites where garnets are found.

274 Rosset, Louis-Felicien. Vers le nord afghan [To the Afghan North]. Af-
    ghanistan 2, no. 4, 24-53. 1947.
    Technical and dull account of observed geology along the route from
    Kabul north to Bactria.

275 Rosset, Louis-Felicien. Les cuvettes d'effondrement du Kaboulistan:
    Lataband hills et terrasses fluviales de Sarobi [The Trench Basins of
    Kabulistan: Lataband Hills and Fluvial Terraces of Sarobi]. Afghan-
    istan 4, no. 2, 1-13. 1949.
    Highly technical account of geological observations in the Lataband
    Pass.

276 Rosset, Louis-Felicien. Prospection paléontologique dans les plissements
    secondaires du Nord Hindu-Koush [Paleontological Exploration in the
    Secondary Foldings of the North Hindu Kush]. Afghanistan 4, no. 4,
    36-47. 1949.

The results of geological observations made at Doab.

277 Rosset, Louis-Felicien. Afghanistan "à la gloire de la Route du Nord"
[Afghanistan: "The Glory of the Northern Route"]. Afghanistan 6,
no. 2, 32-39; no. 3, 11-19. 1951.
A geological tour of the northern Kabul-Doab Route on the Hindu
Kush; with explanations and identifications of the rocks and formations.

278 Rosset, Louis-Felicien. Participation à l'étude tectonique de l'Hindou-
Kouch. Sur "l'anomalie" du déversement des plis en direction nord-
sud [Participation in the Tectonic Study of the Hindu Kush. On the
Anomaly of the Turn of the Ridges in the North-South Direction]. Afghanistan 7, no. 2, 60-64; no. 3, 56-64; no. 4, 1-20; maps; bibliography. 1952.
Research on the tectonic structure of the Hindu Kush.

279 Rosset, Louis-Felicien. Phénomènes volcaniques anciens dans le nord
afghan [Ancient Volcanic Phenomena in the Afghan North]. Afghanistan 8, no. 4, 27-41. 1953.
Research on various geological aspects of the Hindu Kush region.

280 Rosset, Louis-Felicien. Voyages d'étude en Afghanistan [Study-Trips in
Afghanistan]. Afghanistan 8, no. 1, 20-33. 1953.
Report of a geological tour in the Maidan and Angarand valleys and
the Hindu Kush, with notes on the formations found in these regions.

281 Rosset, Louis-Felicien. Nouvelle prospection à Karkar (près Poul-i-khomry)
[New Exploration at Karkar (near Pol-i Khumri)]. Afghanistan 9, no. 1,
11-19. 1954.
Stratigraphic and paleontological description of the region around
Karkar.

282 Rosset, Louis-Felicien. Afghanistan "board de mer" [Afghanistan's "Sea
Coast"]. Afghanistan 9, no. 2, 27-35. 1954.
On the fossil evidence that proves the existence of the triassic Gulf of
Doab.

283 Rosset, Louis-Felicien. Parallèle entre la flore rhétienne du Gondwana
(partie péninsulaire) et celle de même époque (ferghana-angara) du
continent sino-sibérien. (Douab-Eshpochta-Saighan) [A Parallel between the Rhaetian Flora of Gondwana (Peninsular Part) and that of the
Same Epoch of the Sino-Siberian Continent. (Doab-Eshpochta-Saighan)].

Afghanistan 9, no. 3, 56-62; no. 4, 30-47. 1954.
A comparison between fossils of North Afghanistan, India, and South
Africa.

284 Rybitschka, Emil. Im gottgebenen Afghanistan als Gaste des Emirs [In
God-given Afghanistan as the Guest of the Amir]. Leipzig: F. A.
Brockhaus, 1927. Pp. xi, 295; map.

285 Ryshtya, Sayed Qasim. L'Afghanistan au point de vue géographique [Af-
ghanistan from the Geographical Point of View]. Afghanistan 2, no. 1,
16-22. 1947.
A general sketch, with emphasis on the mountain systems.

286 Schefer, Charles H. A. Itinéraires (de Pichaver à Kaboul, de Kaboul à
Qandahar, de Qandahar à Herat) (Extraits du Tarikh-i-Ahmad de
Muhammad Abdul Karim Monshi), trad. du persan [Itineraries (from
Peshawar to Kabul, from Kabul to Qandahar, from Qandahar to Herat)
(Extracts from the Tarikh-i-Ahmad of Muhammad Abdul Karim
Monshi), translated from Persian]. Paris: École Nationale des Langues
Orientales Vivantes, 1878. Pp. iii, 380; map.
The material is found in pages 361-375 of a volume in the series,
Receuil d'Itineraires.

287 Schwarz, Fred. Bakschisch und Feidah. Erinnerungen an Afghanistan
[Bakhshish and Faydeh. Recollections of Afghanistan]. Munich: F.
Bassermann, 1949. Pp. 120.
A general account of the country, apparently designed for younger
readers. The first sentence of the title may be translated as "Present
and Profit."

288 Sedqi, Mohammad Osman. Qandahar [Qandahar]. Afghanistan 7, no. 4,
21-34. 1952.
The situation and history of Afghanistan's second-largest city.

289 Sedqi, Mohammad Osman. La plaine de Herat [The Plain of Herat].
Afghanistan 7, no. 4, 54-55. 1952.
A description of the plain, its appearance, climate, and winds.

290 Sedqi, Mohammad Osman. Les villes d'Ariana [The Cities of Aryana].
Afghanistan 7, no. 1, 5-21; no. 2, 29-41; no. 3, 31-44. 1952.
A list of 140 cities of ancient Bactria, with an explanatory note on
the location and history of each.

II. GEOGRAPHY

291 See Afghanistan. Kabul: Defense Ministry Printing Press, 1959. Pp. 70;
   map.
   A "Short Tourist Guide of Afghanistan, " prepared by the Afghan Tourist Organization and including 51 illustrations.

292 Sellman, Roger R. An Outline Atlas of Eastern History. London: E.
   Arnold Ltd., 1954. Pp. 63.
   Fifty-three maps, chronologically arranged and with historical explanations of each, showing the spread of empires, and of religions,
   etc. Some ten of them are concerned with Afghanistan.

293 Serfaty, A. Au sujet d'un cas tératologique chez un scorpion afghan [On
   a Teratological Case in an Afghan Scorpion] . Afghanistan 3, no. 3,
   18-19. 1948.
   The author lists seven authenticated cases of scorpions with two tails,
   and gives a bibliography.

294 Sheptunov, I. Budni Kabula [Work Days in Kabul] . Sovremenny Vostok,
   no. 7, 33-36. 1958.
   Impressions of a visitor, with emphasis on projects built with Soviet aid.

295 Shor, Jean Bowie. After You, Marco Polo. New York: McGraw Hill Book
   Company, Inc., 1955. Pp. 294.
   Following the route of Marco Polo, the Shors journeyed across Asia,
   through untraveled parts of Afghanistan and the Wakhan Corridor, to
   Hunza. The description tends largely to the personal discomfort of the
   Shors. Their experiences in the huts of the Afghans are interesting,
   though unreliable as to general information.

296 *Shor, Jean Bowie and Franc Shor. We Took the Highroad in Afghanistan.
   National Geographic Magazine 98, 673-706. 1950.
   Lightly written, but very informative, account of a trip into the seldom
   visited Wakhan Corridor. Splendid color photographs.

297 Siiger, Halfdan. Henning Haslund-Christensen: In Memoriam. Afghanistan 3, no. 3, 33-35. 1948.
   A tribute to the head of the Danish Scientific Mission who died at Kabul.

298 Sinclair, Gordon. Khyber Caravan. Through Kashmir, Waziristan, Afghanistan, Baluchistan and Northern India. London: Hurst and Blackett,
   Ltd., 1936. Pp. 278; maps.

An American edition published in 1936 under the same title runs to 316 pages.

299 Singh, Narenderpal. Furrows in the Snow. New Delhi: Vidya Prakashan Bhavan, 1963. Pp. 147.
A record of travel in Afghanistan in 1958. Originally published in Punjabi under the title of Aryana.

300 Snesarev, A. E. Avganistan [Afghanistan]. Moscow, 1921.

301 Sokolov-Strakhov, K. V gornykh dolinakh Afganistana [In the Mountain Valleys of Afghanistan]. Moscow: Mpskovskoe T-vo Pisatelei, 1930. Pp. 78.

302 Spivack, M. R. The Figured Mountains of Afghanistan. Bayonne, N.J.: Y. Seldon (67 W. 37th St.), 1964.

303 Starmuhlner, Ferdinand. Salzseen und Steppen. Eine hindernisreiche Autoreise durch Persien und Afghanistan [Salt Seas and Steppes. An obstacle-filled Auto Tour through Persia and Afghanistan]. Vienna: Büchergilde Gutenberg, 1957. Pp. 208.

304 Stentz, Edward. The Climate of Afghanistan: Its Aridity, Dryness and Divisions. New York: Polish Institute of Arts and Sciences in America, 1946. Pp. 16; map.

305 Stentz, Edward. The Climate of Afghanistan: Its Aridity, Dryness and Divisions. Geographical Review 37, 672. 1947.
A note on Dr. Stentz' climatic-regions map of Afghanistan and his "dryness index."

306 Stentz, Edward. Earthquakes in Afghanistan. Afghanistan 1, no. 1, 41-50. 1946.
Afghanistan considered as part of the Hindu Kush seismic area.

307 Steponov, I. [From Mazar-i-Sharif to Kabul.] Vokrug Sveta, No. 6, pp. 43-48. Moscow, 1952.

308 Stewart, C. E. The Herat Valley and the Persian Border, from the Hari-Rud to Sistan. Proceedings of the Royal Geographical Society, New Monthly Series, 8, 137-156. 1886.
Discursive, disorganized account of wanderings and incidents, mostly on the Iranian side of the frontier. In 1885 he visited Herat and gives

an interesting description of the town. The author was Assistant Com-
missioner of the Afghan Boundary Commission.

309 Stratil-Sauer, G. From Leipzig to Kabul. An Account of my Motor-
Cycle Ride to Afghanistan and my Nine Months' Imprisonment in that
Country. London: Hutchinson, 1929. Pp. 284; map.
A mad idea and a crazy journey. English version of the German
original which had been published a year earlier at Berlin.

310 *Sykes, Christopher. Some Notes on a Recent Journey in Afghanistan.
Geographical Journal 84, 327-336; map. 1934.
A young English writer tells of a trip by private car from Iran to Herat,
and thence via the northern route to Kabul. Well written, keen observations on such subjects as city life at Herat and country life among
the Turkoman along the northern road.

311 Tanzi, Gastone. Viaggo in Afghanistan [Travel in Afghanistan]. Milan:
Maia, 1929. Pp. 267.
The second part of this work by an Italian traveler concerns Afghanistan: Nell'inquiete Afghanistan [In Restless Afghanistan], pp. 135-
267. Rather general travel description, augmented by observations on
the government of King Amanullah.

312 Tarzi, Mahmud. Siyahet-nameh-yi sih git'eh-yi ruy-i zamin [Travel
Account of Three Continents]. Kabul: 'Inayet, 1333 [1915].
Account in Persian of a journey through Asia, Africa and Europe by
the author in the year 1890 A.D. Tarzi, one of the first Afghan
journalists, broadened the local horizon between 1912 and 1916 by
publishing a number of works, including translations from French and
Turkish. He won favor under Amir Amanullah who became his son-
in-law and made Tarzi the principal editor and then Foreign Minister.

313 *Tate, George Passman. The Frontier of Baluchistan. Travels on the Borders of Persia and Afghanistan. London: Witherby and Co., 1909.
Pp. vi, 261; maps.
Professional study by a member of the Survey of India, attached to the
two MacMahon missions of 1884-85 and 1903-04, dealing with the
geography, water supply and population of a part of the Afghan-Indian
frontier.

314 *Tate, George Passman. Seistan. A Memoir on the History, Topography,
Ruins and People of the Country. 2 vols. Calcutta: Superintendent

Government Printing, India, 1910-1912. Pp. (1) 1-272; (2) 272-378. A uniquely detailed and valuable source, although the bulk of the descriptive material concerns territory within Iran rather than in Afghanistan.

315 Thomas, Lowell J. Beyond Khyber Pass into Forbidden Afghanistan. Revised Edition, Illustrated with Many Photographs Taken by Harry A. Chase and the Author. New York: Grosset and Dunlap, 1925. Pp. xvii, 255; maps.
An account of a journey through Afghanistan where, in 1925, few Europeans were admitted. There are vivid characterizations of the Afghans and much informative (and highly-colored) background material.

316 Tichy, Herbert. Zum Heiligstenberg der Welt. Auf Landstrassen und Pilgerfahrten in Afghanistan, Indien und Tibet. Geleitwort von Sven Hedin [To the Holiest Mountain in the World. On Highways and Pilgrimages in Afghanistan, India and Tibet. Foreword by Sven Hedin]. Vienna: W. L. Seidel und Sohn, 1937. Pp. 192; 2 maps.
A young Austrian geologist set out by motorcycle to complement the explorations of Sven Hedin. Afghanistan was the first country visited and the tales from this country set the atmosphere for the balance of the book.

317 Tichy, Herbert. Tibetan Adventure. Travels through Afghanistan, India and Tibet. With a Preface by Sven Hedin. London: Faber and Faber, 1938. Pp. 261; 2 maps.
An English version of the original work in German (see no. 316).

318 *Tichy, Herbert. Afghanistan, das Tor nach Indien [Afghanistan, the Gateway to India]. Leipzig: W. Goldmann, 1940. Pp. 237; bibliography; 4 maps.
Part I is a political and military history of Afghanistan. Part II, more briefly, deals with the people, the present position and the future. Good background material.

319 Tilman, H. W. Wakkan: Or How to Vary a Route. Journal of the Royal Central Asian Society. 35, 249-254. 1948.
Detailed record, with attention concentrated upon topographical features of a trip on horseback from Kashgar through the Afghan corridor to Fayzabad in Afghanistán and thence to Chitral. Date of trip not given, but apparently a number of years prior to this publication.

320 Toynbee, Arnold J. Between Oxus and Jumna. London: Oxford University Press, 1961. Pp. 211.

321 Toynbee, Arnold. A Journey in Afghanistan and in the North-West Frontier. Royal Central Asian Journal 49, no. 3-4, (1962): 277-88.
The author reports that enmity between Afghanistan and Pakistan will inevitably lead to Soviet penetration of both countries unless they compose their differences (which he considers unlikely).

322 Trinkler, Emil. Quer durch Afghanistan nach Indien [Through Afghanistan to India]. Berlin: Kurt Vowinckel, 1925. Pp. 234; sketch map. (See no. 324.)

323 *Trinkler, Emil. Afghanistan. Eine landskundliche Studie auf Grund der vorhandenen Materiel und einiger Beobachtung [Afghanistan: An Informed Study Based on Existing Material and Personal Observation]. Petermanns Mitteilungen, Ergänzungsheft Nr. 196. Gotha: Justus Perthes, 1928. Pp. 80; maps; plates; bibliography.
A fairly comprehensive summary of geographical and anthropological knowledge. Part I deals with the geology and geography of the mountains, the climates, rivers, flora and fauna, etc. Part II deals with racial distribution, cities (with a digression on the probable routes of the early conquerors and explorers), agricultural and natural resources.

324 Trinkler, Emil. Through the Heart of Afghanistan; Edited and Translated by B. K. Featherstone. Boston: Houghton, Mifflin Co., 1928. Pp. 246; map.
The original work in German was published in 1925 (see no. 322). The author was a geologist accompanying members of a German trading company from Russia through Afghanistan to India in 1923. Knowing Persian he acquired and recorded information on a large range of subjects: crossing the heart of the country from Herat to Kabul, he prospected for coal and iron.

325 Vambery, Arminius. Travels in Central Asia, Being an Account of a Journey from Teheran across the Turkoman Desert on the Eastern Shore of the Caspian to Khiva, Bokhara and Samarcand Performed in the Year 1863. London: John Murray, 1864. Pp. xxvi, 443; map.
A member of the Hungarian Academy who undertook a linguistic mission for that Academy in Central Asia. Calls special attention to the advance of Russia in Asia. Chapters XII, XIII, XIV, and XXIV are especially concerned with Afghanistan.

326 Vambery, Arminius. The Geographical Nomenclature of the Disputed
Country between Merv and Herat. Proceedings of the Royal Geographical Society 7, 591-596. 1885.
   A serious attempt, which falls short of a real contribution due to lack
   of support from reliable, earlier sources. In this same volume, F.
   Goldsmid made additions and corrections to the article on pages 823-
   824.

327 Vambery, Arminius, trans. The Travels and Adventures of the Turkish
Admiral Sidi Ali Reis in India, Afghanistan, Central Asia, and Persia,
during the Years 1553-56. London: Luzac and Co., 1899. Pp. xviii,
123.
   The original manuscript of these travels had been published in its native Turkish, in German and in French prior to the English edition.
   This English edition contains notes and a more scholarly appreciation
   of the original text. Two chapters deal with Afghanistan: one with
   the general area of Badakhshan and the other with the region of Kabul.

328 Vertunni, Renato. Afghanistan. Afghanistan 4, no. 2, 18-24. 1949.
   Impressions of landscape, literature, legend and modern Kabul, with
   imagined sound effects of music, airplanes and national songs.

329 Vigne, Godfrey T. A Personal Narrative of a Visit to Ghuzni, Kabul,
and Afghanistan, and of a Residence at the Court of Dost Mohamet;
with Notices of Runjit Sing, Khiva, and the Russian Expedition. London: Whittaker and Co., 1840. Pp. xiii, 479; map.
   From Peshawar the British author crossed into Afghanistan in the
   Gomal area, south of the Khyber Pass, and made his way to Ghazni
   and thence to Kabul before returning to Peshawar. Useful observations made in tribal territory (Sulayman Khel) and a good account of
   the court of Amir Dost Muhammad.

330 Visit Afghanistan. London: Information Bureau, Royal Afghan Embassy,
n.d. Pp. 39.
   Well-illustrated, clearly written presentation of the tourist attractions
   of the country.

331 Wahab Khan, Abdul. Observations concerning Andkhoy Water. Afghanistan 5, no. 2, 36-46; no. 3, 18-24. 1950.
   The rivers and springs that irrigate the agricultural land, including a
   detailed description of the country.

332 Waley, Arthur, trans. The Travels of an Alchemist. The Journey of the
Taoist Ch'and-Ch'un from China to the Hindukush at the Summons of
Chingiz Khan. London: George Routledge and Sons, Ltd., 1931.
Pp. xi, 166; map.
At the end of the long journey from east of Peking the monk and his
companion, who recorded the trip, crossed the Oxus River and passed
through Balkh and then over the Hindu Kush to near the site of Kabul.
Extremely summary account of the route and things observed.

333 Whistler, Hugh. Materials for the Ornithology of Afghanistan. Journal
of the Bombay Natural History Society, 45, 61-72; 106-122; 462-
485. 1945.

334 Williams, Maynard Owen. The Citroen-Haardt Trans-Asiatic Expedition
Reaches Kashmir. National Geographic Magazine, 60, 387-444. 1931.
In this account of a trip across Asia several pages and a number of excellent photographs are devoted to the crossing of Afghanistan following the long route from Herat through Qandahar, Ghazni, and Kabul
to Peshawar.

335 *Williams, Maynard Owen. Afghanistan Makes Haste Slowly. National
Geographic Magazine 64, 731-769. 1933.
Ancient manners and modes of life are contrasted, through illustrations, with the efforts of the Afghan government to modernize the
land.

336 *Williams, Maynard Owen. Back to Afghanistan. National Geographic
Magazine, 90, 517-544. 1946.
After thirteen years the writer returns to Afghanistan and comments
on the far-reaching changes effected during that time. Illustrated
with remarkable color photographs.

337 Wilson, Andrew. North from Kabul. London: George Allen & Unwin
Ltd., 1961. Pp. 190.
According to the dust jacket, "This is Afghanistan as few people have
seen it and come back to tell the story," . . . "a country . . .
filled with rumor and intrigue, and made precarious by the dangerous
political liaison of an autocratic government . . ." The text is somewhat less lurid.

338 *Wood, John. A Personal Narrative of a Journey to the Source of the River
Oxus by the Route of the Indus, Kabul, and Badakhshan, Performed under

the Sanction of the Supreme Government of India in the Years 1836, 1837, and 1838. London: John Murray, 1841. Pp. xv, 424.

Dispatched by the head of the British Mission in Afghanistan, the lieutenant accompanied a British doctor across the Hindu Kush to enter the service of the ruler of Qunduz. That power consenting, the author set out in search of the source of the Oxus and penetrated far into remote territory. The small-scale map in the volume corrects prior versions of this topography. A second edition of 1847 contains additional material on the geography of the Oxus Valley.

339 Yate, Arthur Campbell. England and Russia Face to Face in Asia; Travels with the Afghan Boundary Commission. London: W. Blackwood an Sons, 1887. Pp. vi, 481; folding map.

Covers much the same ground as the account of the work of the Boundary Commission by his brother Charles (see no. 341), but is not as complete, since the author left before the survey work was finished.

340 *Yate, Charles Edward. Notes on the City of Herat. Journal of the Asiatic Society of Bengal 56, 84-106. 1887.

An article of scholarly value for its description of Moslem monuments of Herat and the translation into English of a number of Persian inscriptions on these structures.

341 *Yate, Charles Edward. Northern Afghanistan, or Letters from the Afghan Boundary Commission. With Route Maps. Edinburgh and London: W. Blackwood and Sons, 1888. Pp. viii, 430; maps.

Describes the activity of the commission--by a British officer member--in 1885 in northwestern Afghanistan and then their long trip back to Lahore through Afghanistan. The closing chapters deal with the return of the mission in 1887 for the actual demarcation of the frontier. Includes a plan of Balkh, a map of the northwestern frontier of Afghanistan and sketch maps.

342 Yule, H. Papers Connected with the Upper Oxus Regions. Journal of the Royal Geographical Society, 42, 438-481; map. 1872.

Contains Pandit Manphul's report on Badakhshan, an account of a journey by Munshi Faiz Baksh from Peshawar through Kabul and Badakhshan to Kashgar, and corrections of the editor to erroneous notions on the topography of the Upper Oxus regions.

II. GEOGRAPHY

343 Zachova, Eliska. Tajemny Afghanistan [Mysterious Afghanistan].
Prague: Statni nakladztelstvi detske literatury, 1960.

344 Zaman, Mohammad. The Regions of Drybelts in Afghanistan. Afghanistan 6, no. 2, 63-68. 1951.
The location of the dry-belts, their vegetation, and its uses.

345 Ziemke, Kurt. Als deutscher Gesandter in Afghanistan [As the German
Envoy in Afghanistan]. Stuttgart and Berlin: Deutsche Verlagsanstalt,
1939. Pp. 303; map.
Accounts of travel in Afghanistan in 1933. First from Lahore through
the Khyber Pass to Kabul, and then a "circular tour" of the country.
The closing section deals with life at Kabul and with an estimation
of the character of the Afghans.

346 *Zurmati, Fazl Ahmad. Khosh amadid bah Kabul [Welcome to Kabul].
Kabul: Matba'eh-yi 'umumi, 1330 [1951]. Pp. 1-36; 1-24; plan of
Kabul.
The left-hand cover reads "Welcome to Kabul," followed by 36 pages
in English; the right cover has the Persian title, followed by the Per-
sian text.

III. HISTORY

Pre-Achaemenid; Achaemenid; Parthian;
Sassanian; Buddhistic; Islamic;
Anglo-Afghan and Anglo-Russian
relations; foreign relations

The very names of the historical periods of Afghanistan reflect its focal position in Asia as an area which attracted various ethnic groups, as a corridor for migratory movements and conquering armies, and as a region which in turn was subject and then overlord. Certain of those periods of the thousand or so years prior to the influx of the Moslems into the region have been studied by scholars--the intensive concentration on the Buddhistic by French linguists and archaeologists is an example--but major problems related to chronology, the extent and duration of local kingdoms, the direction and force of artistic and cultural influences, and the origin of ethnic groups remain unresolved. Most welcome for everyone interested in this part of the world would be a fresh, new history of the area prior to Islam. The Afghan scholars are themselves producing such a work in Persian, but it may be too detailed and too unemphatic to fill the gap.

For the Islamic centuries, the source material in Arabic, Persian, and Pushtu is moderately adequate. It should be noted that Afghan scholars are engaged in editing and publishing these manuscripts, a number of which are quite unknown to foreign linguists and historians. In addition, some of these same local scholars are writing accounts of the reigns of noted rulers, based upon this newly available material.

As concerns the history of Afghanistan in the nineteenth and early twentieth centuries, it has been pointed out that British writers publishing in India and England dominated this field, although Russian scholars did produce some important works which failed to have any impact abroad. The contemporary history of the country is not receiving adequate attention: too many current articles are based upon speculation and personal attitudes rather than on documentation. Soviet writers appear to be very active, and some of their material is published in foreign languages when it is regarded advisable to stress certain policy or propaganda lines. What are needed, however, are serious studies based on official documents and reports and on first-hand contact with the officials and individuals now engaged in making the history of the Afghans.

347 Abaeva, T. G. Ocherki istorii Badakhshana [Sketches from the History of Badakhshan]. Tashkent: Izdatel'stvo "Nauka" Uzbekskoy SSR, 1964. Pp. 164; bibliography.

The first comprehensive study of a comparatively little-known area of Afghanistan. Its three chapters concern its geography and resources,

trade routes, and an historical and political outline from ancient
times. Based on original and secondary sources.

348 'Abd al-Karim 'Alavi. Muharabeh-i Kabul va Qandahar [The War of
Kabul and Qandahar]. Lucknow, 1848. Pp. 87.
Lithographed account in Persian of the first British invasion of Afghanistan in 1838-42, based in part on a heroic poem, Akbar nameh, on
the deeds of Akbar Khan, by Qasim Jan. Another edition was put out
at Lucknow in 1850 and one at Cawnpore in 1851.

349 'Abd al-Karim 'Alavi. Tarikh-i Ahmad [History of Ahmad]. Lucknow:
Sultan al-matabi, 1266 [1850]. Pp. 56.
A lithographed work in Persian dealing with the Durrani dynasty from
the reign of Ahmad Shah to the flight of Muhammad Shah in 1797.
Based upon the Husayn Shahi of Imam al-Din Husayn Chishti (see
no. 409).

350 'Abd al-Rahman Khan. Taj al-tavarikh, ya'ni savarat-i 'umri [The
Crown of Histories, or an Account of a Life]. 2 vols., lithographed.
Kabul, 1904.
Apparently a revised Persian edition of no. 536.

351 Adye, John. Sitana: A Mountain Campaign on the Borders of Afghanistan
in 1863. London: Richard Bentley, 1867. Pp. iv, 101; sketch maps.

352 al-Afghani, Jamal al-Din. Tatimmat al-bayan fi tarikh al-Afghan
[Completion of the Exposition of the History of the Afghans]. 'Ali
Yusuf al-Kurdili, ed. Cairo, 1901. Pp. 192.
A little-known work, edited in Arabic by 'Ali Yusuf al-Kurdili, by
the renowned reformer of Islam.

353 Afghanistan. Revue du Monde Musulman 8, 491-498.1909.
Contains informative material on the Amir Habibullah, including the
results of his voyage to India in 1907.

354 Ahmad Jan. Tarikh-i Afghanistan [History of Afghanistan]. Peshawar,
1893.
One of several well-known works by a Pushtu scholar who lived at
Peshawar and taught that language to British personnel.

355 *Aitchison, C. U. A Collection of Treaties, Engagements and Sanads Relating to India and Neighbouring Countries 13, 203-305; appendices
clxxi-ccix. Calcutta: Superintendent of Government Printing, India,
1933.

III. HISTORY

As indicated, this thirteenth volume of the long series contains treaties and state papers relating to Afghanistan.

356 Akhramovich, Roman T. Nezavisimyy Afganistan. 40 let nezavisimosti
[Independent Afghanistan. 40 years of Independence]. Moscow:
Izdatel'stvo Vostochnoy Literatury, 1958. Pp. 269.

357 Akhramovich, Roman T. K kharakteristike vneshney politiki Afganistana
v nachal'nyy period Vtoroy Mirovoy Voyny, 1939-1941gg [On the
characteristics of Afghanistan's foreign policy at the beginning of the
Second World War, 1939-1941]. Kratkiye Soobshcheniya Instituta
Vostokovedeniya 37, 1-8. Moscow, 1960.

358 Akhramovich, Roman T. Afganistan posle vtoroy mirovoy voyny - ocherk
istorii [Afghanistan after World War Two - An Historical Outline].
Moscow: Izdatel'stvo Vostochnoy Literatury, 1961. Pp. 175.
Based primarily on the Afghan press, the work describes the political
and economic situation during World War II, discusses international
relations from 1946 to 1953, characterizes the period of Prime Minister Daud, and closes with a study of developments through 1960.

359 Akhramovich, Roman T. Mirolyubivaya politika Afganistana [Peaceful
policy of Afghanistan], in Bor'ba Narodov Azii za Mir, 1945-1961.
Moscow: Izdatel'stvo Vostochnoy Literatury, 1962. Pp. 41-61.

360 Ali, Mohammed. Aryana or Ancient Afghanistan. Kabul: Government
Printing House, n.d. (1957). Pp. 117.
An account of the ancient history of the region up to the coming of
Islam.

361 Ali, Mohammed. Afghanistan. The National Awakening. Lahore: Punjab Educational Press, 1958. Pp. 142.
Concerns the reigns of the Hotaki and Durrani rulers.

362 Ali, Mohammed. Afghanistan (The Mohammedzai Period). Lahore: Punjab Educational Press, 1959. Pp. 211.
A political history of Afghanistan from the beginning of the thirteenth
century, with emphasis on the foreign relations of the country.

363 Ali, Mohammad. Afghanistan, the War of Independence, 1919. Lahore:
Punjab Educational Press, 1960. Pp. 62; map.

364 Ali, Mohammad. Afghanistan. An Historical Sketch. Kabul: Government Printing House, n.d. Pp. 27.

III. HISTORY

365 Ali Khan, Muhammad. Progress in Afghanistan. Asiatic Review n.s. 32,
863-866. London, 1936.
Praise of the advances made in government and education since the
accession of Nadir Shah in 1930.

366 'Ali Quli mirza. I'tizad al-Saltaneh. Tarikh-i vaqa'i' va Savanih-i
Afghanistan [History of Accidents and Events of Afghanistan]. Tehran:
Muhammad Husayn Mirza, 1273 [1856-57]. Pp. 216; map.
A lithographed work of moderate value in Persian.

367 Allen, R. A. and R. K. Ramazani. Afghanistan: Wooed But Not Won.
Swiss Review of World Affairs 7, no. 7, 16-19. 1957.
A review of Afghanistan's position with respect to Soviet aid and to
relations with the U.S.S.R.

368 Amoss, Harold L. The Story of Afghanistan. Wichita: McCormick-
Mathers, 1965. Pp. 164; index.
One of the Global Culture Series of the publisher. A story line con-
veys an excellent account of the country for young readers.

369 Andrew, Sir William Patrick. Our Scientific Frontier. London: W. H.
Allen and Company, 1880. Pp. 103; appendices.
Covers a number of broad topics such as a description of Afghanistan,
the independent tribes of the Afghan frontier and their relations with
the British, probable routes of attack toward India through Afghanistan, and a consideration of the powindeh, or soldier-merchants of
Afghanistan.

370 Arabadzhyan, A. Z. Vneshnyaya politika i economicheskoye razvitiye
Irana i Afganistana [The foreign policy and economic development of
Persia and Afghanistan]. Problemy Vostokovedeniya, no. 3, 42-54.
Moscow, 1960.

371 Arends, A. K., ed. and trans. Istoriya Mas'uda (1030-1041) [The History of Mas'ud]. Tashkent: Akad. Nauk Uzbekskoy S.S.R., 1962.
Pp. 748.
First translation into a European language of the remarkable history
by Abul Fazl Bayhaqi.

372 Argyll, George Douglas Campbell, 1st duke of. The Afghan Question
from 1841 to 1878. London: Strahan and Company, Ltd., 1879.
Pp. 288.
First-hand knowledge of the area sparingly reflected in a rather pon-
derous and detailed survey of the British position and actions toward

-55-

III. HISTORY

Afghanistan. See also no. 438.

373 Aristov, N. A. Anglo-indiiskii "kavkaz." Stolknoveniia Anglii s
avganskimi pogranichnymi plenenami [The Anglo-Indian "Caucasus."
English Clashes with Afghan Border Tribes]. Zhivaia Starina 10. St.
Petersburg, 1896.

374 Artamonov, E. American Penetration into Afghanistan. New Times,
no. 14, 11-14. Moscow, 1949.
An indignant Soviet protest against "mercenary, military and political imperialist" activities of American interests in Afghanistan;
pointing to the damage already done there and to the rivalry between
the British and Americans for control.

375 Ashe, Waller, ed. Personal Records of the Kandahar Campaign, by Officers Engaged Therein. Edited and Annotated, with an Introduction by
Major Ashe. London: David Bogue, 1881. Pp. lxxvi, 252.
The Second Anglo-Afghan War as reflected in accounts of British participants: the original advance on Kabul, the massacre of the British
at Kabul, and the Qandahar campaign.

376 Atalla, Qazi Khan Sahib. Da Pushtanu tarikh [The Pushtun History]. 2
vols. Peshawar: Manzor Am Press, 1947-1948.
Volume 1 covers the history of Afghanistan from 1622 to 1838 and
vol. 2 from 1838 to 1842. The work is in Pushtu.

377 Atkinson, James. The Expedition into Afghanistan. Notes and Sketches
Descriptive of the Country, Contained in a Personal Narrative during
the Campaign of 1839 and 1840 up to the Surrender of Dost Mohamed
Khan. London: W. H. Allen and Co., 1842. Pp. xx, 428; map.
Of less interest as concerns the account of part of the First Anglo-
Afghan War, by a participant, than for chapters devoted to the
Durrani family and the person of Shah Shoja'.

378 Babakhodzhayev, A. Kh. Iz istorii bukharo-afganskikh otnosheniy, 1920-
1924gg [From the history of Bukhara-Afghan relations, 1920-1924].
Izvestiya Akademii Nauk Uzbekskoy SSR, Seriya Obshchestvennykh
Nauk, no. 4, 8-13. Tashkent, 1960.

379 Babakhodzhayev, Marat A. Bor'ba Afganistana za nezavisimost', 1838-
1842 [Afghanistan in its Struggle for Independence, 1838-1842].
Moscow: Izdatel'stvo Vostochnoy Literatury, 1960. Pp. 160; bibliography.

III. HISTORY

380 Bacon, Elizabeth E. and Alfred E. Hudson. Afghanistan Waits. Asia 41,
31-36. New York, 1941.

381 Badakhshi, Shah Abdullah. Yamgan. Afghanistan 7, no. 4, 56-58. 1952.
A short description of the district and its people.

382 *Bahar, Malik al-Shu'ara', ed. Tarikh-i Sistan, ta'lif dar hudud-i 445-
725 [History of Sistan, Composed between 445-725 A.H.]. Tehran:
Fardin va-bivadar, 1314 [1935].
An excellent contemporary edition of an important work in Persian by
an anonymous historian.

383 al-Balkhi, Abu Bekr ibn 'Abdullah 'Umar ibn Da'ud al-Vayz Safi al-Din.
Faza'il-i Balkh [The Virtues of Balkh].
Translation into Persian of an Arabic manuscript written at the end of
the fifteenth century. The work contains a history of the province, a
description of the town, traditions relating to the superiority of the
town, and the lives of some 70 of the revered inhabitants. Copies of
the manuscript are in the Bibliothèque Nationale and other collections.

384 Ballis, William B. Recent Soviet Relations with Afghanistan. Bulletin of
the Institute for the Study of the U.S.S.R. 13, no. 6, 3-13. 1966.
Traces the nature of these relations from the nineteenth century to the
present.

385 *Barthold, Wilhelm. Turkestan down to the Mongol Invasion. London:
Luzac and Co., 2d ed., 1928. Pp. 513; folding map.
A reference work of great value, displaying vast erudition by the late
Russian scholar. Includes the details of the history of Central Asia in
the Moslem centuries prior to the Mongol invasions, a discussion of
the source material--assembled in a comprehensive bibliography--
and a geographical survey of Transoxiana. The work is in the E. J.
W. Gibb Memorial Series, n.s. 5.

386 Barthold, Wilhelm. Tarikh-i siyasi va ijtima'i Asiya markazi ta qarn
davazdeh [Political and Social History of Central Asia to the Twelfth
Century]. Kabul: Matba'eh Pohantun, 1344 [1965]. Pp. 270.
A Persian translation by Ali Muhammad Rahnuma of no. 385.

387 Beaurecueil, S. de Laugier de. Les Publications de la Société d'Histoire
d'Afghanistan [The Publications of the Historical Society of Afghani-
stan]. Mélanges, Institut Dominicain d'Études Orientales du Cairo 7,
236-240. 1962-1963.

Lists 12 items in European languages and 52 works in Persian or in Pushtu.

388 Bellew, Henry Walter. Journal of a Political Mission to Afghanistan in 1857, under Major (now Colonel) Lumsden; With an Account of the Country and People. London: Smith, Elder and Co., 1862. Pp. xv, 480.
   The first part of the book is the author's maiden effort to describe the history, country and people of Afghanistan--an effort repeated and expanded in his later works. The second part describes the route of the mission and tells of its purpose and results.

389 *Bellew, Henry Walter. Afghanistan and the Afghans. Being a Brief Review of the History of the Country and an Account of its People, with a Special Reference to the Present Crisis and War with the Amir Shir Ali Khan. London: Sampson Low, Marston, Searle and Rivington, 1879. Pp. 230.
   A sketch of the history of the country precedes a rather lengthy summary of Anglo-Afghan relations. The author favors the so-called "Forward Policy" of bold British action to counter the threat of Russian advance in Asia.

390 Bennet. Biographical Sketch of Shah Soojah, Ex-King of Cabul, Written by Himself, at Loodianah, in 1826-27. Translated by . . . Lieutenant Bennet of Artillery. Asiatic Journal n.s. 30, Pt. 2, 6-15. London, 1839.

391 Besant, Annie Wood. England, India and Afghanistan and the Story of Afghanistan; Or, Why the Tory Government Gags the India Press. Madras: Theosophical Publishing House, 1931. Pp. 123.
   First printed in London in 1879.

392 Binava, 'Abd al-Ra'uf. Mir Ways nikeh [Mir Ways the Ancestor]. Kabul: Matba'eh-yi 'umumi, 1325 [1946]. Pp. 114; bibliography.
   An historical study in Pushtu.

393 Binava, 'Abd al-Ra'uf. Hotakiha [The Hotakis]. Kabul: Matba'eh-yi doulati, 1335 [1956]. Pp. 177.
   Deals with the reigns of Shah Muhammad, Shah Ashraf, and Shah Husayn of the Hotaki dynasty in Persian.

394 Biryukor, A. The Soviet Union and Afghanistan. New Times 22, 16-17. 1960.

III. HISTORY

Emphasizes the friendly, selfless attitude of the U.S.S.R. toward Afghanistan, in contrast to the alleged rapacious attitude of the United States.

395 Boldyrev, A. N., ed. Ta'rikh-i-Badakhshan ("Istoriya Badakhshana") [History of Badakhshan]. Leningrad: Izdatel'stvo Leningradskoho universiteta, 1959. Pp. 68 and 253; index.
The second part of the work gives the Persian text of the history.

396 Bosworth, Clifford E. The Imperial Policy of the early Ghaznavids. Islamic Studies 1, no. 3, 49-82. 1962.

397 Bosworth, Clifford E. The Titulature of the Early Ghaznavids. Oriens 15, 210-233. 1962.

398 Bosworth, Clifford E. Early Sources for the History of the first four Ghaznavid Sultans (977-1041). Islamic Quarterly 7, nos. 1/2, 3-22. 1963.

399 *Bosworth, Clifford E. The Ghaznavids. Their Empire in Afghanistan and Eastern Iran 994:1040. Edinburgh: Edinburgh University Press, 1963. Pp. xi, 331; maps; bibliography; index.
Thorough research in original sources, resulting in work of outstanding merit and interest.

400. *Boukhary, Mir Abdoul Kerim. Histoire de l'Asie centrale (Afghanistan, Boukhara, Khiva, Khoqand) depuis les dernières années du règne de Nadir Chah (1153), jusqu'en 1233 de l'Hégire (1740-1818). Publiée, traduite et annotée par Charles Schefer [History of Central Asia (Afghanistan, Bokhara, Khiva, Khoqand) from the Last Years of the Reign of Nadir Shah (1153) to the Year 1233 of the Hegira (1740-1818). Edited, Translated and Annotated by Charles Schefer]. Paris: Leroux, 1876. Pp. vii, 306; map.
Pages 9-92 tell the stories of Ahmad Shah and those of his descendants who ruled in Afghanistan.

401 *Bouvat, Lucien. Essai sur la civilisation timouride [Essay on the Timurid Civilization]. Journal Asiatique 208, 193-299. 1926.
A minutely detailed examination of almost every aspect of life under Timur and his successors.

402 Bushev, P. P. Gerat i anglo-iranskaya voyna 1856-1857 g.g. [Herat and the Anglo-Iranian War of 1856-1857]. Moscow: Izdatel'stvo vostochnoy

literaturī, 1959. Pp. 251; bibliography; index.
The extensive bibliography includes many titles in Russian.

403 *Caroe, Olaf. The Pathans 550 B.C.-A.D. 1957. London: Macmillan
& Co. Ltd., 1958. Pp. xxii, 521; appendices; glossary; maps.
A monumental work by a former British official who was governor of
the Northwest Frontier Province from 1945 through 1947. Concerns
the origins of the "Pakhtu," their history in the Muslim Middle Ages,
the periods of the Durrani and Sikh rulers, and the British period.

404 Caspani, P. E. The First American in Afghanistan. Afghanistan 2, no.
3, 37-42. 1947.
The story of John Harlan (see no. 468).

405 Castagne, Joseph A. Les relations nippo-afghanes [Japanese-Afghan Re-
lations]. France-Japon (Journal) 7, 88-89. Paris, 1935.
A very brief sketch of the subject, with some details on the first representatives from each country to the other.

406 *Castagne, Joseph A. Soviet Imperialism in Afghanistan. Foreign Affairs 13, 698-703. 1935.
An exceedingly well-informed article by a French specialist on Soviet
activities among Moslems within and without the U.S.S.R. Traces
the Soviet attitude toward Afghanistan from 1919 up through their active support of the last days of the reign of Amir Amanullah.

407 Causes of the Afghan War, Being a Selection of the Papers Laid before
Parliament, with a Connecting Narrative and Comment. London:
Chatto and Windus, 1879. Pp. xii, 325.

408 Chatelier, A. le. L'Emir d'Afghanistan aux Indes [The Amir of Afghanistan in India]. Revue du Monde Musulman 2, 35-49. 1907.
Describes the visit paid to India by the Amir Habibullah in 1906.

409 *Chishti, Imam al-Din Husayn. Husayn Shahi [(The Book of) Husayn
Shahi].
An important manuscript, copies of which are found in leading collections. Completed in 1798 A.D., the author writes in Persian of
the times of the first Durrani rulers—Ahmad Shah, Timur Shah, and
Shah Zaman—and of events in which he took part. The work is
named in honor of the author's spiritual guide and literary master.

410 *Chokaiev, Mustafa. The Situation in Afghanistan. Asiatic Review 26,

324-339. 1930.
Contains a detailed analysis of the fall of King Amanullah and of the Soviet attitude toward this event and toward Habibullah.

411 *Churchill, Rogers Platt. The Anglo-Russian Convention of 1907. Cedar Rapids, Iowa: The Torch Press, 1939. Pp. 365.
Of particular interest is Chapter VI: The Convention Respecting Afghanistan, on pages 269-308.

412 La civilisation iranienne (Perse, Afghanistan, Iran Extérieur) [Iranian Civilization (Persia, Afghanistan, Outer Iran)]. Paris: Payot, 1952. Pp. 346.
This general work, produced by some 21 French scholars, is not identified by the name of an editor. Two chapters, comprising some 80 pages, deal specifically with Afghanistan in the sketchy, impressionist manner that characterizes the volume.

413 Clifford, Mary Louise. The Land and People of Afghanistan. New York: J. B. Lippincott, 1962. Pp. 160; index.
A well-written account for younger readers.

414 Correspondence Relating to Persia and Afghanistan. London: J. Harrison and Son, 1839. Pp. xi, 524.
Official correspondence of the British Foreign Office with its representatives in India and elsewhere.

415 Courcy, Kenneth de, ed. Report on India and Afghanistan. Intelligence Digest: Review of World Affairs 9, no. 107, 9-12.
A "special observer's" report on the Northwest Frontier Province: on the political situation there, recommending immediate settlement. Includes a very brief historical sketch of modern Afghanistan.

416 Curzon, George Nathaniel. Russia in Central Asia in 1889, and the Anglo-Russian Question. London: Longmans, Green and Co., 2d ed., 1889. Pp. xiii, 477; folding maps; bibliography.
The second edition of an exhaustive and soundly informative account of the spread of the Russian empire.

417 Dai, Shen-yu. China and Afghanistan. China Quarterly (London) 25, 213-221. 1966.
Traces this history of relations between the two countries from the earliest times to the present.

418 *Davies, C. Collin. The Problem of the North-West Frontier, 1890-1908,
     with a Survey of the Policy since 1849. Cambridge University Press,
     1932. Pp. xii, 220; 3 maps.
     Authoritative study by a former British officer in India who then
     taught the history of India at the University of London. The political
     and human geography of the area is described as is the establishment
     and maintenance of the frontier in question. Pages 153-173 discuss
     the "Afghan Problem," and the bibliography lists Parliamentary Papers
     on Afghanistan.

419 De Croze, Joel. Afghanistan Today. Journal of the Indian Institute of
     International Affairs 3, 29-49. New Delhi, 1947.
     A well-informed, rather broad survey of efforts to bring the country
     abreast of the modern world, with emphasis upon political relations.

420 *Defremery, M. C., trans. Histoire des Sultans Ghourides extraite du
     Rouzet Essefa . . . de Mirkhond; traduite en français, . . . par
     M. C. Defremery [History of the Sultans of Ghor Taken from the
     Ruzeh es-Safa of Mirkhond, Translated into French. . . . by M. C.
     Defremery]. Journal Asiatique, ser. 4, 2, 167-200; 3, 258-291.
     1844.
     (For the complete edition of this work see no. 494.)

421 *Dickson, W. E. R. East Persia. A Backwater of the Great War. London:
     E. Arnold and Co., 1924. Pp. viii, 279; folding map.
     A first-hand account of experiences during World War I. Chapter XII,
     "The Afghan War of 1919," describes the measures taken by the au-
     thor along the Persian-Afghan frontier in anticipation of possible
     fighting.

422 *Dodwell, H. H., ed. The Cambridge History of the British Empire, vol.
     4. British India, 1497-1858. Cambridge University Press, 1929. Pp.
     xxii, 683.
     Chapter XXVII, Afghanistan, Russia and Persia, by W. A. J. Archbold,
     including pages 483-520, deals with the situation in Afghanistan from
     the end of the eighteenth century until 1842. The detailed account
     of political maneuvering and of British military triumphs and disaster
     is documented from official sources. (This same work is Volume 5 of
     the Cambridge History of India.)

423 Dodwell, H. H., ed. The Cambridge Shorter History of India. Cam-
     bridge University Press, 1934. Pp. xix, 970; sketch maps.
     Extraordinarily condensed and crowded account, featuring thousands

of names of people and places. Regarding Afghanistan, the most
pertinent material is in Pt. I, Chapter V: Foreign Invaders of North-
West India and in several chapters within Pt. II: Muslim India.

424 Dollot, Rene. Situation de l'Afghanistan [The Situation of Afghanistan].
Politique Étrangère 23, 353-364. 1958.
A summary of recent events, with emphasis upon foreign relations.

425 *Dorn, Bernhard, trans. History of the Afghans: Translated from the Persian of Neamet Ullah, by Bernhard Dorn. London: Oriental Translation Committee, 1829. Pt. I, xv, 184; Pt. II, viii, 131.
The translation of a manuscript in the library of the Royal Asiatic Society was carried out by the Professor of Oriental Literature of the
Imperial University at Kharkov. The original work was composed in
1609-1611 and as given here--not in its entirety--comprises the history of the Afghans up until the sixteenth century and the biographies
of 68 Moslem saints of Afghan origin. (See also no. 478.)

426 Dupree, Louis. Afghanistan Between East and West. Royal Central Asian
Journal 43, Pt. 1, 52-60; 2 maps. 1956.
Summary of six series of invasions of Afghanistan between the second
century B.C. and 1222 A.D.

427 Dupree, Louis. Afghanistan: The Canny Neutral. The Nation 199, no.
7, 134-137. 1964.

428 Dupree, Louis. Afghanistan in the Twentieth Century. Royal Central
Asian Journal 52, no. 1, 20-30. 1965.

429 Durand, Sir Henry Marion. The First Afghan War and its Causes. London: Longmans, Green and Co., 1879. Pp. xxxviii, 445.
A heavy, detailed account of British-Afghan relations preceding the
war and of the war itself up to March of 1842. The author spent
many years in India as an army officer and administrator.

430 East India (Afghanistan). Papers Regarding Hostilities with Afghanistan,
1919. London: H. M. Stationery Office, 1919. Pp. vi, 36.
Letters from the Amir of Afghanistan to the Viceroy of India, etc.
Text of the Peace Treaty.

431 East India (Military) Report on the Air Operations in Afghanistan between
December 12, 1928 and February 25th, 1929. Presented by the Secretary of State for India to Parliament by Command of His Majesty.

September, 1929. London: H. M. Stationery Office, 1929. Pp. 44.
A report on the Royal Air Force officer commanding (India) on the
evacuation of British civilians from Kabul.

432 Elias, N., ed. The Tarikh-i-Rashidi of Mirza Muhammad Haidar
Doughlat, translated by E. Denison Ross. London: Sampson Low, 1895.
Pp. xxiv, 535; map.
Interesting and trustworthy history of the Moghuls of Central Asia down
to 1541, written by a courtier and cousin of the ruler Babur.

433 Essad Bey, Mohammed. Allah est grand. Décadence et résurrection du
monde islamique. Préface et traduction de G. Montandon [Allah Is
Great! The Decadence and Resurrection of the Islamic World. Preface
and Translation by G. Montandon]. Paris: Payot, 1937. Pp. 355;
maps.
The author's basic concern is with the political renaissance of the
Moslem lands: pages 246-260 deal with Afghanistan.

434 Exchange of Notes between His Majesty's Government in the United Kingdom and the Government of Afghanistan Regarding Treaty Relations
with Afghanistan. London, May 6, 1930. London: H. M. Stationery
Office, 1930. Pp. 2.

435 Exchange of Notes between His Majesty's Government in the United Kingdom and the Government of India and the Government of Afghanistan
in Regard to the Boundary between India and Afghanistan in the Neighbourhood of Arnawai and Dokalim. Kabul, February 3, 1934. London:
H. M. Stationery Office, 1934. Pp. 6; folding map.
With a facsimile in Persian of a note from the Minister for Foreign
Affairs of Afghanistan.

436 Exchange of Official Publications. Agreement between the United States
of America and Afghanistan. Effected by Exchange of Notes, Signed
at Kabul, February 29, 1944, Effective February 29, 1944. Washington: U. S. Government Printing Office, 1944. Pp. 15.

437 Eyre, Vincent. The Military Operations at Cabul, which Ended in the
Retreat and Destruction of the British Army, January 1842. With a
Journal of Imprisonment in Afghanistan. London: John Murray, 1843.
Pp. xxvii, 436; map of Kabul.
A personal narrative of British operations against Kabul, the revolt of
the Afghans, and their destruction of the retreating British forces.
Those pages describing life in Afghan prisons are of interest and less
harrowing than might be expected.

III. HISTORY

438 Farhang, M[ir Muhammad Sadiq], trans. Masaleh-i Afghan az 1841 ta
    1878 [The Afghan Question from 1841 to 1878]. Kabul: Matba'eh-
    yi 'umumi, 1338 [1959]. Pp. 210.
    A translation into Dari of no. 372.

439 *Ferrier, J. P. History of the Afghans. Translated from the Original Un-
    published Manuscript by Captain William Jesse. London: John Murray,
    1858. Pp. xxi, 491; 2 maps.
    General Ferrier came to this part of the world to be Adjutant-General
    to the Persian Army. Traveling extensively from Iran across Afghan-
    istan and Central Asia into India, he developed a masterly knowledge
    of the history, geography, and languages of the area. The present
    work concentrates attention on the period from about 1700 until 1850
    and includes valid critical comments on British policy.

440 *Fletcher, Arnold. Afghanistan: Highway of Conquest; The Position of
    Afghanistan in Relation to East and West. Current History 18, 337-341.
    Philadelphia, 1950.
    Emphasizes the role of the Pushtu-speaking Afghans in determining
    the course of Afghanistan's foreign relations, as well as Afghanistan's
    position in relation to East and West. By a former American teacher
    at Kabul.

441 Fletcher, Arnold. Afghanistan, Highway of Conquest. Ithaca: Cornell
    University Press, 1965. Pp. vii, 325; bibliography; index.
    The history of the country, with emphasis on the Islamic period, and
    particularly the twentieth century.

442 Forbes, Archibald. The Afghan Wars 1839-42 and 1878-80. New York:
    Charles Scribner's Sons, 1892. Pp. 337.
    The operational details of the campaigns of these wars are treated in
    considerable, tedious detail.

443 Friendship and Diplomatic and Consular Representation. Provisional
    Agreement between the United States of America and the Kingdom of
    Afghanistan. Signed March 26, 1936. Effective March 26, 1936.
    Washington: U.S. Government Printing Office, 1936. Pp. 2.

444 *Fufalza'i, 'Aziz al-Din. Timur Shah Durrani [Timur Shah the Durrani].
    Kabul: Matba'eh-yi 'umumi, 1332 [1953]. Pp. 257; genealogical
    table.
    An historical study in Persian.

445 Fulfalza'i, Aziz al-Din Vakili. Dorrat al-Zaman-Tarikh-i Shah Zaman
[The Pearl of the Age. The History of Shah Zaman]. Kabul:
Matba'eh-yi doulati, 1337 [1958]. Pp. 470.

446 Gankovskiĭ, Y. V. Imperiya Durrani: ocherki administrativnoy i voyen-
noy sistemy [The Durrani Empire: Essays on the Administrative and
Military Systems]. Moscow: Izdatel'stvo Vostochnoy Literatury, 1958.
Pp. 170; bibliographical notes; genealogical chart.
Based on the accounts of travelers and on primary sources for the sec-
ond half of the eighteenth century.

447 Gankovskiĭ, Y. V. Missiya Bogdana Aslanova v Afganistan v 1764 g.
[The Mission of Bogdan Aslanov to Afghanistan in 1764]. Sovetskoye
Vostokovedeniye 2, 82-87. 1958.
Tells of the effort by a representative of the government of Catherine
II to establish diplomatic relations with Afghanistan.

448 Gavrilin, V. Na stroĭkakh Afganistana·[Soviet-Afghan Cooperation].
New Times 10, 13-14. Moscow, 1961.
A letter from Kabul describes the value of the Soviet aid programs
and contrasts the projects with such undertakings as the American
built Helmand Canal, adding that "it is not water but unadulterated
whiskey that flows in it."

449 *Ghirshman, Roman. Les Chionites-Hephthalites [The Chionite-
Hephthalites]. Cairo: Imprimerie de l'Institut Français d'Archéologie
Orientale, 1948. Pp. xiii, 156; plates.
Based mainly on numismatics and ancient manuscripts, a history of
the two branches of the Chionites--the Hephthalites in Bactria and
the Zabulites in the South. The volume constitutes Volume LXXX
of the Mémoires de l'Institut Français d'Archéologie Orientale du
Caire and Volume XIII of the Mémoires de la Délégation Archéologique Française en Afghanistan.

450 Ghose, Dilip K. England and Afghanistan: A Phase in Their Relations.
Calcutta: The World Private Press, 1960. Pp. 230; bibliography.
A study of relations in the second half of the nineteenth century.

451 *Ghubar, mir Ghulam Muhammad. Ahmad Shah baba-yi Afghan [Ahmad
Shah, Father of the Afghan]. Kabul: Matba'eh-yi 'umumi, 1322
[1943]. Pp. 352.
A work in Persian, with a list on pages 342-346 of sources used. A
translation into Russian was published at Moscow in 1959.

452 Ghubar, mir Ghulam Muhammad. Afghanistan bi-yak nazar [Afghani-
      stan in One Glance]. Kabul: Matba'eh-yi 'umumi, 1326 [1947].
      Pp. 101.
      A general survey of the country in Persian.

453 Gobj, Robert. Geschichte Afghanistans zwischen Alexander und Moham-
      med [History of Afghanistan between Alexander and Mohammed].
      Bustan (Vienna) 3, 26-31. 1963.

454 Grenard, Fernand. Baber. First of the Moguls. London: Thornton
      Butterworth, 1931. Pp. 253; bibliography.

455 Griesinger, W. German Intrigues in Persia. The Niedermayer Expedition
      through Persia to Afghanistan and India. London: Hodder and Stough-
      ton, 1918. Pp. 39.
      This brief work consists of translations of extracts from the diary of
      the German agent Griesinger.

456 Gul Muhammad. Ayineh-yi jihan-numa [Mirror of the Image of the
      World]. Kabul: Dar al-saltaneh, 1318 [1900]. Pp. 316.

457 Gupta, Harl Ram. Studies in the Later Mughal History of the Panjab 1707-
      1793. Lahore, 1944. Pp. 348.
      Contains considerable material on the activities of Afghan warriors
      and rulers in the Punjab, as seen from the point of view of a contem-
      porary Hindu historian.

458 *Habberton, William. Anglo-Russian Relations concerning Afghanistan,
      1837-1907. Urbana: University of Illinois Press, 1937. Pp. 102;
      bibliography; maps; appendices containing pacts and conventions
      made between Russia and England concerning Afghanistan.
      A sound research study starting from the larger view of over-all rela-
      tions and conflicts between the rival empires and intended to extract
      the single thread from an elaborate pattern of diplomacy. Ends with
      the agreement of 1907, which brought all Afghanistan under British
      influence.

459 *Habib, Mohammad. Sultan Mahmud of Ghaznin. A Study. Bombay:
      D. B. Taraporevala and Co., 1927. Pp. 108; 2d ed. 1951.
      A study from original sources by a professor of History and Politics at
      Muslim University, Aligarh. The interest of the text is enhanced by
      the author's familiarity with the local geography covered by the
      campaigns of Mahmud.

460 Habibi, 'Abd al-Hayy. Loyi Ahmad Shah [Great Ahmad Shah]. Kabul: An historical study in Pushtu.

461 Habibi, 'Abd al-Hayy. Tarikh-i Afghanistan dar 'asr-i Gurgani-yi Hind [History of Afghanistan in the Time of the Ghurids of India]. Kabul: Matba'eh-yi Pohani, 1341 [1962]. Pp. 400.
An important work in Persian, with genealogies, illustrations, and indices.

462 *Habibullah, Amir. My Life: From Brigand to King. Autobiography of Amir Habibullah. London: Sampson Low, Marston and Company, Ltd., n. d. Pp. xiii, 276.
Dictated to a follower by the Bacha Saqqo, during his brief reign. Tales of the early life of a brigand and of the battles that won a throne. A postscript describes his capture and execution.

463 Habibullah, Sardar. Tarikh-i Afghanistan [History of Afghanistan]. Lahore: Matba'eh-yi mufid-i 'amm, 1306, 1929 sic. Pp. 80.
A teacher at the Habibiyah school at Kabul composed in Persian a history, with emphasis upon rulers and events of the eighteenth and nineteenth centuries.

464 Hameed-ud Din. Les Afghans à la conquête du pouvoir en Indie [The Afghans towards the conquest of power in India]. Journal Asiatique 250, no. 2, 191-213. 1962.

465 Hamid Kashmiri, Hamid Allah. Akbar-nameh [The Book of Akbar]. Kabul: Matba'eh-yi 'umumi, 1330 [1951]. Pp. 246.
This work, in Persian verse, is in the form of a mathnavi on the exploits of Akbar Khan, a son of Dost Muhammad. It was completed in 1844. This edition was annotated by 'Ali Akbar Na'imi, with the collaboration of Muhammad Ibrahim Khalil and Muhammad Shafi' Wangazar.

466 *Hanna, Henry B. The Second Afghan War, 1878-79-80. Its Causes, its Conduct, and its Consequences. 3 vols. Westminster and London: Constable and Co., 1899, 1904, 1910. Pp. (1) x, 386; (2) vii, 372; (3) vii, 583; maps; plans.
An exhaustive and elaborately documented study by a witness who also collected material from many others. The first volume sets the background of the so-called Afghan problem, the second carries the war through 1879, and the third finishes it off--at enormous expense.

467 al-Haravi, Sayf ibn Muhammad ibn Ya'qub. Tarikh-nameh-yi Harat
    [History of Herat]. Calcutta: Baptist Mission Press, 1944. Pp. xxvi-i,
    821.
    Edited and with an introduction by Muhammad Zubayr al-Siddiqi.
    Using contemporary and earlier sources, the author covered the years
    from 1221 until the completion of the work in 1320 A.D. Many later
    historians have relied upon this source.

468 Harlan, Josiah. A Memoir of India and Avghanistaun, with Observations
    on the Present Exciting and Critical State and Future Prospects of those
    Countries. Philadelphia, J. Dobson, 1842. Pp. vii, 208; map.
    The author's own account of adventures that are presented in relation
    to their background in a considerably later work (see no. 272). In-
    cludes remarks on the massacre of the British army at Kabul and a re-
    ply to Count Bjornstjerna's work on British India. See also no. 404.

469 Hasan, K. Pakistan-Afghanistan Relations. Asian Survey 2, 14-19. 1962.

470 Hashim Khan, mir. Tarikhcheh-yi Afghanistan [Short History of Afghan-
    istan]. Kabul.
    A work in Persian by an Afghan writer now deceased.

471 Hasrat, Aman Allah. Afghanistan va milal-i mottahid [Afghanistan and
    the United Nations]. Kabul: Doulati matba'eh, 1342 [1963]. Pp. 162.

472 Hauser, Ernest O. Afghan Listening Post. Saturday Evening Post 216,
    no. 39, 19ff. March 25, 1944.
    The uneasy position of Afghanistan during World War II, when both
    sides in the conflict tried to sway the chosen course of neutrality.

473 Havelock, Henry. Narrative of the War in Affghanistan, 1838-1839.
    2 vols. London: Henry Colburn: (2d ed.) 1840. Pp. (1) xix, 336;
    (2) 324; appendix.
    Still another personal narrative of the First Anglo-Afghan War. Of
    moderate interest.

474 Herati, Muhammad Husayn. Vagi'at-i Shah Shoja' [The Events of Shah
    Shoja']. Kabul: Matba'eh-yi 'umumi, 1333 [1954]. Pp. 162.
    The first section of the work contains the memoirs of Shah Shoja',
    the second is material supplied by the author on the events of his reign.

475 Heravi, Ghulam Riza Mayil. Montakhab-i ash'ar Sayyid Mir Heravi
    [Selections from the Poems of Sayyid Mir Heravi]. Kabul: Vizarat-i

etala'at va Kultur, 1344 [1965]. Pp. 63.
Selections, with commentaries, of the work of a nineteenth-century Afghan poet, in Dari.

476 Holdich, Thomas Hungerford. The Indian Borderland, 1880-1900. London: Methuen and Co., 1901. Pp. xii, 402; folding map; appendix. The appendix gives a chapter on the history of Afghanistan.

477 Hough, W. Narrative of the March and Operations of the Army of the Indus, in the Expedition to Afghanistan in the Years 1838-1839. Comprising Also the History of the Dooranee Empire from its Foundation to the Present Time, and an Appendix. London: W. H. Allen, 1841. Pp. xl, 443; 95 pages of appendices; map.
A member of the British force describes the route followed to Qandahar, Ghazni and Kabul. Noteworthy is Chapter XVII, which deals with the history of the Durranis from the founding of the dynasty in 1747.

478 *Hughes, Thomas P., ed. Tarikh-e-Morassa' [The Gem-Studded History]. Peshawar, 1872.
This edition presents a translation, with additions, into Pushtu of the Makhzan-i Afghani (see no. 425). The version is by Afzal Khan Khatak, grandson of the Pushtu poet Khushhal Khatak.

479 Imamuddin, S. M. The Tarikh Khan-i-Jahani wa-Makhzan-i-Afghani. Islamic Culture 22, 128-142. Hyderabad: Islamic Culture Board, 1948. Discusses this important history of the Afghans (see no. 425), in its two editions, and gives an account of the historian's life.

480 In Whose Benefit? New Times 28, 17. Moscow, 1955.
An editorial claiming that American militarists are obstructing efforts to settle the Afghanistan-Pakistan conflict, hoping to "bludgeon Afghanistan into abandoning its policy of non-participation in aggressive blocs. "

481 Istoriya tadzhikskogo naroda. Tom 1: S drevneyshikh vremen do U. v. n. e. [The History of the Tadzhik people. Vol. 1: From Ancient Times to the 5th Century]. Moscow: Izdatel'stvo Vostochnoy Literatury, 1963. Pp. 595.

482 Jalabert, Louis. Du roman en pleine histoire: L'aventure de quelques allemands en Afghanistan et en Perse pendant la guerre [Historical Romance: The Adventures of Some Germans in Afghanistan and Persia during the War]. Études, 20 mars, pp. 744-755; 5 avril, pp. 57-70. Paris, 1937.

III. HISTORY

A summary account of the German mission of Niedermayer,
Schunemann, and Zugmayer, which failed to arouse the Afghans in
World War I. These articles also mention the activity of Wassmuss
in Iran.

483 Jalalabadi, Shir Ahmad. Fath-nameh-yi Kafiristan [Account of Victory
in Kafiristan]. Lahore, 1896. Pp. 16.
A poem in Persian on the conquest of this region by the Afghans in
1896.

484 Jawzjani, Minhaj al-Din ibn Serraj al-Din Tabaqat-i Nasiri [Compendium
of Nasiri]. Kabul: Matba'eh-yi doulati. Vol. 1, 1342 [1963],
pp. 501, vol. 2, 1343 [1964], pp. 507.
Important history, in Dari, of the Ghurid period. Edited by 'Abd al-
Hayy Habibi.

485 Kamel, Dost Muhammad Khan, ed. Kolliyat-i Khushhal Khan Khattak
[The Collected Works of Khushhal Khan Khattak]. Peshawar. 2d ed.,
1920.

486 Kapur, Harish. Soviet Russia and Asia 1917-1927. A study of Soviet
Policy towards Turkey, Iran and Afghanistan. Geneva: M. Joseph,
1966. Pp. 266; map.
Based primarily on Russian source material.

487 Khafi, Mirza Yacub 'Ali. Padshahan motakher [Recent Rulers]. 2 vols.
Kabul: Matba'eh-yi doulati, 1334 [1955], 1336 [1957]. Pp. (1)
246; (2) 196.
An important work in Persian, dealing primarily with rulers of the
nineteenth century.

488 Khalfin, N.A. Proval britanskoy agresii v Afganistane, 19v.-nachalo 20v.
[Downfall of British aggression in Afghanistan, 19th century to the beginning of the 20th Century]. Moscow: Izdatel'stvo Sotsial'no-
ekonomicheskoy Literatury, 1959. Pp. 208; maps; index.

489 Khalil, Muhammad Ibrahim. Amir Khosro. Kabul: Doulati matba'eh,
1340 [1961]. Pp. 91.

490 *Khalili, Khalilullah. Saltanat-i Ghaznaviyan [The Empire of the
Ghaznavides]. Kabul: Matba'eh-yi 'umumi, 1333 [1954]. Pp. 371;
bibliography.
A work in Persian by a contemporary scholar; compiled from Persian
and Arabic sources.

491 Khan, Ghulam Mustafa. A History of Bahram Shah of Ghaznin. Lahore:
Caravan Press, 1955. Pp. 99.
Includes an account of the Shah's career, his literary interests, and a
record of his sons and courtiers in the early twelfth century.

492 Khan, Said Alim, S. H. l'Emir de Boukharie. La Voix de la Boukharie
Opprimeé [The Voice of Oppressed Bokhara]. Paris: Maisonneuve
Frères, 1929. Pp. 71; map.
Describes the unsuccessful resistance to the Bolshevik advance into
Bokhara, details military aid given by Afghanistan, and concludes
with the amir fleeing to Afghanistan in 1921.

493 Khaturvatana, Najibullah. Aryana [Aryana]. Kabul.
An historical study in Persian.

494 *Khwand-Amir, Ghiyas al-Din ibn Humam al-Din. Dastur al-vuzara';
shamil ahval-i vuzara-yi islam ta inqiraz-i Timuriyan [Instruction of
the Viziers; Containing the Conditions of the Viziers of Islam til the
Extinction of the Timurids]. Tehran: Kitab-furushi va chapkhaneh-
yi Iqbal, 1317 [1938]. Pp. 514.
An edition of this important work by Sa'id Nafisi. See also no. 420.

495 Kieffer, Charles M. Les Ghorides Une Grande Dynastie Nationale [The
Ghurides. A Great National Dynasty]. Kabul: Historical Society of
Afghanistan, No. 71, 1962. Pp. 50.

496 King, David Wooster. Living East: Photographs by Lowell Thomas. New
York: Duffield and Co., 1929. Pp. 265.
A record of the author's adventures in India and Afghanistan.

497 Klimburg, Max. Afghanistan. Das Land im Historischen Spannungsfeld
Mittelasians [Afghanistan. Land in the Historical Area of Discord of
Middle Asia]. Vienna: Österreichischer Bundesverlag, 1966. Pp. 313;
plates; index; bibliography.
A comprehensive study of history, social structure, and modern de-
velopment.

498 Kohzad, Ahmad Ali. In the Highlights of Modern Afghanistan. Kabul:
Government Printing House, n.d. Pp. 144.
Articles drawn from documentary sources on the history of Afghanistan
in the nineteenth century, translated from Persian.

499 Kohzad, Ahmad Ali. Men and Events through 18th and 19th Century Afghanistan. Kabul: Government Printing House, n.d. Pp. 179.

III. HISTORY

Translations of 49 short articles originally written in Persian and embodying documentary research.

500 Kohzad, Ahmad Ali. Rijal va-ruydadha-yi tarikhi [Historical Personalities and Events]. Kabul: Matba'eh-yi 'umumi, n.d. Pp. 146.
A number of short sketches in Persian on individuals such as Ahmad Shah, Timur Shah, and Sardar Muhammad Azim Khan and on important historical incidents.

501 Kohzad, Ahmad Ali. Cultural Relations between Afghanistan and India. Afghanistan 1, no. 2, 12-30. 1946.
The emphasis is on place names found in the Vedas and the Avesta, on the development of Buddhism, and on the influence of Islam in India.

502 Kohzad, Ahmad Ali. Les Ratbils Shahs de Kaboul [The Ratbil Shahs of Kabul]. Afghanistan 5, no. 2, 1-18. 1950.
About the Kings of Kabul, who governed a large territory in Central Asia in the first two centuries of the Hijreh.

503 Kohzad, Ahmad Ali. Two Coronations. Afghanistan 5, no. 3, 38-40. 1950.
The story of the coronation of Ahmad Shah with an ear of wheat, and of Dost Mohammed with an ear of barley.

504 Kohzad, Ahmad Ali. Two of the Last Buddhist Rulers of Ghazni and Bamian. Afghanistan 5, no. 4, 37-39. 1950.
The fall of the Ruler of Bamiyan (nameless) and of the Ruler of Ghazni (variously named) to Eleptagin in the fourth century of the Hijreh.

505 Kohzad, Ahmad Ali. Huit légendes concernant la fondation de la ville de Herat [Eight Legends about the Founding of the City of Herat]. Afghanistan 6, no. 4, 11-21. 1951.
A recounting of the legends, followed by a comment on their possible historical foundations.

506 Kohzad, Ahmad Ali. Afghanistan, A Great Mountainous Mesopotamia. Afghanistan 7, no. 4, 49-53. 1952.
A short sketch of Afghan history.

507 A(hmad Ali) K(ohzad). Émir Cher Ali Khan en face de la diplomatie anglaise, la fidélité des tribus [Amir Sher Ali Khan, in the Face of English Diplomacy, the Fidelity of the Tribes]. Afghanistan 7, no. 4, 59-66. 1952.

A history of the relations between Sher Ali Khan and the British administrators in India.

508 Kohzad, Ahmad Ali. Sher Shah Souri: A Representative of the Afghan Spirit in India. Afghanistan 7, no. 4, 35-40. 1952.
The life of Sher Shah, showing him as the embodiment of the finest Afghan traits.

509 Kohzad, Ahmad Ali. Dar zavaya-yi tarikh-i mu'asir-i Afghanistan [On Aspects of the Contemporary History of Afghanistan]. Kabul: Matba'eh-yi 'umumi. 1331 [1952]. Pp. 148.
A compilation of articles written in Persian.

510 Kohzad, Ahmad Ali. Les capitales de l'empire afghan koushanide au temps de Kanischka [The Capitals of the Afghan Kushanid Empire at the Time of Kanishka]. Afghanistan 8, no. 2, 22-30. 1953.
On Kanishka's summer capital, Capici, excavated at Begram near Alexander's Nicea, and on Poura-Shapoura (Peshawar), a prosperous city and a center of Buddhism.

511 Kohzad, Ahmad Ali. Zaman Shah et l'activité des puissances coloniales [Zaman Shah and the Activity of Colonial Powers]. Afghanistan 8, no. 4, 5-26. 1953.
A history of the embattled reign of Zaman Shah. The author accuses the British, particularly the Directors of the East India Company, of fomenting strife and insurrection in Afghanistan in order to keep Zaman Shah out of India.

512 Kohzad, Ahmad Ali. Bala Hesar Kabul va pish amadhayi tarikhi [The Bala Hesar at Kabul and the Related Events of History]. Kabul: Matba'eh-yi doulati, 1336 [1957]. Pp. 316.
A history of the renowned fortification at Kabul.

513 Kohzad, Mohammad Nabi. Les événements de Shah Shodjaa [The Events of Shah Shoja'] . Afghanistan 9, no. 3, 45-48. 1954.
On the appearance of a book edited by the Society of Historical Studies of Afghanistan, and written by Shah Shoja' and Mohammad Husayn Herati. The review gives a brief sketch of the Shah's life and an uncomplimentary note on the collaborator, Mohammad Husayn.

514 Konow, Sten. A Note on the Sakas and Zoroastrianism. In Jal Dastur Cursetji Parry, ed., Oriental Studies in Honor of Cursetji Erachji Parry. London: Oxford University Press, 1933. Pp. 220-222.

The author considers a few facts which indicate that the Sakas made no attempts to propagate Zoroastrianism outside Sistan.

515 Kushan, Hazrat G., trans. Khatareh-yi Salferinu. Kabul: Matba'eh-yi dafa' melli, 1343 [1954]. Pp. 160.
Bears the English subtitle: "A Memory of Solferino, J. Henry Dunant, translated into Durri by G. Hazrat Koshan. "

516 *Kushkaki, Burhan al-Din. Nadir-i Afghan [Nadir the Afghan]. Kabul: Matba'eh-yi 'umumi, 1310 [1931]. Pp. 611; maps.
The life of Nadir Shah, from his birth until his ascent to the throne in 1929, written in Persian by an Afghan scholar. Well documented and with a score of fascinating contemporary photographs. The work is labeled Volume 1, but others have not appeared.

517 *Lal, Mohan. Life of the Ameer Dost Mohammed Khan of Kabul, with his Political Proceedings towards the English, Russian and Persian Governments, Including the Victories and Disasters of the British Army in Afghanistan. 2 vols. London: Longman, Brown, Green and Longman, 1846. Pp. (1) 399; (2) 497.
A work of first importance, written by the Indian clerk of Sir Alexander Burnes, who accompanied the latter to Kabul and gathered material directly from the courtiers and relatives of Dost Mohammad. Includes a comprehensive account of relations between Afghanistan and the rival Russian and British empires.

518 Lamb, Harold. Babur the Tiger. New York: Doubleday & Co., 1961. Pp. 336.
Historical novel, drawn from the autobiography of the conqueror of India who was fondest of his years at Kabul.

519 Lee, Vladimir. Storm Clouds over the Khyber Pass. New Times 51, 27-28. Moscow, 1961.
A belligerent defence of the Afghan position on the Pushtunistan issue. Probably only an electronic computer could interpret this statement: "Most of them (the Pushtus) live in Afghanistan, the rest (estimated at 7,000,000) in Pakistan. "

520 Levine, J. O. L'Angleterre, la Russie et l'Afghanistan [England, Russia and Afghanistan]. Monde Slave 1, 336-363. Paris, 1931.
Traces the relationships between Afghanistan and its powerful neighbors in the nineteenth century, concluding with a brief resumé of contemporary relations.

521 Levine, J. O. L'U.R.S.S. et l'Afghanistan [The U.S.S.R. and Afghan-
istan]. Affaires Étrangères, 6e année, pp. 283-289. 1936.
An article giving the history of the amicable political and economic
relations between Russia and Afghanistan and pointing out the advantage to the Soviet of a Communist Afghanistan and Russia's hopes for
a "social revolution" there.

522 Lobanov-Rostovsky, A. Russia and Asia. Ann Arbor: Wahr, 1951.
Pp. 342.
Attention is concentrated on Afghanistan in Chapter 8: "The Afghan
Question and the Kulja Incident," pages 177-192. This volume is a
revision of the 1933 edition.

523 *Lockhart, Laurence. Nadir Shah. A Critical Study Based Mainly upon
Contemporary Sources. London: Luzac and Co., 1938. Pp. xv, 344;
bibliography; maps.
The story of the life of this eighteenth-century ruler of Iran includes
his campaigns which drove the Afghans from Iran, and his passage
through Afghanistan as he marched into India. For some years a resident of Iran, the British author knows the topography of much of this
story.

524 *Lockhart, Laurence. The Fall of the Safavi Dynasty and the Afghan Occupation. Cambridge: Cambridge University Press, 1958. Pp. xiii;
584; map; appendices; bibliography; index.

525 Mackenzie, C. F. and Sir H. M. Elliot, trans. Tarikh-i Salatin-i Afghana
by Ahmad Yadgar and Makhzan-i Afghani and Tarikh-i Khan Jahan Lodi
by Ni'amatullah. Calcutta, 1955. Pp. 152.
A reprint of the well-known history of India by Elliot and Dowson.

526 *MacMunn, George Fletcher. Afghanistan, from Darius to Amanullah.
London: G. Bell and Sons, 1929. Pp. xii, 359; 9 maps.
A British Lieutenant-General conducts a fairly detailed survey of the
history of the area throughout the ages. Emphasis is on the earliest
Afghan-British relations and on contacts with India at all periods. In-
cludes genealogical tables of the Durrani and Barakzai families.

527 Macrory, Patrick A. Signal Catastrophe. The Story of the Disastrous Re-
treat from Kabul 1842. London: Hodder and Stoughton, 1966.
Pp. 288; maps; bibliography.
Also published under the title, "The Fierce Pawns." New York:
J. B. Lippincott, 1966. An extremely detailed, well-written, and

interesting account of the First Anglo-Afghan War.

528 Malleson, George Bruce. History of Afghanistan. From the Earliest
Period to the Outbreak of the War of 1878. London: Allen, 1879.
Pp. xxviii, 453; map.
A popular, narrative history of Afghanistan from the Ghaznavid period,
comprising a series of brief chapters on various dynasties and rulers.

529 *Malleson, George Bruce. Herat: The Granary and Garden of Central
Asia. London: Allen and Co., 1880. Pp. vi, 196.
A valuable work of observation and compilation. The history of Herat
is traced by interesting excerpts from earlier historians. Routes leading from Herat are described.

530 Mann, Oskar. Quellenstudien zur Geschichte des Ahmed Sah Durrani
(1747-1773) [Source Studies on the History of Ahmed Shah Durrani
(1747-1773)]. Zeitschrift der deutschen morgenlandischen Gesellschaft
52, 97-118; 161-186; 323-358. 1898.
A study of coins, and manuscripts to trace the history of Ahmad Shah;
with a history of, and comment on, the manuscripts, some of which
appear translated into German, with portions of the original Persian.
An offprint of the article was published in Leipzig by G. Kreysing,
1898, containing 84 pages.

531 Masson, Vadim M. and Vadim A. Romodin. Istoriya Afganistana [History
of Afghanistan]. 2 vols. Moscow: "Nauka," 1964-65. Pp. (1) 464
(1964); (2) 551 (1965).

532 Melia, J. Visages royaux d'Orient [Rulers of the East]. Paris: Bibliothèque Charpentier, 1930. Pp. 228.
The pages dealing with Amanullah, 5-72, represent a definite contribution to the study of his successes and impending failure.

533 Memoirs of Zehir-ed-din Muhammed Babur, Emperor of Hindustan, Writ-
ten by himself, in the Chagatai Turki and Translated . . . by J.
Leyden . . . and W. Erskine . . . Annotated and Revised by Sir Lucas
King. 2 vols. Oxford, 1921. Pp. (1) cxi, 324; (2) 471; map.
Excellent edition of one of the most fascinating and revealing of auto-
biographies.

534 Miles, C. V. The Zakka Khel and Mohmand Expeditions. Rawalpindi,
1909. Pp. 66.

535 Mir-Khwand (Muhammad ibn Khawand-Shah ibn Mahmud). Rawzat al-
safa [Garden of Purity]. Tehran: 1853-56.
A general history in seven parts, composed in Persian by a writer long
resident at Herat. Parts Four through Six include material on the
rulers and dynasties of this area, while the Seventh--by another hand--
deals with the patrons of the author, the Sultan Husayn and his sons.

536 *Mir Munshi, Sultan Mohomed Khan, ed. The Life of Abdur Rahman,
Amir of Afghanistan. 2 vols. London: John Murray, 1900. Pp. (1)
295; (2) 319; map in pocket to scale 1:1, 520, 640.
The first volume contains the ruler's own narrative of his early life
and final accession to the throne. The second volume details his efforts as a ruler, taken down in his own words on various occasions by
the editor, his former State Secretary. Fascinating account of a reso-
lute, determined, cruel, and superstitious man. See also no. 350.

537 Mohebi, Ahmad Ali. Samanian [The Samanids]. Kabul: Matba'eh-yī
'umumi, 1334 [1955]
A history of the Samanid dynasty.

538 Molesworth, Lieut.-General George N. Afghanistan 1919. An Account
of Operations in the Third Afghan War. Bombay: Asia Publishing
House, 1962. Pp. 183; maps; index.

539 Moorish, C. Afghanistan in the Melting Pot. Lahore: Civil and Military
Gazette Press, 1930. Pp. 61.
From the vantage point of Peshawar, the author kept track of the overthrow of Amanullah and the campaign for the re-establishment of law
and order by Nadir Shah and his brothers.

540 *Morley, William Hook, ed. Tarikh-i-Baihaqi. Containing the Life of
Massaud, Son of Sultan Mahmud of Ghaznin; Edited by W. H. Morley
and Printed under the Supervision of Capt. W. N. Lees. Calcutta:
College Press, 1862. Pp. 868.
The title comes from the birthplace of the author Abu Fazl Baihaqi,
the village of Baihaq, near Nishapur in Iran. The work is a history
of the Ghaznavid dynasty up to the lifetime of the author. Other editions have been published at Delhi, Cairo, and Bombay.

541 Morrison, Ronald M. S. H. M. King Mohammad Nadir Shah-i-Ghazi of
Afghanistan. Naji-i-Millat (Savior of the Nation). Journal of the
Royal Central Asian Society 21, 170-175. 1934.
A tribute to Nadir Shah, written after the assassination of that ruler.
Includes material covering an Afghan law on citizenship.

542 Muhammad Abu'l-Fayz. Mukhammas-i Saghar-i bazm-ashub. (The
title is not translatable.) Gujranwala, 1902. Pp. 16.
A lithographed work in Persian dealing with the warfare between Dost
Muhammad Khan and Sardar Hari Singh.

543 *Muhammad Hayat Khan. Hayat-i Afghan [Life of Afghans]. Lahore,
1867. Pp. 17, 1, 1-696; folding maps.
On the history of the country, with special emphasis on accounts of
the principal tribes. Includes a table of contents in English, a key
to each chapter, and a page of the Persian text.

544 Muhammad Kabir ibn Shaykh Isma'il. Afsaneh-yi Shahan [Tale of the
Kings].
An undated manuscript in Persian composed of anecdotes collected
by the author about the Afghan rulers of India. Copies exist in the
British Museum and elsewhere.

545 *Muhyi al-Din. Burhan va-najat [Crisis and Salvation]. Kabul:
Matba'eh-yi anis, 1310 [1931]. Pp. 288; map.
A work in Persian describing the overthrow of Amir Amanullah and
the final restoration of order by Nadir Shah and his brothers.

546 Nafisi, Sa'id. Asar-i gum shudeh-yi Abu Fazl-i Bayhaqi [Lost Works of
Abu Razl Bayhaqi]. Tehran: Mihr, 1315 [1936]. Pp. 108.
An Iranian scholar and editor writes in Persian of little-known works
by one of the most reliable historians of Islam.

547 Naimi, Ali Ahmad. Un regard sur Ghor. Préambule: la géographie,
l'histoire, et les sites historiques [A Look at Ghor. Preamble: Geography, History and Historic Sites]. Afghanistan 4, no. 4, 1-23. 1949.
Useful and important article, with some documentation. Follows
the history of the various rulers and includes brief descriptions of
some thirteen historical sites.

548 Naimi, Ali Ahmad. Gauhar Shad, une reine afghane du neuvième siècle
de l'hégire [Gowhar Shad, an Afghan Queen of the Ninth Century of
the Hegira]. Afghanistan 7, no. 1, 22-34. 1952.
Gowhar Shad--of whom little is known--was the wife of Shah Rokh,
son of Tamerlane. The article deals with her father-in-law, her
husband, and the probable events of her own life, with notes on her
sons, her mausoleum, and her mosque at Mashhad.

549 Naimi, Ali Ahmad, ed. Akbar nameh [The History of Akbar]. Kabul:

Matba'eh-yi doulati, 1337 [1958]. Pp. 246.

An edition of a work by Hamid Kashmiri, apparently a translation from Persian into Pushtu, describing the struggles of a member of the family of Dost Muhammad against the British in Afghanistan. The exact date of publication is open to question.

550 Najibadadi, Akbar Shah Khan. Khan Jahan Ludi. Kabul: Matba'eh-yi 'umumi, 1326 [1947]. Pp. 94.

A translation of a Persian text into Pushtu by Aziz al-Rahman Sayfi.

551 Narimanov, L. Afganistan v ogne grazhdanskoi voiny [Afghanistan in the Flame of the Civil War]. Leningrad: Priboi, 1929. Pp. 98.

552 al-Narshakhi, Abu Bakr Muhammad ibn Ja'far. Tarikh-i Bukhara [History of Bokhara]. Translated into Persian by Abu Nasr Ahmad ibn Muhammad al-Qubavi, abridged by Muhammad ibn Zufar ibn 'Umar. Tehran: Sana'i (n.d.). Pp. 128.

The manuscript was completed prior to 959 by a scholar at the Samanid court; translated into Persian in 1128 and abridged in 1178 A.D.

553 *Nazim, Muhammad. The Life and Times of Sultan Mahmud of Ghazna. Cambridge University Press, 1931. Pp. xv, 271; map.

Emphasis is placed on the military campaigns and conquests of Mahmud. References are to primary sources.

554 Nazim, Muhammad. Hayat va-awqat-i Sultan-i Mahmud-i Ghaznavi [Life and Times of Sultan Mahmud of Ghazni]. Kabul: Matba'eh-yi 'umumi, 1318 [1939]. Pp. 209; bibliography.

A translation into Persian, by 'Abd al-Ghafur Amini, of a work written in English and published in 1931 (see no. 553). The bibliography lists works in European languages, both in the Latin alphabet and in Persian translation.

555 *Niedermayer, Oskar von. Unter der Glutsonne Irans. Kriegserlebnisse der deutschen Expedition nach Persien und Afghanistan [Under Iran's Scorching Sun. War Experiences of the German Expedition to Persia and Afghanistan]. Dachau/Munich: Einbornverlag, 1925. Pp. 331; sketch map.

Narrative of a "political and military" mission through India, Afghanistan, and Persia in 1915-1916. Pages 126-182 deal with the journey through Afghanistan--observations on the country and meetings with Afghan officials.

556 Niedermayer, Oskar von. Im Weltkrieg vor Indiens Toren. Der Wüsten-
zug der deutschen Expedition nach Persien und Afghanistan [At the
Gates of India in the World War. The Desert Passage of the German
Expedition to Persia and Afghanistan]. Hamburg: Hanseatische
Verlagsanstalt, 1936. Pp. 228; map.
A later edition of the same author's Unter der Glutsonne Irans (see
no. 555).

557 Nollau, Günther and Hans J. Wiehe. Russia's south flank; Soviet operations in Iran, Turkey, and Afghanistan. New York: Praeger, 1963.
Pp. 171.

558 Nukhovich, Eduard S. Vneshnyaya politika Afganistana [The Foreign
Policy of Afghanistan]. Moscow: Izdatel'stvo Instituta mezhdunarod-
nikh otnosheniy, 1962. Pp. 108.
Stress is placed upon Afghanistan's relations with the U. S. S. R. and
the United States, and on the country's policy of definite neutrality.

559 Nur-Muhammad, Hafez. Tarikh-i Mazar-i Sharif vaqe' Balkh [The History of Mazar-i Sharif, Balkh Locality]. Kabul: Matba'eh-yi 'umumi,
1325 [1946].

560 Ocherki po novoi istorii stran Srednego Vostoka. Pod red. I. M. Reisnera
i N. M. Gol'dberga [Sketches on Modern History of the Middle Eastern
Countries. Edited by I. M. Reisner and N. M. Gol'dberg]. Moscow:
Izdatel'stvo Moskovskogo Universiteta, 1951.
The section dealing with Afghanistan (pp. 53-81) is by Reisner and is
useful, recognition being given by the foreign reader to the Marxist
bias.

561 *Operation in Waziristan 1919-1920. London: His Majesty's Stationery
Office, 1924. Pp. viii, 194.
A detailed account of one section of the operations incidental to the
Third Anglo-Afghan War.

562 Osctrov, N. Za dal'neysheye razvitiye sovetsko-afganskogo sotrudnich-
estva [On the further Development of Soviet-Afghan Cooperation].
Sovremenniy Vostok 2, 17-18. 1957.
A stereotyped account of Soviet-Afghan diplomatic relations since
1919.

563 Osipov, A. M., ed. Indiya i Afganistan [India and Afghanistan].
Moscow: Izdatel'stvo vostochnoy literaturï, 1058. Pp. 290.
This work is subtitled, "Sketches of History and Economics." On

pages 57-87, Yu. V. Gankovskiĭ discusses "The Army and Military System of the Durrani Shahs," and on pages 284-290 he reviews recent Afghan writing on the history of the Durrani Shahs.

564 'Osman, Shir Muhammad. Yaftaliyan [The Yaftalites]. Kabul: Matba'eh-yi 'umumi, 1326 [1948]. Pp. 40.

565 Pandey, Awadh B. The First Afghan Empire in India (1451-1526). Calcutta: Bookland Ltd., 1956. Pp. 320.
   An account of the Lodi Afghans, based on sources in Persian and Sanskrit.

566 Panjshiri, Safdar. Mobarezeh-yi Sayyid Jamal al-Din Afghan [The Combat of Sayyid Jamal al-Din Afghan]. Kabul: Matba'eh-yi ma'aref, 1342 [1963]. Pp. not numbered.

567 Peers, Ellis Edward. 'Uruj-i Barakza'i [Barakzai Ascendency]. Kabul: Matba'eh-yi 'umumi, 1333 [1954]. Pp. 187; bibliography.
   A translation into Persian by 'Abd al-Rahman Pazhwak and Muhammad 'Usman Sidqi of a work in English entitled "Afghanistan in the Nineteenth Century." The bibliography is taken from the original work and is reproduced in the Latin alphabet.

568 Peter of Greece and Denmark, Prince. Post-War Developments in Afghanistan. Journal of the Royal Central Asian Society 34, 275-286. 1947.
   A brief history of Afghanistan since 1838, and general remarks on, and an explanation of, economic and political conditions and foreign relations. Prince Peter was at the time a correspondent of The Times, and was intimate with members of the Afghan Royal Family.

569 *Philips, Cyril Henry. Handbook of Oriental History. London: Royal Historical Society, 1951. Pp. vii, 239.
   Section II: India and Pakistan, includes on pp. 87-88, under the heading Muslim Dynasties, a list of the Ghaznavids and the Rulers of Ghur; and on pages 93-94, a list of the Amirs of Afghanistan.

570 Priestly, H., trans. Afghanistan and its Inhabitants, by Sirdar Muhammad Hayat Khan. Lahore, 1874.
   A translation of the Hayat-i Afghan (see no. 543).

571 The Problem of Afghanistan. Journal of the Central Asian Society 13, 187-204. 1926.

This article contains the account of a meeting held at London and
attended by many British authorities on Afghanistan and India. The
subject for discussion was the threatened annexation of Afghan Turkestan by the U.S.S.R. and the possibility of a Russian move as far
as Herat. Some urged that the British government take urgent measures if the Russians intervened directly in Afghan affairs.

572 Qandahari, Ghulam Morteza Khan. Halat-i valahazrat Amir 'Abd al-
Rahman Khan [The Times of His Royal Highness Amir 'Abd al-Rahman
Khan]. Mashhad, 1319 [1901]. Lithographed.

573 Qanungo, K. R. Sher Shah and His Times. Calcutta: Orient Longmans,
1965. Pp. 459.

574 Qasim 'Ali Khan. Muharabeh-yi Kabul [The Battle of Kabul]. Agra:
Sulaymani, 1272 [1856]. Pp. 535.
An epic poem in Persian, dealing with the exploits of Shah Shoja'.
The work is lithographed.

575 Rahim, M.A. History of the Afghans in India A.D. 1545-1631, with
Especial Reference to their Relations with the Mughals. Karachi:
Pakistan Publishing House, 1961. Pp. 326.

576 Rahmany, Magdalina. La reine Razia: Impératrice afghane aux Indes
[Queen Razia: Afghan Empress of India]. Afghanistan 3, no. 3, 13-
17. 1948.
An Amazon queen of Ghurid line, who reigned at Delhi from 1210-
1235 A.D.

577 Rahmany, Magdaline. La reine Gawarchade [Queen Gowhar Shad].
Afghanistan 4, no. 2, 14-17. 1949.
Sketch of the issue of this queen, wife of Shah Rokh, son of Timur.

578 Ramazani, R. K. Afghanistan and the U.S.S.R. Middle East Journal 12,
no. 2, 144-152. 1958.
An account of Soviet aid to Afghanistan and the attitudes of both nations to this aid and to each other.

579 Rao, J. Sambashiva, King Amanullah. Madras, 1929.

580 Rastogi, Ram S. Indo-Afghan Relations 1880-1900. Lucknow: Nav-
Jyoti Press, 1965. Pp. 256; bibliography.
A descriptive account of Indian (British)-Afghan relations, including

a full treatment of the delimitation of Afghanistan's frontiers with
Russia and India.

581 Rebuff. New Times 25, 20-21. Moscow, 1954.
An editorial commenting on an editorial in the New York Times,
and including an answer to the Times by an Afghan attaché in Washington.

582 *Reisner, Igor Mikhailovich. Razvitie feodalizma i obrazovanie gosudar-
stva u Afgantsev [Development of Feudalism and Formation of the Afghan State]. Moscow: Izdatel'stvo Akademii Nauk S.S.S.R., 1954.
Pp. 415.
A careful and thorough study of the formation of the Afghan state under Mir Ways and his successors. Completely Marxist in approach and
deductions.

583 Reissner, Larissa. In Karl Radek, ed., Oktober: Ausgewahlte Schriften.
Berlin: Neuer deutscher Verlag, 1930. Pp. 294; 309-437.
Sections entitled Vanderlip in Afghanistan (page 294) and Afghanistan
(pages 309-437).

584 *Reynolds, James, trans. The Kitab-i-Yamini, Historical Memoirs of the
Amir Sabaktagin, and the Sultan Mahmud of Ghazna . . . Translated
from the Persian Version of the Contemporary Arabic Chronicle of Al
Utbi, by the Rev. J. Reynolds. London: Oriental Translation Fund, 1858
(For the original Arabic text see no. 616.)

585 Rishtin, Sadiqullah. Da pushtanu mojahedi [The Pushtu Pioneers]. Kabul: Matba'eh-yi 'umumi, 1331 [1952]. Pp. 93.
Parallel columns of Persian and Pushtu give accounts of Afghans who
fought for independence in the period following the arrival of the
British in India.

586 *Rishtiya, Sayyid Qasim. Afghanistan dar garn-i nuzdahum [Afghanistan
in the Nineteenth Century]. Kabul: Matba'eh-yi 'umumi. 1329
[1950]. Pp. 256. Second edition 1336 [1957].
The work, in Persian, is the most ambitious effort in the field of contemporary history by an Afghan scholar. The source material, reflected in the bibliography, includes works in Persian, Pushtu, French,
and English. The book has been printed at Moscow in Russian translation (see no. 587).

587 Rishtiya, Sayyid Qasim. Afganistan v XIX v. [Afghanistan in the Nineteenth Century]. Gankovskiy, Yuriy V., ed., L. N. Dorofeyevnaya,

M. K. Kurkin, and Muhammad Rahim Khan, trans. Moscow: IIL, 1958. Pp. 487; bibliography.

A Russian translation of no. 586.

588 Roberts, Frederick Sleigh, 1st earl of. Forty-One Years in India. 2 vols. New York: Longmans, Green and Co. London: Richard Bentley and Son, 1897. Pp. (1) xx, 511; (2) xii, 522; appendices; numerous maps. A Field-Marshal reports on his long career in India and adjacent countries. The second volume is nearly entirely devoted to Anglo-Afghan relations and conflicts of these years. In the 1898 one-volume edition, the material on Afghanistan, corresponding to Volume 2 of the first edition, begins on page 280.

589 Roos-Keppel, George Olof. Translation of the Tarikh-i-Sultan Mahmud-i-Ghaznavi. Allahabad: Pioneer Press, 1901. Pp. 65.

590 Roskoschny, Hermann. Afghanistan und seine Nachbarländer [Afghanistan and her Neighbors]. 2 vols. Leipzig: Gressner und Schramm, 1885. Pp. (1) 1-176; (2) 177-336.

Discusses Afghanistan as the scene of the presumed final conflict between Russia and England in Central Asia.

591 Rosset, Louis-Felicien. Le Padishah Baber--1483-1530. Son passage à Kaboul [The Padishah Babur--1483-1530. His Visits to Kabul]. Afghanistan 1, no. 3, 36-46. 1946.

Tells of the ruler's trips from India back to his beloved Kabul.

592 Rosset, Louis-Felicien. Afghanistan, carrefour de l'Asie, terre de contrastes d'histoire [Afghanistan, Crossroads of Asia, Land of Historic Contrasts]. Afghanistan 6, no. 4, 27-51. 1951.

Highlights of Afghan history, with emphasis on the invaders: Alexander in Bactria, Chengiz Khan in Bamiyan and Babur.

593 Roy, Nirodbhusan. Niamatullah's History of the Afghans. Makhzan-i-Afghani. Part I: Lodi Period. Santiniketam (West Bengal): Bidyut Ranjan Basu, 1958. Pp. 211.

594 Rubinstein, Alvin Z. Afghanistan and the Great Powers. United States Naval Institute Proceedings, 83, pp. 62-68. 1957.

The background and present status of Afghanistan's major foreign relations.

595 *Sale, Lady Florentia. A Journal of the Disasters in Attghanistan, 1841-2. London: John Murray, 1843. Pp. xvi, 451; map.

·The wife of the British commander at Kabul, General Sale, describes
the revolt of the Afghans at Kabul in 1841, the British retreat, and
her own captivity of eight months in Afghan hands. Her frankness
gives the work a value beyond its account of personal experiences.

596 Salimi, Muhammad Arslan and Muhammad Shah Arshad. Zama ya dana
mu'alef valahazrat Marshal Shah Wali Khan Ghazi fateh Kabul [Of
Myself, or two Recollections of His Highness Marshal Wali Khan Ghazi,
Victor of Kabul]. Kabul: Matba'eh-yi doulati, 1339 [1960]. Pp. 97.
Two reminiscences of Marshal Shah Wali, in Pushtu.

597 Salisbury, Harrison E. Peaceful Competition along Russia's Border. New
York Times Magazine, p. 294. April 8, 1962.
Includes a discussion of Afghan-Soviet relations.

598 Saljuqi, Fekri. Gazargah, qesmat-i az tarikh-i Herat-i bastan [Gazargah,
a Part of the History of Ancient Herat]. Kabul: Matba'eh-yi doulati,
1341 [1962]. Pp. 91.
An account, in Persian, of the history of the shrine of Khwaja 'Abd
Allah Ansari at Gazargah, adjacent to Herat.

599 Savad-i mu'ahadeh-yi dawlatayn-i 'aliyatayn-i Afghanistan va-Iran
[Transcript of the Agreement between the Sublime Governments of
Iran and Afghanistan]. Kabul, 1921. Pp. 11.
Text of the agreement in Persian.

600 Schwarzenhach, Annemarie Clark. Military Importance of Afghanistan.
Living Age 358, 577-581. New York, 1940.
Afghanistan's uneasy Tribal Territory and the difficulty of maintain-
ing its uncertain loyalty against Russia.

601 *The Second Afghan War. 1878-80. Official Account. Produced in the
Intelligence Branch Army Head-Quarters, India. London: John Murray,
1908. Pp. x, 734; 40 appendices; maps; plans.
An exhaustive, pedestrian account of the British military operations
against the Afghan forces. Originally treated as a secret work, its
publication was held up for years until time had dulled the spirit of
controversy.

602 Seifi, Aziz al-Rahman, trans. Delhi da pushtunwzheh wakhtaki [Delhi
in the Time of the Pushtuns]. Kabul: Matba'eh-yi doulati, 1338
[1959]. Pp. 79.
A translation from the Persian text of Khan Ghazi.

III. HISTORY

603 Shah Shoja' al-Molk Saduza'i. Sawanih Shah Shoja' [The Accidents of
Shoja'] . Kabul.
An important work in Pushtu by a ruler of Afghanistan.

604 Shah Sirdar Ikbal Ali. Bolshevism in Central Asia. Edinburgh Review
234, 136-146. 1921.
A succinct account of Russian expansion in Central Asia is followed
by a summary of the unsuccessful efforts of Russian agents to involve
Afghanistan in World War I.

605 *Shah Sirdar Ikbal Ali. Modern Afghanistan. London: Sampson Low and
Co., n.d. [1939]. Pp. x, 342.
The first part of this work repeats background material familiar from
other works by this Afghan writer. Then attention is concentrated
upon the person and the government of Nadir Shah. Useful pages describe the political and social structure at this period.

606 Shcherbinovsky, N. Soviet Scientists in Afghanistan. New Times 25,
29-31. Moscow, 1953.
A review of M. S. Dunin's Afghanistan, Pakistan and India (see no.
146). According to the reviewer, Professor Dunin recalls with pride
Russia's efforts toward friendship with Afghanistan, and regrets the
backwardness and misery brought about there by British and American
imperialists.

607 *Shir Muhammad Khan. Tavarikh-i Khorshid-i jahan [Histories of the
Sun of the World] . Lahore: Islamieh, 1311 [1894] . Pp. ix, 320.
A genealogical history of the Afghans, written in Persian and litho-
graphed.

608 Siddiqi, Iqtidar Husain. Advent of the Afghans to Power. Studies in Islam
1, 4, 213-37. 1964.

609 Siddiqi, Iqtidar Husain. The Army of the Afghan Kings in North India.
Islamic Culture 39, 3, 223-43. 1965.

610 Sidqi, Muhammad 'Usman. Yaftaliyan [Ephthalites] . Kabul: Matba'eh-
yi 'umumi, 1326 [1948] . Pp. 40.
A treatment in Persian of the arrival of the Ephthalite Huns, of their
activity, and of their disappearance from the region.

611 Singh, Ganda. Ahmad Shah: The Man and His Achievements. Afghanistan 8, no. 1, 1-19. 1953.

A glowing portrait, with much personal detail about the Shah's appearance, his dress, his taste in literature and art, and his government policy.

612 *Singh, Ganda. Ahmad Shah Durrani. Father of Modern Afghanistan. Bombay: Asia Publishing House, 1959. Pp. 475; appendices; chronology; bibliography; index.
A comprehensive, documented study based on manuscript sources in Persian, on material in Indian languages, and on works by European writers. The extensive bibliography is uniquely valuable.

613 Singhal, D. P. India and Afghanistan 1876-1907. A Study in Diplomatic Relations. St. Lucia, Queensland: University of Queensland, 1963. Pp. 216; appendices; index.
A documented study, drawing on British source material.

614 Sokolov-Strakhov, K. I. Grazhdanskaya voyna v Afganistane, 1928-1929gg. [Civil War in Afghanistan, 1928-1929]. Moscow: Voyenizdat, 1931. Pp. 79.

615 Sperling, O. Mein Traum indien [My Indian Dream]. Berlin, 1934. Pp. 430.
Deals with plans to incite India to revolt against the British Empire during World War I.

616 Sprenger, A. and Maulawi Mamluk al-'Ali, eds. Tarikh Yamini. Delhi, 1847.
An edition of the history in Arabic of the Amir Subuktigin and Sultan Mahmud of Ghazni by Abu Nasr Muhammad b. 'Abd al-Jabbar al-'Utbi, one of the secretaries of Sultan Mahmud.

617 Squire, Sir Giles. Recent Progress in Afghanistan. Journal of the Royal Central Asian Society 37, 6-18. 1950.
An Englishman who was first British Minister, then Ambassador, at Kabul from 1943 to 1949, summarizes his impressions of the varied progress and change achieved during his residence.

618 Sultan Muhammad ibn Musa Khan. Tarikh-i Sultani [The Sultani History]. Bombay: Muhammadi, 1298 [1881]. Pp. 291.
A lithographed work in Persian, written about 1865 A.D. and dealing with the history of Afghanistan up to 1862.

619 Sykes, Sir Percy M. Sir Mortimer Durand, A Biography. London: Cassel, 1926. Pp. xi; 356.

III. HISTORY

The life of the delineator of the Durand Line, who served several
times in Kabul.

620 *Sykes, Sir Percy M. Afghanistan: The Present Position. Asiatic Review.
36, 279-310. 1940.
A recapitulation of Afghan political history and relations with Russia,
Britain, and Germany from the middle of the nineteenth century to
the present--with a strong British bias. Sir Percy spent almost 50 years
in the British Consulate in Persia. Discussion follows the paper.

621 Tabibi, Doktur Abd al-Hakim. Hoquq al-doval va monasabat-i an ba
mamalek-i mohafez bekhoskeh [International Law and its Relation to
Landlocked Countries]. Kabul: Matba'eh-yi doulati, 1337 [1958].
Pp. 59.
A study of this subject in Persian by a member of the delegation of
Afghanistan to the United Nations, who has specialized in this field.

622 Taillardat, C. F. Révolte afghane [The Afghan Revolt]. L'Asie
Française, pp. 15-20; 50-55. 1929.

623 Tarikh-i Afghan [Afghan History]. Constantinople: Jarideh Khaneh,
1277 [1861]. Pp. 174.
A reprint in Persian of a basic work by a Jesuit, Father J. T.
Krusinski, resident at Isfahan in the early eighteenth century.

624 Tarikh-i Afghanistan [History of Afghanistan]. 3 vols. Kabul: Matba'ch-
yi 'umumi, n.d. and 1325 [1946]. Pp. (1) 495; (2) 600; (3) 150.
An important work in Persian, for which additional volumes are con-
templated. The first volume, from earliest times to the period of
Alexander, is by A. A. Kohzad and M. U. Sidqi; the second continues to the rise of Islam and is by A. A. Kohzad. The third volume,
through the Taharid dynasty, is by M. Ghubar and A. A. Na'imi.
Only the first volume has an index.

625 Tarikh-i Afghanistan. Jeld-i sevum [History of Afghanistan. Volume
Three]. Kabul: Matba'eh-yi doulati, 1336 [1957]. Pp. 669.
This work, part of a semi-official history of the country in Persian,
appears to overlap sections of no. 624. M. Ghubar deals with the influence of Islam, A. A. Na'imi with the Taharid dynasty, M. M. S.
Ferhang with the Safarid dynasty, A. Mohebi with the Samanid dynasty, and K. Khalili with the Ghaznavid period. There is no index.

626 Tarikh-i Khayran; shamil avakhir-i safaviyeh fitneh-yi Afghan saltanet-i

Nadir Shah va ahval-i jam'i az buzurgan [History of Khayran (?);
Comprising the End of the Safavids, the Afghan Revolt, the Reign of
Nadir Shah and Biographies of a Number of Important People].
Isfahan: Ta'yid, 1332 [1953]. Pp. 140.
The second printed edition of an apparently obscure work in Persian.

627 *Tarn, W. W. The Greeks in Bactria and India. Cambridge University
Press, 1938. Pp. 539; bibliography; maps.
A masterly account of the Greek kingdoms set up in Afghanistan,
Central Asia, and India following the death of Alexander. All perti-
nent sources are clearly presented: Bactria is given a prominent
place, and the nomadic conquest of this region is discussed.

628 Tarzi, Mahmud, trans. Tarikh-i muharabeh-yi Rus va-Zhapan [History
of the Russo-Japanese War]. 3 vols. Kabul: 'Inayet, 1334-5 [1916-
17]. Pp. (1) 296; (2) 260; (3) 304.
Translation from Turkish into Persian of a history compiled by officers of the Turkish General Staff.

629 Tarzi, Mahmud. Siraj al-tavarikh [The Luminary of Histories]. Kabul.

630 *Tate, George Passman. The Kingdom of Afghanistan. A Historical
Sketch. Bombay and Calcutta: The Times of India Offices, 1911.
Pp. 224.
Attention is concentrated on the modern history of the country, be-
ginning with the period of Mir Ways. Includes an account of the
Pushtu language and a map of the "three cities" of Qandahar.

631 Tavakkuli, Ahmad. Ravabat-i siassi Iran va Afghanistan [Political Relations of Iran and Afghanistan]. Tehran: Mehr, 1327 [1948].
Pp. 135.

632 Tavakkuli, Ahmad. Afghanistan [Afghanistan]. Tehran, 1328 [1949].
Pp. 135.
A general survey in Persian, with the emphasis on Irano-Afghan rela-
tions.

633 Teplinskiy, Leonid B. Sovetsko-Afganskiye Otnosheniya 1919-1960;
Kratkiy ocherk [Soviet-Afghan Relations 1919-1960; a short Essay].
Moscow: Izdatel'stvo sotsial'no-ekonomicheskoy literatury, 1961.
Pp. 214; bibliography; indices.
Stresses the thesis of coexistence between two countries with different
social systems. Includes texts of agreements and an account of Soviet
aid to Afghanistan.

III. HISTORY

634 Terenzio, Pio-Carlo. La rivalité anglo-russe en Perse et en Afghanistan
     jusqu'aux accords de 1907. [The Anglo-Russian Rivalry in Persia and
     Afghanistan prior to the Agreements of 1907]. Paris: Rousseau, 1947.
     Pp. 178.
     Chapters 3 and 4 are concerned with the rivalry over Afghanistan.

635 Thabet, Muhammad Ibrahim. Sultan Shahab al-Din Ghuri. Kabul:
     Matba'eh-yi doulati, 1344 [1965]. Pp. 162.
     A work in Pushtu on the kingdom of this ruler.

636 *The Third Afghan War. 1919. Official Account. Compiled in the Gen-
     eral Staff Branch, Army Headquarters, India. Calcutta: Government
     of India, Central Publication Branch, 1926. Pp. ii, 174; maps; plans.
     The detailed accounts of military operations which lasted from May
     6th until June 2nd, 1919, are preceded by a number of pages describ-
     ing the composition of the Afghan forces at that period: their advan-
     tages and their disabilities.

637 Tissot, Louis. Un grain de blé entre deux meules, l'Afghanistan [A Grain
     of Wheat between Two Mill-Stones--Afghanistan]. Revue de défense
     nationale, n.s. 6, 597-606. 1948.
     An examination of Afghanistan's history in foreign relations, her pres-
     ent economic situation, and her position between Iran, India, Baluch-
     istan, and Soviet Russia.

638 Toynbee, Arnold J. Survey of International Affairs 1920-1923. Oxford
     and London, 1925. Pp. xv, 526; appendices; maps.
     Pages 376-378--"Relations between British India, Soviet Russia and
     Afghanistan, 1912-1923"--give a history of the brief Afghan War of
     1919 and a text of the Treaty of August 8, 1919. There is an expla-
     nation of the ensuing agreements with the British and of the Russo-
     Afghan and Turko-Afghan treaties of 1921.

639 Toynbee, Arnold J. The Islamic World since the Peace Settlement. In
     Survey of International Affairs 1925, Vol. 1. London and Oxford, 1927.
     Pp. xv, 587; appendices; folding map.
     Pages 546-569--"India, Afghanistan and the Frontier Tribes"--give a
     history of the troubles with the rebellious tribes on either side of the
     Durand Line and of the attempts of the British in India and of the Af-
     ghan government's less enthusiastic attempts to subdue them.

640 Toynbee, Arnold J. Impressions of Afghanistan and Pakistan's North-West
     Frontier: In Relation to the Communist World. International Affairs 37,
     2, 161-69. London, 1961.

641 Trever, K. V. Kushany, khionity i eftality po armianskim istochnikam
IV-VII vv; K istorii narodov Srednei Azii [The Kushans, Chionites
and Ephthalites according to Armenian Sources of the Fourth to the
Seventh Centuries; History of the Peoples of Central Asia]. Sovetskaia
Arkheologiia 21, 131-147. Moscow, 1954.

642 Tucci, Guiseppe. Une lettre [A Letter]. Afghanistan 9, no. 2, 59.
1954.
A letter from the president of the Italian Institute for the Middle and
Far East, thanking the Afghan Minister of Foreign Affairs for the offer
of a visit from Ahmad Ali Kohzad.

643 'Utbi, Muhammad. Tarikh-i Yamini [History of Yamin (al-Dawleh)].
Translated into Persian by Abu'l-Sharaf Nasih Jarfadaqani. Tehran,
1856. Pp. 460.
A lithographed translation into Persian from the Arabic by Abu'l-
Sharif Nasih Jarfadaqani. The text is a history of Amir Sabuktagin
and Mahmud of Ghazni.

644 Vali, Marshal Shah. Yaddashtha-yi man [My Memoirs]. Kabul:
Matba'eh-yi doulati, n.d. Pp. 108.
The important recollections of one of the heroes and builders of mod-
ern Afghanistan, in Persian.

645 Vaqat-i Shah Shuja' [The Events of Shah Shuja']. Kabul: Matba'eh-yi
doulati, 1333 [1954]. Pp. 162.

646 Vaqi 'at-i Durrani [The Events of the Durranis]. Cawnpore, 1875.
A translation into Urdu of the Tarikh-i Ahmad by 'Abd al-Karim
'Alavi (see no. 349). Translated by Mir Varis 'Ali Sayfi.

647 Viollis, Andrée. Tourmente sur l'Afghanistan [Storm over Afghanistan].
Paris: Libraire Valois, 1930. Pp. 240.
A French woman writer arrives at Kabul by Soviet plane to find her-
self plunged into the fury of the hectic days following the capture of
the capital by Nadir Khan. Other chapters concern the errors of King
Amanullah and the brief power of Habibullah.

648 Volsky, D. The Soviet Union and Afghan Progress. New Times 22, 18-
19. Moscow, 1962.
A description of Soviet aid programs in the fields of highway construction and irrigation facilities, as contrasted with American aid which
is concerned with "pumping money out of the Afghan treasury."

III. HISTORY

649 Weston, Christine. Afghanistan. New York: Charles Scribner's Sons,
1962. Pp. 162; map; glossary; index.
A personalized account of Afghan life and history.

650 Wheeler, Stephen. The Ameer Abdur Rahman. London: Bliss, Sands
and Foster, 1895. Pp. xvi, 251.
A study of contemporary history is followed by a detailed account of
the reign of this Afghan ruler, based almost exclusively on the ruler's
autobiography.

651 Wilber, Donald N. Afghanistan, Independent and Encircled. Foreign Affairs 31, no. 3, 486-494. 1953.
An examination of the modern political scene, with emphasis on Afghanistan's relations with the U.S.S.R., the U.S., and Pakistan.

652 Wild, Roland. Amanullah, Ex-King of Afghanistan. London: Hurst and
Blackett, 1932. Pp. 228.
Journalistic style and approach, with a certain amount of valuable
material such as a description of the "great council" held in 1928.

653 Yapp, M. E. Disturbances in Western Afghanistan, 1839-41. Bulletin of
the School of Oriental and African Studies 26, 2, 288-313. 1963.

654 Yuldashbayeva, Fatima K. Iz istorii angliyskoy kolonial'noy politiki v
Afganistane i Sredney Azii, 70-80 gody XIX v. [On the History of
British Colonial Policy in Afghanistan and West Asia, during 70-80
years of the Nineteenth Century]. Tashkent: Gos. Izd-vo Uzbekskoy
S.S.R., 1963. Pp. 189; bibliography.

655 Zaidi, Manzur. Afghanistan: Case Study in Competitive Peaceful Co-
Existence. Pakistan Horizon 2, 93-101. 1962.
Outlines the disputes between Afghanistan and Pakistan, and states
that Afghanistan profits by dealing with both the United States and
the U.S.S.R.

656 Zur-Muhammad, Hafiz. Tarikh-i Mazar-i Sharif va-vaqi'-i Balkh [His-
tory of Mazar-i Sharif and the Situation of Balkh]. Kabul: Matba'eh-
yi 'umumi, 1325 [1946].

IV. SOCIAL ORGANIZATION

Character of society; size and
geographical distribution of
population; ethnic groups;
social structure

The coverage on this basic subject is definitely inadequate. The Afghan government does not possess reliable figures on the total size and geographical distribution of the population and has no prospect of obtaining those figures in the near future. Existing material relating to the ethnic groups is most unsatisfactory. The commonly accepted picture of these groups dates from the nineteenth century, and in certain cases the studies done at that time merely compound confusion. It does appear that careful examination of those manuscripts recently edited by Afghan scholars should provide the sources for clarifying the situation as regards ethnic elements and social structure. However, the long-established structure of tribal and settled life is currently in a state of flux, with new patterns about to emerge.

Anthropologists, ethnologists, and sociologists are beginning to do fundamental work in the country, willingly assisted by the facilities of the Afghan government. However, far too little work of this nature is being carried on by the Afghans themselves—given the hundreds of Afghans now studying abroad it should be possible to develop a few sociologists.

657 Ali, Mohammad. Manners & Customs of the Afghans. Lahore: The Punjab Educational Press, 1958. Pp. 81.
     Short chapters on hospitality, tribal codes of conduct, nomadic life, ceremonies at the New Year, typical Afghan names, sports, and folklore.

658 Aristov, N. A. Zametki ob etnicheskom sostave tiurkskikh plemen i narodnostei i svedeniia ob ikh chislennosti [Remarks about the Ethnic Composition of the Turkic Tribes and Nationalities and Information about their Number]. Zhivaia Starina, 6. St. Petersburg, 1896.

659 Bacon, Elizabeth E. A Preliminary Attempt to Determine the Culture Areas of Asia. Southwestern Journal of Anthropology 2, 117-132. 1946.
     Deals with sedentary and nomadic cultures of southwestern Asia, including Afghanistan.

660 *Bacon, Elizabeth E. The Hazara Mongols of Afghanistan: A Study in Social Organization. Unpublished Ph.D. Thesis. University of California. Graduate Division, Northern Section, 1951. Pp. 144; bibliography.

IV. SOCIAL ORGANIZATION

661 *Bacon, Elizabeth E. An Inquiry into the History of the Hazara Mongols of Afghanistan. Southwestern Journal of Anthropology 7, 230-247. 1951.

The author examines the usually-held belief that the Hazaras are descended from military garrisons left in Afghanistan by Ghengis Khan in the early thirteenth century by consulting contemporary sources and concludes that the region was populated by Chagatai, moving in between 1229 and 1447 A.D.

662 Bacon, Elizabeth E. Obok. A Study of Social Structure in Eurasia. Viking Fund Publications in Anthropology 25. New York: Wenner-Gren Foundation for Anthropological Research, Inc., 1958. Pp. 235; bibliography; index.

Pages 1-65 deal with the social organization and the cultural relatives of the Hazara Mongols of Afghanistan.

663 Bellew, Henry Walter. A General Report on the Yusufzeis in Six Chapters. Lahore: Government Press, 1864. Pp. ix, 266.

664 Bellew, Henry Walter. The Races of Afghanistan, Being a Brief Account of the Principal Nations Inhabiting that Country. Calcutta: Thacker, Spink and Co., 1880. Pp. 124.

A preliminary study in preparation for the later work by this author: An Inquiry into the Ethnography of Afghanistan (see no. 665).

665 *Bellew, Henry Walter. An Inquiry into the Ethnography of Afghanistan. Woking: The Oriental University Institute, 1891. Pp. iv, 208.

Crowning work of a retired Surgeon-General of the Bengal Army: a monument of effort and application. Material drawn from sources of unestablished reliability, or doubtful reliability, in such a complex manner as to be without present-day value.

666 Benjamin, J. J., II. Eight Years in Asia and Africa from 1846 to 1855. Hanover, 1859. Pp. xv, 332; map.

An ardent Jewish traveler visited his co-religionists in many parts of the world. In this work, first published in German in 1857, two chapters are devoted to the manners and customs of the Hebrew community at Kabul.

667 Biddulph, J. Tribes of the Hindoo Koosh. Calcutta: Office of the Superintendent of Government Printing, 1880.

A rare work which treats the subject in a most detailed and thoroughly confusing manner.

668 Bravin, N. and I. Beliaev. Ukazatel' plemennykh imen k stat'e N. A. Aristova: "Zametki ob etnicheskom sostave tiurkskikh plemen i svendeniia o okh chislennosti." Izdano pod redaktsiei P. M. Melioranskogo [An Index of Tribal Names to the Article by N. A. Aristov: "Remarks about the Ethnic Composition of the Turkic Tribes and Nationalities and Information about their Number." Edited under the Supervision of P. M. Melioranskii]. Zapiski Imp. russk. geogr. obshchestva po otdel. etnografii 28, no. 2, St. Petersburg, 1903.

669 *Broadfoot, J. S. Reports on Part of the Ghilzai Country, and on Some of the Tribes in the Neighbourhood of Ghazni, and on the Route from Ghazni to Dera Ismail by the Ghwalari Pass. Journal of the Royal Geographical Society, Supplementary Papers 1, 1-60. 1885.
Notes taken by a Lieutenant Broadfoot in 1839 were finally edited and published by Major W. Broadfoot. Most useful for the account of tribes found around Ghazni.

670 Burnes, Alexander. On the Siah-Posh Kaffirs with Specimens of their Language and Costume. Journal of the Asiatic Society of Bengal 7, 325-333. 1838.
Captain Burnes interviewed several Kafirs, a Mohammedan and a Hindu--both of whom had traveled among the Kafirs--from whom he learned of their customs. There is a short vocabulary of the Kafir language, with sentences, and a shorter one of the Pushye dialect, with sentences.

671 Cagatay, B. and A. F. Sjoberg. Notes on the Uzbek Culture of Central Asia. The Texas Journal of Science 7, no. 1, 72-112. 1955.
A study based on observations of the Uzbek community at Kabul.

672 Carless, Hugh. The Tajiks of the Panjshir valley of the Hindu Kush. Revue Iranienne d'Anthropologie 1, no. 4/5, 40-54. 1956.

673 Collin-Delavaud, M. C. Deux exemples de mise en valeur dans l'Afghanistan septentrional [Two Examples of (Land) Improvement in northern Afghanistan]. Bulletin de l'Association de Géographes Français, 1958.
Factual information on Hazara society collected in the field in 1956.

674 Cunningham, George. Tribes of the North-West Frontier of India. World Review 2, 23-29. London, 1947.
The author, governor of the North-West Frontier Province from 1937 to 1946, writes informatively, indicating that the large tribes along the frontier would rather remain undeveloped and free than governed and developed.

675 *Dames, M. Longworth. The Baloch Race. A Historical and Ethnological Sketch. In Asiatic Society Monographs 4. London: Royal Asiatic Society, 1904. Pp. 90; bibliography; appendices.

On the divisions and subdivisions of the Baloch tribes living in India, Baluchistan and Sistan, their probable origin and their history in poetry and legends.

676 Darmesteter, James. Lettres sur l'Inde: À la frontière afghane [Letters on India: On the Afghan Frontier]. Paris: Lemerre, 1888. Pp. xxix, 355.

A noted French comparative philologist describes a stay of seven months in 1887 in the area of Northwestern India and Afghanistan.

677 Davydov, Aleksandr D. Sel'skaya obshchina u Khazareytsev tsentral'-nogo Afganistana [The Rural Community of the Hazaras of Central Afghanistan]. In: Kratkiye Soobshcheniya Instituta Narodov Azii. Moscow: "Nauka," 1964. No. 77, pp. 1-19.

A resumé of field research by Western scholars. An English translation appears in the Central Asian Review 14, 1, pp. 32-44. 1966.

678 *Datta, Bhupendra Nath. An Enquiry into the Racial Elements in Beluchistan, Afghanistan, and the Neighbouring Areas of the Hindu Kush. Man in India 19, 174-186, 218-273; 20, 1-43. 1939, 1940.

A careful compilation and analysis of historical data on the ethnic groups of the area and of available physical anthropological measurements. This study is an English translation and elaboration of a doctoral dissertation submitted to the University of Hamburg in 1923. Relevant works published after 1923 have been made use of in the revision.

679 Dianous, Hugues Jean de. Hazars et Mongols en Afghanistan [Hazaras and Mongols in Afghanistan]. Orient 19, 71-98 and 20, 91-113. 1961.

680 *Dictionary of the Pathan Tribes on the North-West Frontier of India, Compiled under the Orders of the Quarter-Master General in India. Calcutta: Government Printing Office, 1890. Pp. viii, 239.

A complex study, produced by the Intelligence Branch at Simla, dealing with tribal groups, subgroups, habitat, intra-tribal relations, leadership, etc. A map in color illustrates the areas of important groups.

681 Dupree, Louis. The Changing Character of South-Central Afghanistan Villages. Human Organization 14, no. 4, 26-29. 1956.

IV. SOCIAL ORGANIZATION

682 Dzhafarova, A. A. Iz istorii zhenskogo voprosa v Afganistane [From the History of the Position of Women in Afghanistan]. In: Kratkiye Soobshcheniya Instituta Narodov Azii. Moscow, 1963. No. 73, pp. 23-28.

683 Edwardes, Herbert Benjamin. A Year on the Punjab Frontier in 1848-49. 2 vols. London: Richard Bentley, 1851. Pp. (1) xiv, 608; (2) xiv, 734.

> Only a limited part of this work is related to tribal elements on the Afghan side of the frontier; pages 385-369 describe the people of Murwat and their life.

684 *Fazy, Robert. L'Exploration du Kafiristan par les Européens [The Exploration of Kafiristan by Europeans]. Asiatische Studien, pp. 1-25; appendices. Bern, 1953.

> Brief accounts of the Europeans who have traveled in Kafiristan (Nuristan) with notes on their publications, of which the appendices contain extracts.

685 Ferdinand, Klaus. Afghanistans Nomader [Afghan Nomads]. Fra Nationalmuseets Arbejdsmark (Copenhagen). Pp. 61-70. 1956.

> Material similar to that contributed by this author to no. 183.

686 Ferdinand, Klaus. Nomadestudier i Afghanistan. In: Menneskets Mangfoldighed (Copenhagen). Pp. 126-41. 1957.

687 Ferdinand, Klaus. The Baluchistan Barrel-vaulted Tent and its Affinities. Folk 1, 27-50. 1959.

688 Ferdinand, Klaus. Preliminary Notes on Hazara Culture. Det Kongelige Danske Videnskabernes Selskab, Historisk-filosofiske Meddelelser, Bd. 37, Nr. 5. Copenhagen: Ejnar Munksgaard, 1959. Pp. 51; bibliography.

> Material collected on the Mongol tribes of Afghanistan between 1953 and 1955 by the Danish Scientific Mission to Afghanistan.

689 Ferdinand, Klaus. Nomad Expansion and Commerce in Central Afghanistan. A Sketch of Some Modern Trends. Folk 4, 123-59. 1962.

690 Ferdinand, Klaus. Ethnographical Notes on Chahar Aimaq, Hazara, and Moghol. Acta Orientalia 28, no. 3-4, 175-204. 1965.

691 Field, Claud H. A. With the Afghans. London: Marshall Brothers, n. d. (1908). Pp. 221.

An account of missionary work with Afghans at Peshawar, in the tribal areas, and with Afghans from across the frontier.

692 Gafferberg, E. G. Formy braka i svadebnye obriady u dzhemshidov i
khezare [Forms of Marriage and Wedding Rituals among the Jemshin
and Khezar]. Sovetskaia etnografiia. Leningrad, 1936.

693 Gafferberg, E. G. Khazareiskaia (Afganistan) iurta khanaikhyrga; k
voprosu ob istorii kochevogo zhilishcha [Hazara (Afghanistan) Yurt
"Khanai Khyrga"; History of Nomadic Dwellings]. Akademiia nauk
S. S. S. R. Muzei antropologii i etnografii. Sbornik 14, 72-92. Moscow, 1953.

694 Gharzi, General Muhammad Safar Vakil. Nuristan [Nuristan]. Kabul:
Matba'eh-yi doulati, 1338 [1960]. Pp. 88.
An account in Persian of travels in Nuristan and observations of the
so-called Baluris by an Afghan army general.

695 Hackin, Joseph. Les idoles du Kafiristan [The Idols of Kafiristan].
Artibus Asiae, No. 4, 258-262. 1926.
Five illustrations show as many idols in the Kabul Museum, while the
text describes how the conventionalized figures were executed solely
by knives and hatchets, and tells of their roles in pagan beliefs.

696 *Hackin, Ria and Ahmad Ali Kohzad. Légendes et coutumes afghanes
[Afghan Legends and Customs]. Paris: Imprimerie nationale, presses
universitaires de France, 1953. Pp. xxvi, 204.
The bulk of the volume consists in material collected during a decade
by Mme. Hackin and Kohzad, an outstanding Afghan scholar. The
popular stories were gathered in the neighborhood of famous archaeological sites and relate to these sites. Material of quite another type
is found in the pages devoted to popular customs and beliefs.

697 *Herrlich, Albert. Land des Lichtes. Deutsche Kundfahrt zu unbekannten
Völkern im Hindukusch [The Land of Light. German Research with the
Unknown Peoples of the Hindu Kush]. Munich: Knorr und Hirth, 1938.
Pp. 177; sketch maps.
A member of the German expedition of 1935 describes the trip from
Kabul into Nuristan (Land of Light). Valuable account of little-known
areas, with a route map of the expedition.

698 Holdich, Thomas Hungerford. Origin of the Kafirs of the Hindu-Kush.
Geographical Journal 7, 42-49. 1896.

IV. SOCIAL ORGANIZATION

A discussion of the historical background of the region leads to the conclusion that this group is of Iranian stock and moved from Badakhshan into their present habitat.

699 *Ivanov, W. Notes on the Ethnology of Khurasan. Geographical Journal 67, 143-158. 1926.

The author, who lived for several years in Iran, discusses the population of a region which includes parts of both Iran and Afghanistan. He describes Persian stock, Turks, Kurds, Baluchis, Timuris, Barbaris (Hazaras), with the Afghan elements either overlapping the border as emigrants from Afghanistan in recent years, or as nomads moving across frontiers. A most informative article.

700 Jarring, Gunnar. An Uzbek's View on his Native-Town and its Circumstances. Ethnos 4, 73-80. Stockholm, 1939.

Is concerned with the town of Andkhui and its immediate vicinity. Reflects a visit made by the author in 1935. At that time he asked his local Uzbek informant to describe this town, its people, manners and customs and the article is a translation of that account.

701 Jarring, Gunnar. On the Distribution of Turk Tribes in Afghanistan: An Attempt at a Preliminary Classification. In Lunds Universitets Arsskrift, N. F., Ard. 1, Bd. 35, Nr. 4. Lund (Sweden): C. W. K. Gleerup, 1939. Pp. 104; bibliography.

A preliminary attempt to classify these tribes in Afghanistan by a Scandinavian diplomat and scholar who has specialized on the Turks of Central Asia. Attention is centered on the tribes of the center and north of the country. Supported by a valuable bibliography, including works in Russian.

702 Jeanneret, André. Contribution a l'étude des boulangers de Kaboul (Afghanistan) [A Contribution towards the Study of the Bakers of Kabul (Afghanistan)]. Bulletin Annuel du Museé et Institut d'Ethnographie de la Ville de Genève 7, 35-48. 1964.

A study of baking methods, including kinds of ovens and types of bread.

703 Jenkins, Robin. Some Kind of Grace. London: Macdonald, 1960.

A novel by an Englishman who was resident at Kabul for several years.

704 Jenkins, Robin. Dust on the Paw. New York: G. P. Putnam's Sons, 1961. Pp. 384.

A perceptive novel, with modern Kabul as its setting.

IV. SOCIAL ORGANIZATION

705 Karpov, G. Turkmeniia i turkmeny [Turkmeniya and the Turkmen].
Turkmenovedenie, No. 10 and 11. Ashkhabad, 1929.
Useful work by a trained ethnologist who worked in Turkmeniya.

706 Karpov, G. Plemennoi i rodnoi sostav turkmen [Tribal and Family Composition of the Turkmen]. Poltoratsk, 1925.

707 Karpov, G. I. and P. V. Arbekov. Salyry (Salory) [Salyr (Salor) People].
Turkmenovedenie, No. 6 and 7. Ashkhabad, 1930.

708 *Khadem, Qiyam al-Din. Pushtunwali [Pushtun Code]. Kabul:
Matba'eh-yi 'umumi, 1331 [1952]. Pp. 204.
An uniquely valuable account of the laws and customs of the so-
called true Afghans, written in Pushtu.

709 Khan, Ghani. The Pathans. A Sketch. Peshawar: University Book
Agency, 1958. Pp. 58.
A light-hearted account by a Pathan, with chapters on history, cus-
toms, folk songs and tales, and tribal patterns of behavior.

710 Kislyakov, N. A. and A. I. Pershits, eds. Narodī Peredney Azii [The
Peoples of the Middle East]. Moscow: Izdatel'stvo Akademii Hauk
SSR, 1957. Pp. 614; bibliography.
Pages 53-72 deal with the ethnic groups of Afghanistan; a map of
population density is included.

711 Kohzad, Ahmad Ali. Recherches sur l'étymologie et les origines des
Ephthalites [Research on the Etymology and Origins of the Hephtha-
lites]. Afghanistan 7, no. 3, 1-5. 1952.
The names by which the Hephthalites were known in Europe, their
possible origin, and a few words on their empire and fall.

712 A(hmad Ali) K(ohzad). The Nuristanis Are Aryans and Not Greek Rem-
nants. Afghanistan 9, no. 2, 36-40. 1954.
A refutation of the theory that the Nuristanis are the descendants of
Alexander's Greeks.

713 Komarov. Kratkiie statisticheskiie svedeniia o plemenakh ersari, obita-
iushchikh levyi bereg Amu-Dar'i ot pogranichnogo s Afganistan om
seleniia Bossagi do Chardzhuia. 1886 [Brief Statistical Data about the
Tribes of the Ersar who Live on the Left Bank of the Amu Darya, from
the Settlement Bossag on the Border of Afghanistan to Charjuia. 1886].
Sbornik geograficheskikh, topograficheskikh i statisticheskikh mate-
rialov po Azii, Pt. 25, 278-97. St. Petersburg, 1887.

714 Kussmaul, Friedrich. Badaxshan und seine Tagiken [Badakhshan and its
 Tajiks]. Tribus 14, 11-99. 1965.
 Account of a trip made in 1962/63 through the Panshir valley to
 Badakhshan. Valuable material on the life and customs of remote
 peoples.

715 Ligeti, L. Le lexique moghol de R. Leech [The Moghal Vocabulary of
 R. Leech].
 A study of a vocabulary of the language of the Moghal Aimaks pub-
 lished by R. Leech in 1838.

716 Ligeti, L. Recherches sur les dialects mongol et turcs de l'Afghanistan
 [Researches on the Mongol and Turkish Dialects of Afghanistan]. Acta
 Orientalia 4, 93-117. 1954.
 Summary in French of an account in Russian of field work conducted
 prior to World War II.

717 Logofet, D. N. Bukharskoe Khanstvo pod russkim protektoratom [The
 Khanate of the People of Bukhara under a Russian Protectorate]. 2 vols.
 St. Petersburg, 1913.

718 *Lumsden, Sir Peter. Countries and Tribes Bordering on the Koh-i-Baba
 Range. Proceedings of the Royal Geographical Society 7, 561-583;
 map. 1885.
 Lively, entertaining description of the country north of Herat, and
 particularly of the life, habits and customs of the Saryk Turkoman;
 with duller quotations from other travelers in the same country. The
 discussion of the paper included some remarks read by Sir Henry
 Rawlinson on the two ancient cities called Merv.

719 Meakin, Annette M. B. Quelques races indigènes de l'Asie centrale
 [Some Native Races of Central Asia]. Revue Anthropologique 38,
 241-245. 1927.
 Emphasis upon the position of the female sex in a brief review of the
 Uzbek, Tajik, Kirghiz and Turkoman population elements.

720 Michener, James. Caravans. New York: Random House, 1963. Pp. 341.
 A novel, not highly regarded by the Afghans nor those familiar with
 the country, since "his highly stereotyped characterizations never re-
 motely penetrate the psychology of the Kabuli, the villager, or the
 nomad."

721 Mo'tamedi, Ahmad Ali. Iqtisad-i rustayi Nuristan [The Rural Economics

of Nuristan]. Kabul: Puhantun, 1335 [1956]. Pp. 76.
A first-hand study, illustrated with photographs and sketches, in Persian by a graduate of Kabul University.

722 Mumand, Muhammad Gol. Landda Kay pushtu aw pushtunwaleh [Brief Account of Pushtu and Pushtunwali]. Kabul: Matba'eh-yi 'umumi, 1327 [1948]. Pp. 53.
A general treatment of the subject in Pushtu.

723 Oliver, Edward Emmerson. Across the Border; or, Pathan and Biloch. London: Chapman and Hall, Ltd., 1890. Pp. xi, 344; folding map.
The map shows the locations of all the tribes discussed.

724 The Non-Pathan Tribes of the Valley of the Hindu-Kush. Journal of the Royal Central Asian Society 21, 305-308. 1934.
The tribes and their dialects, divided geographically by rivers.

725 Pennell, Theodore L. Among the Wild Tribes of the Afghan Frontier. A Record of Sixteen Years' Close Intercourse with the Natives of the Indian Marches. London: Seeley and Co., Ltd., 1909. Pp. xvi, 324; maps.
A British medical missionary, conversant in Pushtu, reports on years of close association with the Afghans of the region between Peshawar and the Afghan frontier. While the story takes place outside of Afghanistan, there is a great deal of valuable material related to the Afghan character and modes of life. The book was well received: a fourth edition appeared in 1912.

726 Petermann, August Heinrich. Völker- und Sprachenkarte des Vorderen Orient [Peoples-and-Languages Map of the Near East]. Petermanns Geographische Mitteilungen 90, Tafel 2. 1944.
A facsimile of a map which shows the racial distribution of tribes in Afghanistan; unfortunately so reduced that much of it is illegible.

727 Peter of Greece and Denmark, Prince. Jars Built without a Wheel in the Hazarajat of Central Afghanistan. Man: A Monthly Record of Anthropological Science 54, no. 73. 1954.
A brief letter describing the life of Dai Zangi people near Herat, especially their method of making clay jars.

728 *Peter of Greece and Denmark, Prince. The Abul Camp in Central Afghanistan. Journal of the Royal Central Asian Society 41, 44-53. 1954.
An ethnographical mission, led by Prince Peter, followed up rumors

of a huge nomadic camp which met to elect kings and to trade; found
the camp and were entertained there.

729 Pikulin, M. G. Beludkhi [Baluchi]. Moscow: Izdatel'stvo Vostochnoy
Literatury, 1959. Pp. 210; bibliography.

730 Rand, Christopher. From the Sweet to the Bitter. New Yorker 31, no. 1,
100-115. February 19, 1955.
A colorful account of a visit to the Fakir of Ipi in his canyon strong-
hold. With descriptions of the Pathans, their feasts and dances; the
biography and thumb-nail sketch of the Fakir himself. Although the
Fakir lives in Pakistan, he sides with Afghanistan on the Pushtunistan
issue.

731 *Robertson, George S. The Kafirs of the Hindu-Kush. London: Lawrence
and Bullen, Ltd., 1896. Pp. xx, 658; map.
A British army officer, interested in linguistics and ethnography, tells
in narrative form of his trip through Kafiristan in 1889 and 1890. Important treatment of the Siah Push branch of the Kafirs and valuable
comments on three local languages. A second edition appeared in
1900.

732 Robinson, Nehemiah. Persia and Afghanistan and their Jewish Communities. New York: Institute of Jewish Affairs, 1953. Pp. 31.
The economic, social and political situation of these communities is
analyzed.

733 Romodin, Vadim A. Sotsial'no-ekonomicheskiy stroy yusufzayskikh
plemen v XIX veke (sravitel'no s drugimi afganskimi plemenami)
[Social-economic system of the Yusufzai tribes in the 19th century
(compared with the other Afghan tribes)]. In Ocherki po novoy istorii
stran Srednego Vostoka. Moscow: MGU, 1951. Pp. 99-124.

734 *Schurmann, H. F. The Mongols of Afghanistan. Hague: Mouton & Co.,
1961. Pp. 435; 14 figures; ethnographical map; glossary; bibliography; indices.
A very comprehensive and informative ethnography of the Moghols
and related peoples of Afghanistan.

735 *Scott, George Batley. Afghan and Pathan--A Sketch. London: The
Mitre Press, 1929. Pp. 188; map.
The first half of this work is given over to a general account of Afghanistan and the North-West Frontier Province during the nineteenth
century. The second part is devoted to the border tribes, with

valuable material on geographical distribution, characteristics of various groups, and conflicts between tribes and authorities. A sketch map shows tribal locations.

736 *Shah, Sirdar Ikbal Ali. Afghanistan of the Afghans. London: The Diamond Press, 1928. Pp. 272; map.

A brief historical sketch is followed by a collection of moderately effectively assembled material on folklore and customs, religious beliefs and superstitions, and on the life of various ethnic groups.

737 Shakur, M. A. The Red Kafirs. Peshawar: Imperial Press, 1946. Pp. v, 42; folding sketch map; bibliography.

A first-hand survey of part of the region by the Curator of the Peshawar Museum resulted in this description of the topography, history, and social life of these little-known people. There are several illustrations of the characteristic carved wooden statuary.

738 *Slousch, N. Les Juifs en Afghanistan [The Jews in Afghanistan]. Revue du Monde Musulman 4, 502-511. 1908.

739 Snoy, Peter. Nuristan und Mungan [Nuristan and Mungan]. Tribus 14, 101-148. 1965.

Observations in Nuristan, especially interesting for its photographs and account of the songs and dances of this region.

740 Spain, James W. The Way of the Pathans. London: Robert Hale, 1962. Pp. 190.

There is also an American edition under the title of "The People of the Khyber: The Pathans of Pakistan." New York: Praeger. Describes the tribal affiliations of the tribes to the east of the Durand Line.

741 Spain, James W. The Pathan Borderland. The Hague: Mouton and Co., 1963. Pp. 293; map; bibliography; index.

An excellent study of these tribes, their internal rivalries, and their opposition to outside interference.

742 Temple, R. C. Rough Notes on the Distribution of the Afghan Tribes about Kandahar. Journal of the Asiatic Society of Bengal 48, Pt. 1, 181-185; map. 1879.

While Lieutenant Temple was on foraging and reconnaissance expeditions, he took brief notes on the tribes, their subdivisions and locations.

IV. SOCIAL ORGANIZATION

743 Temple, R. C. Remarks on the Afghans Found along the Route of the
Tal Chotaili Field Force, in the Spring of 1879. Journal of the Asiatic
Society of Bengal 49, 91-106; 141-180; maps. 1880.
Notes on the habitat and divisions of Pathan tribes within Afghanistan
and languages spoken by these groups.

744 Thesiger, W. The Hazaras of Central Afghanistan. Geographical Journal
121, no. 3, 312-319. 1955.
Report on a tour of the Hazarajat in 1954.

745 Thorburn, S. S. Bannu; or Our Afghan Frontier. London: Trubner and
Co., 1876. Pp. x, 480; map; appendices.
A British officer, resident in the area for several years prior to publication, writes of a Pushtun element in the area just west of Waziristan
and hence outside of Afghanistan. The title is included because the
work contains valuable material on Pushtu proverbs, popular stories,
ballads and riddles.

746 Vakil, Safar. Le Nouristan [Nuristan]. Afghanistan 3, no. 4, 3-7.
1948.
Sketchy survey of topography, ethnic divisions, possible ethnic origin,
idol worship; diet and local sports.

747 Vambery, Arminius. Das Türkenvolk in seinen ethnologischen und ethno-
graphischen Beziehungen [The Turkish People in their Ethnological and
Ethnographical Relations]. Leipzig: F. A. Brockhaus, 1885. Pp. xii,
638; bibliography.

748 Voigt, Martin. Kafiristan. Versuch einer Landes Kunde auf Grund einer
Reise im jahre 1928 [Kafiristan. Attempt at a Geography of a Country
from the Basis of a Journey in the year 1928]. Bresleau: F. Hirt, 1933.
Pp. 119; maps.

749 Waleh, A. H. Nooristan. Afghanistan 6, no. 3, 20-29. 1951.
A sketch of Nuristan life, describing houses, customs, agriculture,
religion, language, etc.

750 Zarubin, I. I. Spisok narodnostei Turkestanskogo Kraia [A List of Na-
tionalities of the Turkestan Region]. Leningrad: Rossiiskaia akademiia
nauk. Trudy Komissii po izucheniiu plemennogo sostava naseleniia
Rossii'i sopredel'nykh stran, 9. 1925.
Zarubin was a gifted linguist who was in his element in studies of
Iranian dialects.

V. SOCIAL EVOLUTION AND INSTITUTIONS

Cultural development and expression; applied
sciences; education; religion; public
information; press and publications;
health and public welfare;
social attitudes

A considerable number of titles appear under this heading, but they are of uneven merit and importance, and some of the subjects listed have been almost entirely neglected. There is, for example, very little reliable and up-to-date material on religion in Afghanistan and just as little on the subjects of health and public welfare. Once again, it is necessary to distinguish between writings by foreigners and by Afghan authors. Foreign publications reflect a fairly clear picture of trends in contemporary education, as well as of current attitudes of various elements of the population toward change and "modernization," whereas the articles by Afghans are rather less precise and conclusive.

The listing of newspapers, periodicals, and serial publications given in this section may be considered to be comprehensive--possibly exhaustive--and should indicate what enormous strides have been taken in the field of public information within the last few decades.

751 'Abd al-Qaddus. Taftish-i Amaniyeh [The Amani Investigation]. Dehra Dun: Bahariyeh, 1927. Pp. 20.
A short treatise on education, written in Persian and compiled with special reference to the reforms of Amir Amanullah. The work is lithographed.

752 'Abd al-Rahman Khan, amir. Kalimat amir al-bilad fi'l-targhib ila'l-jihad [Words of the Ruler of the Countries Concerning Instigation to Holy War]. Kabul: Humayun, 1304 [1887]. Pp. 40.
A lithographed work in Arabic by a ruler of Afghanistan concerning the duties and merits of conducting holy wars.

753 'Abd al-Rahman Khan, amir. Sar-rishteh-yi islamiyeh-yi Rum [The Islamic Competence of Turkey]. Kabul: 1304 [1887]. Pp. 8.
A lithographed proclamation in Persian from the Amir to his Moslem subjects, regarding the attitude of Turkey toward European powers.

754 'Abd al-Rahman Khan, amir. Mir'at al-'uqul va kalimat-i maw'izat-i asas [The Mirror of Intellects and Words of Fundamental Admonition]. Kabul: Dar al-Saltaneh, 1311 [1894]. Pp. 28.
A lithographed work in Persian, in which an Afghan ruler discusses this

subject and concludes with advice to his people concerning their religious duties.

755 The Afghan Student.
News bulletin of the Associated Students of Afghanistan in the United States. First issued in 1956, it appears irregularly from different addresses.

756 Afghanistan. Washington, D.C.: Division of International Health, 1960. Pp. 171; tables; bibliography.
Reproduced by mimeograph, this work is one of a series known as the International Epidemiology Series, which describes the state of the people's health in various countries.

757 Afghanistan Ariana.
A bimonthly which began publication at Kabul in June 1961. Described in the first issue as a pictorial representation of Afghanistan's developments in educational, technical, industrial, and social fields, the text is in English and the illustrations in black and white and color. Publisher: Publicity Section of the Department of Press and Information.

758 Da Afghanistan Bank Majeleh [The Magazine of Da Afghanistan Bank]. Began publication as a monthly in 1957. Text in Persian and Pushtu.

759 L'Afghanistan nouveau [The New Afghanistan]. Paris: Royal Legation of Afghanistan, 1924. Pp. 95.
A general survey of the country, covering such subjects as history, international relations, and recent political and economic moves, with emphasis on French participation in archaeology and education within the country.

760 Akhtar, S.A. On Some Nematode Parasites from Afghanistan. Proceedings of the Indian Academy of Sciences, Section B, 10, no. 5, 287-291. Bangalore; 1939.
A list and description, with two illustrations, of several parasites.

761 Ali, Mohammad. A Cultural History of Afghanistan. Lahore: Punjab Educational Press, 1964. Pp. 255.
A general survey of considerable interest and value, including material on some contemporary writers.

762 Aman-i Afghan [Afghan Peace].

The official daily paper published in Persian at Kabul during the reign of Amir Amanullah and for a part of this time under the editorship of Mahmud Tarzi.

763 Angar [Imagination].
Privately published biweekly newspaper, issued in Persian and Pushtu in 1951 at Kabul by Fayz Muhammad Angar.

764 *Anis [Companion].
Began publication at Kabul as a fortnightly newspaper in 1927. In recent years it has become the "national" evening daily, largely in Persian, with an estimated circulation of 5,000.

765 Ansari, Mir Amin al-Din. Dar justajuy-i kamiya [In Search of Alchemy]. Kabul: Matba'eh-yi 'umumi, 1318 [1939]. Pp. 86.
An original work in Persian by an American-educated official of the Ministry of Education.

766 Ansary, Mir A. Buzkashi: Sport of the Asian Khans. Viewpoints 5, no. 10, 28-32.
Excellent account of an Afghan game played on horseback.

767 Arberry, A.J. and R. Landau, eds. Islam Today. London: Faber and Faber, Ltd., 1943. Pp. 258.
Chapter 14, by Sir Percy M. Sykes, is on Afghanistan and places emphasis on the resources of the country and the program of modernization.

768 Arshad, Muhammad Shah. Dimukrasi Islam [The Democracy of Islam]. Kabul: Matba'eh-yi doulati, 1343 [1964]. Pp. 66.
In this work in Persian, the author defines the pillars of Islam as brotherhood, cooperation, social solidarity, consultation, justice, and equality and relates these to basic human rights.

769 Badakhshan [Badakhshan].
A Persian-language weekly paper published at Fayzabad.

770 Bakhtiari, 'Abdullah. Pushtana da Iqbal pa nazar Kishi [Afghans from Iqbal's Point of View]. Kabul: Doulati matba'eh, 1335 [1956]. Pp. 68.

771 Balkh [Balkh].
Founded in 1949, this periodical is printed in Persian and published

at Mazar-i Sharif by the Matba'eh-yi Mazar-i Sharif. Hand-set and hand-printed, the periodical appears monthly--or less frequently-- and features short articles on the history and monuments of the province of Masar-i Sharif.

772 Barg-i sabz [Green Leaf].
A monthly magazine, established at Kabul in 1948. Sponsored by the Marestun [Social Service Center], the periodical runs articles in Persian on child care, hygiene, and allied subjects, most of which are translations from the foreign press.

773 Baudet, Roger. La philatélie en Afghanistan [Philately in Afghanistan]. Afghanistan 5, no. 3, 10-17; 6, no. 1, 41-47. 1950, 1951.
After some advice to young philatelists, a description of Afghan issues from the first in 1868 to the present.

774 Baudet, Roger. Les journées philatéliques de Kaboul [The Philatelic Days of Kabul]. Afghanistan 7, no. 2, 54-59. 1952.
Report of a Philatelic Exhibition, describing several notable collections that were on display.

775 Baudet, Roger. Les émissions commémoratives afghanes [Commemorative Afghan Issues]. Afghanistan 8, no. 4, 51-53. 1953.
Some remarks on special commemorative issues and on Afghan stamps in general--their rarity and the difficulties involved in collecting them.

776 Baudet, Roger. Aérophilatélie [Air-Philately]. Afghanistan 9, no. 1, 58-61. 1954.
On the rare and valuable stamps of the Afghan airmail service.

777 Baum, F. L. Trachoma in Afghanistan. South African Medical Journal 23, 214-215. Capetown, 1949.

778 Beck, Sebastian. Das afghanische Strafgesetzbuch vom Jahre 1924 mit dem Zusatz vom Jahre 1925. Aus dem persischen übersetz und mit einer allgemeinen Einleitung in die afghanische Strafgesetzgebung-Versehen [The Afghan Penal Code for the Year 1924 with Supplement for 1925. Provided with a Translation from Persian and a General Introduction of Afghan Penal Legislation]. Berlin, 1928.

779 *Bell, Marjorie Jewett, ed. An American Engineer in Afghanistan: From the Letters and Notes of A.C. Jewett. Minneapolis: Minnesota University Press, 1948. Pp. 335; map.

Letters written home by an American engaged in the arduous and frustrating task of introducing and installing engineering and power equipment in Afghanistan. Complements Frank A. Martin's Under the Absolute Amir (see no. 855).

780 Berke, Zuhdi. Inoculation Experiments against Typhus in Afghanistan. British Medical Journal 2, no. 4485, 944-945. 1946.

781 Berke, Zuhdi. La santé publique et l'hygiène en Afghanistan [Public Health and Hygiene in Afghanistan]. Afghanistan 1, no. 3, 1-9. 1946. An account of current problems, with emphasis on the most prevalent diseases, and attempted solutions.

782 Bidar [Vigilant].
A newspaper founded in 1921 at Mazar-i Sharif and published biweekly in Persian, with occasional material in Pushtu.

783 Bigham, mir 'Abd al-Rashid. Atlilik baray-i javan-i Afghan [Athletics for the Afghan Youth]. Kabul: Matba'eh-yi 'umumi, 1325 [1946]. Pp. 134.
A history of sports and games by the Director of Sports in the Ministry of Education.

784 Bleiber, F. Afghanistan und die Sowjetunion [Afghanistan and the Soviet Union]. Osteuropa, pp. 322-331. Stuttgart, October 1953.
Political and economic relations viewed from West Germany.

785 *Bogdanov, L. Notes on the Afghan Periodical Press. Islamic Culture 3, 126-152. Hyderabad, 1929.
A very informative article by a scholar resident at Kabul. Describes the twelve newspapers and periodicals of the years 1919-1928 in considerable detail. Titles are given in Arabic characters and in transliteration and translation. In addition, a variety of general information, such as sketches of editors.

786 Borhani, Mo'in al-Din, ed. Ershadat-i dini [Religious Instructions]. Kabul: Doulati matba'eh, 1342 [1963]. Pp. 302.
Guidance on religion from six writers, some contemporary.

787 Boulanger, M. Allocution du doyen de la Faculté de Médecine a l'occasion de la commémoration de la création de la Faculté de Médecine de Kaboul [Address of the Dean of the Faculty of Medicine on the Anniversary of the Creation of the Faculty of Medicine at Kabul]. Afghanistan 3, no. 3, 54-62. 1948.

V. SOCIAL EVOLUTION AND INSTITUTIONS

A resumé of the status of the Faculty is followed by an account of the needs of the school--in equipment and for improvements in curriculum.

788 Boulenger, P. M. La Faculté de Médecine de Kaboul, Afghanistan [The Medical Faculty at Kabul, Afghanistan]. Semaine des Hopitaux de Paris 26, 1627-1631. 1950.

789 *Burnes, Sir Alexander. Cabool: A Personal Narrative of a Journey to, and Residence in, that City, in the Years 1836, 7 and 8. London: John Murray, 1842. Pp. xii, 398.

Casual and informal account of life at Kabul by a British officer with years of travel and experience in the region. Many other subjects are treated in some detail, such as the Siah Push Kafirs.

790 Castagne, Joseph A. Le mouvement d'émancipation de la femme musulmane en Orient. III. Afghanistan [The Movement for the Freedom of Moslem Women in the Orient. III. Afghanistan]. Revue des Études Islamiques 2, 163-226. 1929.

The reference is to several pages in a long article on the general subject. Pertinent material includes an article by a Soviet feminist, the marriage regulations in effect in 1921, and a brief discussion of clothing reform and the veil.

791 *J(oseph) C(astagne). Notes sur l'Afghanistan. I. La revue afghane "Kabul" II. Poètes afghans III. Note sur une brochure afghane IV. Bibliographie V. L'Ouverture du Conseil des Nations (6-7-1931) VI. Le développement économique de l'Afghanistan [Notes on Afghanistan. I. The Afghan Periodical "Kabul" II. Afghan Poets. III. Note on an Afghan Pamphlet IV. Bibliography V. The Opening of the National Assembly (6-7-1931) VI. The Economic Development of Afghanistan]. Revue des Études Islamiques 6, 545-561. 1932.

Section I gives the contents of the periodical for two issues; II, the summary of an article in "Kabul, " with brief sketches of eight poets; III is on a pamphlet issued on Independence Day; IV is a note of an Afghan book dealing with the overthrow of Amir Amanullah and the restoration of order by Nadir Khan; V details opening ceremonies, and VI quotes local papers on this subject.

792 Cervin, Vladimir. Problems in the Integration of the Afghan Nation. Middle East Journal 6, 400-416. 1952.

The author, a social scientist, was resident in Afghanistan between 1938 and 1944. His article deals with the problems incidental to bringing such diverse elements as the ethnic groups, tribes, village communities, and the finance group within the framework of a modernized Afghanistan.

793 Cresson, Rebecca A. American Family in Afghanistan. National Geographic Magazine 104, 417-432. 1953.
   Informal account of an American housewife's efforts to run a household at Kabul.

794 Cutler, J.C. Survey of Venereal Diseases in Afghanistan. Bulletin of the World Health Organization 2, 689-703. Geneva, 1950.

795 Daiwa [Lamp].
   A newspaper published at Shiberghan in Juzjan province. Began as a weekly in 1951, became a semiweekly in 1963, and a daily in 1965.

796 Daly, Kate. Eight Years among the Afghans. London, 1905.
   The trials and tribulations of a courageous British woman doctor, Mrs. Daly, at Kabul: complements other accounts of the reign of Amir Habibullah.

797 De Croze, J. Berjane. Tourism in Afghanistan for the Student. Afghanistan 2, no. 2, 15-20. 1947.
   An investigation of how to attract student-tourists to Afghanistan, together with a suggested itinerary.

798 Delor, J. Musique afghan [Afghan Music]. Afghanistan 1, no. 3, 24-29. 1946.
   Illustrated description of local instruments and a brief account of the character of the music.

799 Dianous, Hugues Jean de. Note sur la presse Afghane [A Note on the Afghan Press]. Orient 15, 177-184. 1960.
   Traces the history of newspapers and periodicals and cites numerous titles. Very valuable for its references.

800 Dupree, Louis. Tribal Traditions and Modern Nationhood: Afghanistan. Asia 1, 1-12. New York, Spring, 1964.
   Identifies and examines the divisive and cohesive factors active in the process by which the country is reaching for nationhood.

801 Education in Afghanistan during the last Half-Century. Munich: Royal Afghan Ministry of Education [1956]. Pp. 96.

802 *Educational Mission--4. Report on Afghanistan. Paris: UNESCO, 1952. Pp. 87.

Conclusions of a team of UN specialists who studied the educational system of Afghanistan with a view toward suggested reforms, innovations, and changes required to relate this system to Western concepts. Some of these suggestions may be ill-related to current attitudes and customs of the Afghans. Other pages contain general material descriptive of certain aspects of present-day life.

803 El-Hashimi, Sayed. Afghanistan Revisited. Contemporary Review 1039, 21-24. London, 1952.

Generalized travel impressions, ending with the conclusion that "Afghanistan is certainly the happiest, least divided country in Asia that I have seen. "

804 Faryab [Faryab--place name].

A daily newspaper published at Maimana.

805 Feroz. Bakhter News Agency. Afghanistan 3, no. 3, 20-21. 1948.

An account of the official news agency since its creation at the end of 1939, written by its director.

806 Finley, Mark. Afghanistan. Contemporary Review 1000, 225-230. 1949.

A brief survey of the contemporary economic and political structure of the country.

807 Fucik, Julius. Na Piandzhe, kogda stemneet [On the Panj When Darkness Falls]. V Zashchitu Mira 28, 34-40. Moscow, 1953.

808 A R(aymond) F(uron). René Grousset et l'Afghanistan [René Grousset and Afghanistan]. Afghanistan 7, no. 3, 65-67. 1952.

A tribute to the late René Grousset and his work on Afghan history.

809 Furon, Raymond. L'Afghanistan [Afghanistan]. Paris: Albert Blanchard, 1926. Pp. 133; 3 maps.

A general account of the geography, history, ethnography, and progress in modern times.

810 Ghubar, M. The Role of Afghanistan in the Civilization of Islam. Afghanistan 1, no. 1, 26-32. 1946.

Lists and describes briefly numbers of Afghan theologians, scribes, translators, scientists, and historians who contributed to the rise of Islamic culture.

V. SOCIAL EVOLUTION AND INSTITUTIONS

811 Gosti iz Afganista [Guests from Afghanistan]. Ogonek 32, no. 3, 12. Moscow, 1954.

812 Gray, John Alfred. At the Court of the Amir. London: Macmillan and Co., 1901. Pp. xxi, 523.
An Englishman who lived for several years at Kabul, close to Amir Abdul Rahman, tells of a time of political and economic change.

813 Habibiyeh 1282-1322 [Habibiyeh 1903-1943]. Kabul: Matba'eh-yi 'umumi, n.d. Pp. 36.
A commemorative volume in Persian, marking the first 40 years in the life of this school. Numerous articles and lists of former students comprise the work.

814 Haddad, Nikulay. Da zhwandaheh lari [The Roads of Life]. Kabul: Matba'eh-yi 'umumi, 1326 [1947]. Pp. 93.
A general discussion of contemporary civilization and its aspects by an Egyptian author: translated into Pushtu by 'Aziz al-Rahman Sayfi.

815 Hadiyeh bi-dustan [An Offering to Friends]. A monthly in Persian, sponsored by the newspaper Anis, which began its publication at Kabul in 1945.

816 Hakim, Abdul. L'Organisation de l'instruction publique et des écoles en Afghanistan [The Organization of Public Education and Schools in Afghanistan]. Afghanistan 4, no. 1, 4-18. 1949.
Technical and detailed: a study of the composition of the Ministry of Education, an account of subjects of study at the primary level, and a description of all the higher institutions of learning.

817 Hannah, Norman B. Afghanistan--A Problem of Timing and Balance. Asia 2, 18-37. New York, 1964.
An American diplomat, who served in Afghanistan, discusses the concept of fixing the country in time and space and then of interpreting its role on the Asian stage.

818 Harat [Herat]. An independent monthly periodical, founded at Herat in 1932 and printed in Persian.
The name of the periodical has changed from time to time; it is also called Adabi, or Adabi Harat [Literary Herat], in reference to the fact that it is the organ of the Literary Society of Herat.

819 *Harris, Fred et al. Public School Education in Afghanistan. (Kabul):

The Public School Survey and Planning Team, United States Operations Mission to Afghanistan, n.d. Pp. 173.

A mimeographed survey of needs in this field and proposals for developments.

820 Hawa [Air].

Quarterly journal of the Afghan Air Authority, which began publication at Kabul in 1957; articles in Pushtu and Persian.

821 Heras, Henri. Les Jésuites en Afghanistan [The Jesuits in Afghanistan]. New Review Vol. 1, Calcutta, 1935.

822 Hufford, Donald. Afghan Hospitality. Geographical Magazine 24, 128-137. 1951.

823 Hudson, Alfred E. and Elizabeth E. Bacon. Inside Afghanistan Today. Asia 40, 118-122. 1940.

824 *Huffman, Arthur V. The Administrative and Social Structure of Afghan Life. Journal of the Royal Central Asian Society 38, 41-48. 1951.

An American who taught for six years in an Afghan secondary school at Kabul crowds these pages with facts on politics, ethnic elements, economic progress, and the changing system of education.

825 Huquq [Laws]. A quarterly of the Faculty of Law of Kabul University, with articles in Persian. First appeared in 1945.

826 International Educational, Cultural and Related Activities for Afghanistan. Washington, D.C.: Bureau of Cultural Relations, Department of State, 1960. Pp. 52.

Lists and describes activities in Afghanistan under the auspices of agencies of the American government, of other governments, and of the specialized agencies of the United Nations.

827 'Irfan [Knowledge].

Began publication in 1924 at Kabul under the name of Ayineh-yi 'irfan [Mirror of Knowledge] and continued irregularly, taking its present name in 1936. As an organ of the Ministry of Education it publishes articles on teaching, literature, history, and science, many of which are translations from the foreign press.

828 *Islah [Reform]. Founded in 1929 at Kabul.

Semiofficial morning daily, primarily in Pushtu, with an estimated 5,000 circulation.

829 Ittifaq-i Islam [Concord of Islam]. Founded at Herat in 1920.
This newspaper has appeared daily at some periods and weekly at
others. Most of its contents are in Persian.

830 Ittihad [Union]. A biweekly newspaper published at Baghlan.
In its earlier years, when it was printed at Khanabad, most of its articles were in Pushtu, while later on more Persian has been used.

831 Ittihad-i mashriqi [Eastern Union]. Founded in 1919 at Jalalabad and
published weekly in Pushtu.

832 Janssens, B. Busson de. Les wakfs dans l'Islam contemporain [Waqfs in
Contemporary Islam]. Revue des Études Islamiques (no volume number), pp. 13-14. 1951.
Within this long article, the pages indicated supply a brief indication
of the fact that the waqfs--religious endowments--of Afghanistan were
taken over by the State under Amir Abdur Rahman. Mosques, shrines,
and religious schools are now supported privately and by state and
municipal donations.

833 Jarring, Gunnar. The New Afghanistan. Svenska Orientsallskapets arsbok,
pp. 131-145. Stockholm, 1937.

834 Jeffrey, Thomas E. Educational Testing in Afghanistan. Human Organization 24, no. 1, 83-88. 1965.

835 Da Kabul Puhantun Khabaruneh [The Kabul University News].
A monthly which began publication in 1960, with articles in Persian.

836 Kabul Times.
Began publication at Kabul in March 1962 as a four-page daily paper
in English, with emphasis upon foreign news. Publisher: Bakhtar News
Agency.

837 Khalil, Muhammad Ibrahim. 'Arof va nozul-i Islam [The Ascending and
Descending of Islam]. Kabul: Doulati matba'oh, 1336 [1957].
Pp. 58.
A religious treatise in Dari.

838 Khawganani, Muhammad Amin. Hayat-i sayyid-i Jamal al-Din-i Afghani
[Life of Jamal al-Din Afghani]. Kabul: Matba'eh-yi 'umumi, 1318
[1939]. Pp. 204.
A study in Persian by a contemporary Afghan writer.

839 A(hmad) K(ohzad). L'Afghanistan modern [Modern Afghanistan]. Afghanistan 4, no. 4, 54-55. 1949.

A brief review of a publication with the above title issued in April 1949 by La Documentation Française: certain errors are pointed out.

840 Kohzad, Ahmad Ali. Allocution prononcée à l'occasion du millénaire de la naissance d'Avicenne [Address Delivered on the Thousandth Anniversary of the Birth of Avicenna]. Afghanistan 7, no. 3, 51-65. 1952.

The life and work of Avicenna, the "Aristotle of Islam."

841 Kohzad, Ahmad Ali. L'Afghanistan au point de vue de la religion [Afghanistan from the Point of View of Religion]. Afghanistan 8, no. 3, 1-17. 1953.

A history of Afghan religion from prehistoric times to the present-- from the pre-Aryan worship of the mother goddess, through the Vedic cult, Zoroastrianism, Buddhism, Greek mythology, the Brahman sun-worship, and Nestorianism to Islam.

842 Kohzad, Ahmad Ali. Indo-Afghan Cultural Relations. Afghanistan 9, no. 1, 1-10. 1954.

The exchange of cultural and religious influences between Afghanistan and India in the prehistoric, Vedic, Zoroastrian, Buddhist, and Moslem periods.

843 Kohzad, Ahmad Ali. Un mois en Italie [A Month in Italy]. Afghanistan 9, no. 3, 1-7. 1954.

A summary of Mr. Kohzad's articles on his Italian visit, giving various traditions of the founding of Rome, accounts of his conferences at the Italian Institute for the Middle and Far East, and accounts of visits to Ostia Antiqua and Pompeii. He discusses the similarity between the art of Pompeii and the Greco-Buddhistic art of Bactria, mentions the likeness between the statue of St. Peter in Rome and a statue found at Charsada, and finishes with a note on the Etruscans. He adds that the Italian Institute will be allowed to excavate at Ghazni and Laghman.

844 Kukhtina, Tat'yana I. Prosveshcheniye v nezavisimoy Afganistane [Education in Independent Afghanistan]. Moscow: Izdatel'stvo Vostochnoy Literatury, 1963. Pp. 131.

845 Latifi, 'Abd al-Baqi. Afghanistan va yak nigah-i ijmali bah awza' va shu'un-i mukhtalifeh va halat-i 'umumiyet [Afghanistan: A Brief Look into Various Conditions and Public Affairs]. Kabul: Matba'eh-yi

'umumi, 1326 [1947]. Pp. 136.
A number of chapters on the subject by different authors.

846 Leyden, J. On the Rosheniah Sect and its Founder Bayezid Ansari. Asiatic Researches: or, Transactions of the Society Instituted in Bengal 11, 363-428. London, 1812.

The story of a horse dealer turned prophet, whose heretical sect had great power in Afghanistan in the sixteenth and seventeenth centuries A.D. The first part of the article is a history of the sect, taken largely from Akhund Darvizeh's Makhzan al-islam (see no. 865)-- which is highly unsympathetic. The second part is a translation from Mohsani Fani's Dabistan, on Bayezid's education, teachings, and successors; the third explains the Shi'a sect Ismailiyah, to which the Rosheniah sect bears a close resemblance.

847 Lindberg, K. Le paludisme in Afghanistan [Malaria in Afghanistan]. Rivista de Malariologia 28, 1-54. Rome, 1949.

848 *Magnus, Julius. Die höchsten Gerichte der Welt [The Highest Courts of the World]. Leipzig: W. Moeser, 1929. Pp. xii, 634.

Within Part IV of this work, under the heading "Afghanistan," may be found a reliable description of the judicial system, jurisdiction of the courts and administration of the courts under the ruler Amanullah.

849 Mahfouz, Imza. En Asie. II. Afghanistan [In Asia. II. Afghanistan]. Revue des Études Islamiques 11, 405-412. 1937.

A series of brief reviews and notes from local-language papers in Afghanistan, Iran, and India are grouped under such headings as Afghanistan Moves towards Modernism, Afghan-Japanese Relations, Afghan Wage Scales, Governmental Appointments, Afghan Independence Day, etc.

850 La Maison des Français [The House of the French]. Afghanistan 4, no. 1, 36. 1949.

Describes the activities of a cultural center newly opened at Kabul-- a library, lectures, national dances, and plays.

851 Majum'eh-yi sihhet [Health]. A monthly revue of hygiene published in Persian at Kabul by the Ministry of Public Health.

852 Malakhov, M. Afghanistan. Geographical Sketch. New Times 7, 23-29. Moscow, 1946.

.A Soviet reporter in Afghanistan views the situation with a jaundiced eye: Socialism is completely lacking and everything seems disorganized and backward. There is an "unexampled confusion of tribes and peoples," while "agriculture cannot keep the mass of the population above the starvation level. "

853 Malik al-Shu'ara, Bitab. 'Elm-i ma'ani [The Meaning of Knowledge] . Kabul, n.d. Pp. 92.

854 Malik al-Shu'ara, Bitab. Guftar-i ravan dar 'elm [Discourse of the Soul in the Rhetoric] . Kabul, 1334 [1955] . Pp. 23.
A study of rhetoric, in Persian.

855 *Martin, Frank A. Under the Absolute Amir. London and New York: Harper and Brothers, 1907. Pp. xii, 330.
Observations on private and public life at Kabul by an Englishman who was for eight years chief engineer to the Amirs Abdur Rahman and Habibullah. Displays an intimate knowledge of manners and customs, prisons and punishments, soldiers and their arms, and of the daily conduct of government by Amir Abdur Rahman.

856 Matthews, Herbert L. Beyond the Khyber Pass. New York Times Magazine, July 18, 1943. Pp. 17f.
Ancient, secluded Afghanistan becoming modern Afghanistan, with a characterization of the Afghans and a little of their history and culture.

857 Merman [Ladies] . First appeared at Kabul in 1953.
A quarterly designed for the feminine reader, with articles in Persian and Pushtu.

858 Naim, Elizabeth. "Élan Féminin" ["Feminine Spirit"] . Afghanistan 1, no. 3, 47-48. 1946.
Concerns the establishment of a feminine society for assisting the poorer girl students at Kabul.

859 Najaf 'Ali Khan. Maw'izeh-yi nadireh [Admonition of Nadir] . Lahore: Firuz, 1311 [1932] . Pp. 48.
A lithographed work in Persian, consisting of letters addressed to Nadir Shah concerning the modernization of Afghanistan.

860 Najib-ullah Khan. Speech Delivered by Dr. Najib-ullah Khan at Delhi Province Post Graduate Teachers' Club. Afghanistan 5, no. 2, 47-62. 1950.

V. SOCIAL EVOLUTION AND INSTITUTIONS

On the progress of modern education in Afghanistan since 1905, and its present condition.

861 Nangrahar [Nangrahar--place name].
A daily newspaper published at Jalalabad.

862 Nendari [Exhibition]. First appeared at Kabul in 1953.
A monthly in Persian published by the Kabul Cinema.

803 Nida'-i Khalq [The Voice of Creation].
A privately-sponsored, biweekly paper in Persian and Pushtu, which was published by a duplication process at Kabul in 1951 and then closed by official action.

864 Nilab [Nilab].
A privately-sponsored weekly, which began publication in Persian and Pushtu in 1952, and was printed by the Government Central Press.

865 *Ningarhari, 'Abd al-Karim ibn Makhdum, Akhund Darvizeh. Makhzan al-islam [Treasury of Islam]. Delhi, 1877.
A famous encyclopedia of observances, rites, and dogmas of the Sunni sect of Islam, compiled in Pushtu about 1615 A.D.

866 Nizam-nameh-yi tashkilat-i asasi-yi Afghanistan [Regulation of the Principal Difficulties of Afghanistan]. Kabul, 1921.

867 Open Doors, a Report on Three Surveys: Foreign Students in U.S. Institutions of Higher Education, Foreign Faculty Members at U.S. Colleges and Universities, Foreign Doctors Training at U.S. Hospitals, 1954-55. New York: Institute of International Education, 1955. Pp. 56.
Tables indicate the number of Afghan students in the U.S., their academic status, sources of financial support, and fields of major interest.

868 Parwan [Parwan--place name].
A daily newspaper published at Charikar in Parwan province.

869 Pamir [Pamir]. A biweekly paper which began publication at Kabul in late 1951.
Some issues were printed and some produced by a duplication process. Articles in Persian and Pushtu.

870 Payam-i Imruz [Today's Message].
A privately owned biweekly, which began publication at Kabul in

1966 with material in both Dari and Pushtu.

871 Payam-i Tandurusti [Message of Health]. A monthly issued at Kabul
     in Persian by the Publicity Section of the Ministry of Public Health.
     Occasionally issues bear the title Tandurust [Healthy].

872 Poullada, L. B. Problems of Social Development in Afghanistan. Royal
     Central Asian Journal 49, no. 1, 33-39. 1962.

873 Price, M. Philips. A Visit to Afghanistan. Journal of the Royal Central
     Asian Society 35, 124-234. 1949.
     Stresses the fascination and appeal of changeless aspects, while em-
     phasizing progress toward national unity and economic improvements.

874 *Pushtun zhagh [The Pushtun Voice]. A monthly magazine published at
     Kabul by Kabul Radio.
     Each issue contains the program of the station for the coming month,
     as well as articles in Persian and Pushtu.

875 Qawa'id-i Siraj al-Milleh dar Kharidari-yi mal az duval-i Kharijeh [Reg-
     ulations of the "Luminary of the Nation" concerning Imports from For-
     eign Countries]. Kabul: Dar al-saltaneh, 1321 [1904]. Pp. 2, 66.
     A lithographed work in Persian, which includes decrees of Amir
     Habibullah concerning foreign imports.

876 Qur'an. 3 vols. Kabul: Matba'eh-yi 'umumi, 1324-28 [1945-49].
     Edited in Arabic and with translation and commentary in Pushtu by
     Mahmud Hasan Diwabandi and Shabir Ahmad Diwabandi.

877 Rahmani, Magdeline. La société féminine de Bien-Faisance [The
     Women's Society of Good Work]. Afghanistan 9, no. 4, 56-59. 1954.
     Discusses an Afghan women's organization, which aims to educate
     poor women and to raise their standard of living by selling their em-
     broideries and handiwork.

878 Rahnuma-yi tadavi va-viqayeh az maraz-i trakhom [Guide to the Treat-
     ment and Protection from Trachoma]. Kabul: Matba'eh-yi 'umumi,
     1321 [1942]. Pp. 18.
     A pamphlet published in Persian by the Ministry of Health.

879 Rashad, Shah Muhammad. Irshadat-i dini [Guidance in Religion]. Ka-
     bul: Matba'eh-yi doulati, n.d. Pp. 196.
     The text in Persian of 59 talks delivered over Radio Kabul.

V. SOCIAL EVOLUTION AND INSTITUTIONS

880 Rashad, Shah Muhammad, trans. Siassat-i shar'ieh [Islamic Methods of Politics]. No publisher, no date. Pp. 191.
A translation into Persian of a work written in Arabic.

881 Reports of the Member States. Afghanistan. UNESCO Document 5C/4 Afghanistan. Florence, 1950. Pp. 7.

882 Reshtia, Said Qassim. Journalism in Afghanistan: A Brief Historical Sketch. Afghanistan 3, no. 2, 72-77. 1948.
A description and record of the various newspapers and periodicals published in the country, and an account of the establishment of the Department of Press and Publication in 1939. By a former director of that Department.

883 Rishtia, Sayyid Qasim. Education in Afghanistan. Afghanistan 1, no. 1, 20-25. 1946.
A sketchy account of the history of modern education. Current statistics are lacking.

884 Rishtya, Said Qasim. Kabul Calling. Afghanistan 1, no. 2, 1-3. 1946.
Sketch of the history of radio broadcasting in Afghanistan and of the installation of Radio Kabul.

885 Roghtia [Health]. An illustrated monthly published at Kabul in Persian and Pushtu by the Ministry of Public Health.

886 Sadoi Sharq.
A periodical published at Dushanbe, formerly Stalinabad, in Soviet Tajistan. Prior to 1964 it was called Sharqi Surkh. It presents material on Afghan poets and folklore.

887 Safa, Muhammad Ibrahim. Mukhtasar-i mantiq; bahis az ta'lil-i istoriqra' va mitudaluzhi [Outline of Logic; Investigation of Deduction and Methodology]. Kabul: Matba'eh-yi 'umumi, 1332 [1953]. Pp. 200.
An original work in Persian, based upon European sources.

888 Saint-Brice. Le voyage du roi d'Afghanistan [The Travels of the King of Afghanistan]. Correspondance d'Orient 20, no. 361, 1-9. 1928.
Amir Amanullah in France.

889 Saint-Brice. La nouvelle ère afghane [The New Afghan Era]. Correspondance d'Orient 21, no. 383, 193-200. 1929.

V. SOCIAL EVOLUTION AND INSTITUTIONS

A short account of Nadir Khan and the revolution of 1928-29 which gave him the throne.

890 Saljuqi, Salah al-Din, trans. 'Ilm-i akhlaq-i "Nikumakusi" az Aristu [Aristotle's Nichomachean Ethics]. Kabul: Matba'eh-yi 'umumi, n.d. Pp. 330.
A translation into Persian from the work in English, "Nichomachean Ethics, " by D.P. Chase.

891 Saljuqi, Salah al-Din. Muqaddimeh-yi 'ilm-i mantiq [Introduction to Logic]. 2 vols. Kabul: Matba'eh-yi 'umumi, 1331 [1952]. Pp. (1) 412; (2) 413-764.
A compilation into Persian from an extensive range of sources.

892 Saljuqi, Salah al-Din. Jabireh [Compensation]. Kabul: Matba'eh-yi doulati, 1335 [1956]. Pp. 324.
A study in Persian of psychological and sociological aspects of behavior.

893 Saljuqi, Salah al-Din. Tajalli dar afaq va anfas [The Manifestation in the Worlds and the Individuals]. Kabul; 1344 [1965]. Pp. 443.
A philosophical and religious treatise in Dari.

894 Sami, Mahmud. Tarbiyeh-i 'askariyeh [Military Drill]. Kabul: Mashin Khaneh, 1327 [1909]. Pp. 15.
A lithographed text in Persian, containing a manual of infantry drill for the Afghan army.

895 Samylovskiy, I. V. Nauchnyye i kulturnyye svyazi S.S.S.R. so stranami Azii i Afrikii [Scientific and cultural communications of the U.S.S.R. with the countries of Asia and Africa]. Moscow: Izdatel'stvo Vostochnoy Literatury, 1963. Pp. 67.
Text of cultural agreements between the U.S.S.R. and Afghanistan, pp. 25-29.

896 Sana'i [Sana'i--pen name of a poet].
A daily newspaper at Ghazni, which began publication in 1952.

897 *Sassani, Abul K. Education in Afghanistan. Washington, D.C.: U.S. Government Printing Office, 1961. Pp. 55; tables; bibliography.
A study, reproduced by mimeograph, by the Division of International Education of the U.S. Department of Health, Education, and Welfare, on the subjects of preprimary, primary, secondary, higher, and

teacher's training education. Numerous ephemeral items in the accompanying bibliography are not included in this bibliography.

898 *Schlegelberger, Franz. Rechtsvergleichendes Handwörterbuch für das Zivil- und Handelsrecht des in-und auslandes [A Dictionary of Comparative Law for Civil and Commercial Law, Domestic and Foreign]. Berlin: F. Wahlen, 1927.
Under the heading "Afghanistan," beginning on page 291, may be found a comprehensive account of the laws in force during the reign of Amanullah.

899 Seraj ul-Akbar [Torch of the News].
Began publication as a bimonthly in Persian, edited by the leading Afghan reformist and writer, Mahmud Tarzi. It ceased publication in 1918.

900 Sereh miyasht [Red Crescent]. Illustrated quarterly published at Kabul by the Afghan Red Crescent Society.
Publication began in 1955 and articles were in Persian, Pushtu, and English.

901 Sérignan, Claude. La condition des femmes en Afghanistan et son évolution récente [The Status of Women in Afghanistan and its recent development]. Orient 4, no. 2, 33-56. 1960.
Describes steps taken to improve the status of women, and states that their inferior position remains as the major problem of the country.

902 Simmons, J. S., T. F. Whayne, et al., eds. Global Epidemiology: A Geography of Disease and Sanitation. Volume III. The Near and Middle East. Philadelphia: J. P. Lippincott Co., 1954.
This extensive survey includes some material concerned with public health in Afghanistan.

903 Simpich, Frederick. Every-Day Life in Afghanistan. National Geographic Magazine 39, 85-110. 1921.
Frederick Simpich, formerly American consul at Tehran, translated and published the notes made by an unnamed European diplomat to the court of the new ruler, Amanullah.

904 Sistan [Sistan]. A biweekly in Persian and Pushtu, poorly printed at Fareh.

905 *Stolz, Karl. Le théâtre afghan [The Afghan Theater]. Afghanistan 9, no. 3, 36-44. 1954.
The article describes the plays, the entr'actes, and the audiences of

the Afghan theater and mentions favorite actors (men play the feminine parts), with an account of the Afghans' efforts to develop a modern theater on European models.

906 Storai [Star]. A biweekly published in Persian and Pushtu at Maymaneh.

907 Surkhakan va-suret-i tadabir-i sihhi-yi an [Measles and the Manner of Sanitary Inoculation]. Kabul: Matba'eh-yi 'umumi, 1315 [1936]. Pp. 6.
A pamphlet in Persian issued by the Ministry of Public Health.

908 Tafsir sharif [Commentary on the Qur'an]. 3 vols. Kabul: Matba'eh-yi doulati, 1323 [1954], 1326 [1957], 1327 [1958]. Pp. (1) 1196; (2) 2470; (3) 3521.
A translation into Pushtu, prepared by a group of religious leaders.

909 Taillardat, C.F. Le voyage du roi Amanu-Ullah. Le roi Amanu-Ullah en Angleterre. La fin du voyage du roi Amanu-Ullah [The Journey of King Amanullah. King Amanullah in England. The End of King Amanullah's Journey]. L'Asie Française, pp. 53-54; 67-69; 184-188; 320-323. 1928.

910 Taraki, Muhammad Qadir. Mafhum-i dawlat az nuqteh-yi nazar-i huquq-i ijtima'yat va-falsafeh [The Purpose of the State from the Points of View of Social Justice and Philosophy]. Kabul: Matba'eh-yi 'umumi, 1326 [1947]. Pp. 68.
An original work in Persian by a writer on the subjects of philosophy and law.

911 Thornton, Ernest. Leaves from an Afghan Scrapbook: The Experiences of an English Official and his Wife in Kabul. London: J. Murray, 1910. Pp. xvi, 225.
Valuable chapters are devoted to descriptions of daily and family life at Kabul.

912 Toloi Afghan [The Afghan Awakener].
A daily newspaper published at Qandahar in Pushtu.

913 Tulu'-i afghan [Afghan Sunrise]. A newspaper founded at Qandahar in 1921 and currently published daily in Pushtu.

914 Urdu-yi afghan [The Afghan Army]. A monthly periodical issued in Persian and Pushtu at Kabul by the Ministry of War.

First appeared in 1921. The name has changed several times: it has been Urdu [Army] and Da Urdu Majalleh [The Army Magazine].

915 Urmanova, Rukiya K. Reformy afganskogo pravitel'stva v 1919-1925 gg. [The reforms of the Afghan Government, 1919-1925]. Tashkent: Izvestiya Akademii Nauk Uzbekskoy SSR. No. 2, pp. 65-75. 1958.

916 Vatan [Homeland]. A privately-sponsored weekly paper, which began publication at Kabul in 1951.
Produced by a duplication process. The paper was closed down by official action in 1952. Claimed a circulation of 1,500 copies.

917 Velichkovsky, Y. Kabul Impressions. New Times 5, 28-30. Moscow, 1955.
A glowing report by the Director of the Moscow Institute for Advanced Training of Teachers, who was a member of a Soviet delegation invited to visit the University of Kabul. He describes briefly Kabul City, its schools, the University, Afghan art and drama, and the hospitality of the Afghan intellectuals.

918 Wahdat [Unity].
A privately-owned weekly, which began publication at Kabul in 1966 with material in both Dari and Pushtu.

919 Wala. We Want Peace and Security. Afghanistan 3, no. 3, 22-23. 1948.
The author advocates universal friendship and moral armament.

920 Walus [Community]. A weekly in Pushtu which began publication at Kabul in 1951.

921 Warangeh [Beam of Light]. A weekly in Pushtu published at Gardiz: began publication in 1941.

922 Watta.
Monthly publication of the Ministry of Finances, which first appeared in 1954. Articles are in Persian and in Pushtu.

923 Wilber, Donald N. Matbu'at-i Afghanistan. [The Press of Afghanistan]. Danesh 3, 485-487. Tehran, 1330 [1951].
A general survey in Persian of contemporary Afghan publications: newspapers, periodicals and historical studies.

924 *Wilber, Donald N. The Structure of Islam in Afghanistan. The Middle

V. SOCIAL EVOLUTION AND INSTITUTIONS

East Journal 6, no. 1, 41-48. Washington, 1952.

A description of contemporary Moslem institutions and practices and an examination of local statements regarding the future role of Islam in the country.

925 Wolanga [Progress].

A daily newspaper published in Pushtu at Gardez.

926 Zahir Shah. Discours inaugural prononcé par S. M. le Roi a l'occasion du 33ème anniversaire des fêtes de l'indépendence [Inaugural Address Delivered by H. M. the King on the Thirty-Third Anniversary of Independence Day]. Afghanistan 6, no. 3, 36-37. 1951.

On the Afghan government's plans, domestic and foreign, with the inevitable reference to Pakistan.

927 Zahir, Payendeh Muhammad and Sayyid Muhammad Yusuf 'Elmi. Da Afghanistan da ma'raef tarikh [History of Education in Afghanistan]. Kabul: Ministry of Education, 1339 [1960]. Pp. 177 and 184.

A work with the text in parallel columns of Dari and Pushtu.

928 Zahma, 'Ali Muhammad. Maqalat-i ijtima'i va falsafi [Talks on Sociology and Philosophy]. Kabul, 1339 [1960]. Pp. 196.

929 *Zhwandun [Life]. Illustrated periodical published weekly at Kabul in Persian and Pushtu by the Department of Press.

930 Zirai [Good News]. A weekly paper published in Pushtu at Kabul and sponsored by the Pushtu Tolaneh of the Afghan Academy.

VI. POLITICAL STRUCTURE

Constitutional system; structure of government;
political dynamics; public order; foreign
policies; subversive potentials;
official propaganda, including
material on Pushtunistan

Material on the constitution, the structure of government, and the organization of ministries and provincial organizations is rather extensive, but the coverage of the legislative bodies, of the laws passed by these bodies, and of functions and operations of the Ministry of Justice is definitely inadequate. Items on the operation of the government on the level of the general public are also lacking. There is no material on political parties (since there are no active parties), and for somewhat the same reason there is scanty documentation on subversive potentialities.

Users of the bibliography may well be struck by the amount of material in a number of languages which the Afghan government has published on the Pushtunistan issue—enough material to establish a separate chapter for this subject, if it were thought that the issue was even a semipermanent one. The effort to distinguish between publications on foreign policies and on foreign relations presented problems: in case of doubt, the reader should refer back to Chapter III for additional items on the foreign affairs of Afghanistan.

931 Aerial Bombardment of the Tribal Area by Pakistan Government Causing the Death of Hundreds of our Afghan Brothers. Afghanistan 4, no. 1, 41-42. 1949.
   Deplores this action and warns Pakistan of the danger of arousing tribal enmity.

932 The Afghan-Pakistan Conflict. New Times 16, 22-23. Moscow, 1955.
   An editorial charging that Pakistan's attacks on Afghanistan are American-sponsored attempts to coerce Afghanistan into a Middle East military alliance.

933 Afghanistan dar dowreh-i hekumat-i entaqali, hut-1341-mizan 1344 [Afghanistan in the Period of the Transitional Government, March 1963-October 1965]. Kabul: Imprimerio d'État [1965]. Pp. 340.

934 *L'Afghanistan moderne [Modern Afghanistan]. Documentation Française 1112, 3-39. 1949.
   An authoritative survey of the political and social institutions of the country, including the text of the Afghan constitution.

935 Afghanistan and Pakistan, by S. K. Afghanistan 4, no. 2, 25-27. 1949.
The Pushtunistan issue, with reference to a bombing of Waziristan in
February 1949.

936 *Ahmad, Mohammad B. Constitutions of Eastern Countries. In Select
Constitutions of the World, Vol. I. Karachi: Governor General's
Press and Publications, 2d ed., 1951. Pp. 403.
Page 43 begins a few pages describing the Afghan government, followed, on pages 48-59, by an English translation of the constitution
of 1931, with the addendum of 1933. On pages 379-385, the features
of this constitution are summarized.

937 Akhramovich, R. T. Novyye yavleniya v razvitii obshchestvennoy mysli v
Afganistane v svyazi s problemoy Pushtunistana [New Statements in the
Development of Popular Opinion in Afghanistan in Connection with the
Problem of Pushtunistan]. Sovetskoye Vostokovedeniye 4, 155-161.
1958.
A presentation of articles in the Afghan press on Pushtunistan as illus-
trative of new trends of popular opinion.

938 Armstrong, H. F. North of the Khyber. Foreign Affairs 34, no. 4, 603-
619. 1956.
A detailed discussion of Afghanistan's domestic and foreign policies,
including one of the first efforts to underline Soviet economic penetration of the country.

939 *Asas-nameh [Fundamental Law]. Kabul: Matba'eh-yi 'umumi.
A series of leaflets of various dates, containing basic laws and regulations, presented in parallel columns of Persian and Pushtu.

940 Benava. Pashtoonistan. Afghanistan 5, no. 1, 10-24. 1950.
A highly partisan history of the Pushtunistan movement.

941 Beneva. Les leaders actuels du Pashtounistan [The Real Leaders of Pushtun-
istan]. Afghanistan 7, no. 3, 6-32. 1952.
Brief biographies of the Fakir of Ipi, Khan Abdul Ghafar Khan, and
several other leaders of the movement.

942 *Binava, 'Abd al-Ra'uf. Pushtunistan [Pushtunistan]. Kabul: Matba'eh-
yi 'umumi, 1330 [1951]. Pp. 480; folding map; bibliography.
A very lengthy work in Pushtu, tracing the history of the area of so-
called Pushtunistan from early times to the present. A host of inadequately transliterated or transcribed references are given in the

bibliography, and the folding map illustrates the maximum area claimed for Pushtunistan. The most pertinent interest lies in the account of individuals currently active in the movement.

943 Bujtar, August von. Ob Mann Afghanistan Kritizieren Darf? [Dare One Criticize Afghanistan?]. Afghanistan 4, no. 2, 32-33. 1949.
Stresses the need to know the country and its people before passing judgments.

944 Caroe, Olaf. The North-West Frontier, Old and New. Royal Central Asian Journal 48, no. 3/4, 289-298. 1961.
A discussion of the Pathan character and the origins of the Pushtunistan dispute, related to the genealogy of the Afghans.

945 Castagne, Joseph. Notes sur la politique extérieure de l'Afghanistan. Missions et traites, étude accompagnée d'annexes importantes, constitutions, monnaies, ordres afghans [Notes on the Foreign Policy of Afghanistan. Missions and Treaties, a Study Accompanied by Important Annexes, Constitutions, Monetary System, Afghan Decorations]. Revue du Monde Musulman 48, 1-74. 1921.
A reliable and thorough study. The second part stems directly from an official Afghan work of 1921.

946 Concerning a Statement Made by the Governor-General of Pakistan. Afghanistan 4, no. 1, 43-44. 1949.
Questions whether the speaker could have made the "astounding and deeply regrettable" statement that "the Government of Pakistan considers that the Tribal Area form a part of Pakistan."

947 Constitution of Afghanistan. 9 Mizan 1343-1 October 1964. Kabul: Education Press, 1964. Pp. 62.
Also available, but not separately listed, are editions in Pushtu, in Dari (Afghan Persian), and in French.

948 Current Afghan Observations on Pashtoonistan. Kabul: The Government Central Press, n.d. (1955?). Pp. 14.
Contains statements made to the press in 1954 by the Prime Minister and the Minister of Foreign Affairs of Afghanistan on the subject of Pushtunistan.

949 English Historian's Verdict on Durand Line. Afghanistan 4, no. 3, 36-38. 1949.
A solicited statement from Dr. Codrington of London University, stressing the fact that the Durand Line divided the Pathan tribes and adding that the present attitude of Pakistan is inexplicable.

VI. POLITICAL STRUCTURE

950 Far Eastern News Letter. A New State--Pakhtunistan Emerges in Asia. Afghanistan 5, no. 4, 17-30. 1950.
Another view of the Afghan-Pakistan dispute.

951 Fayz Muhammad Khan, molla. Siraj al-tavarikh [The Luminary of Histories]. Kabul, 1331 [1913].
A history of Afghanistan down to the accession of Amir 'Abd al-Rahman.

952 Firoz, M. M. Journey to Moghalgai of the Observer's Mission. Afghanistan 4, no. 3, 26-35. 1949.
An account of a trip made to escort representatives from ten countries to a site inside Afghanistan which had been attacked and bombed by a plane from Pakistan.

953 *Franck, Dorothea Seelye. Pakhtunistan--Disputed Disposition of a Tribal Land. Middle East Journal 6, no. 1, 49-68. Washington, 1952.
A history of the territory separated from Afghanistan by the Durand Line and the cases for partition, independence, and federation. Includes a map.

954 *Fraser-Tytler, Sir W. Kerr. The Expulsion of Axis Nationals from Afghanistan. In George Kirk, ed., The Middle East in the War (Survey of International Affairs 1939-1946), pp. 141-146. Oxford University Press, 2d ed. 1953.
The most authoritative account of this action taken under pressure from the Western powers, as witnessed by the author, who was a British Minister at Kabul until October 1941.

955 Da Gharbi Pakistan Yunitt [The Western Unit of Pakistan]. (Kabul), 1333 [1954]. Pp. 38.
A pamphlet in Pushtu.

956 Ghosh, K. P. Afghanistan in World Affairs. Contemporary Review 1073, 325-327. 1955.
Touches on Afghan government and relations with the United States and the Soviet Union, ending with a pro-Afghan resumé of the Pushtunistan issue.

957 Ghosh, K. P. Afghanistan in World Affairs. Afghanistan 9, no. 4, 51-55. 1954.
Afghanistan's efforts to become financially and culturally modernized and to maintain friendly relations with the larger powers, though remaining always independent.

VI. POLITICAL STRUCTURE

958 Ghubar, M. The Eastern Provinces of Afghanistan. Afghanistan 2, no. 3, 22-36. 1947.
Discusses the separation of these regions from Afghanistan and the current situation in the area.

959 Gillett, Sir Michael. Afghanistan. Royal Central Asian Journal 53, no. 3, 238-244. 1966.
A review of political developments from September 1953 to October 1964.

960 Gochenour, Theodore S. A New Try for Afghanistan. Middle East Journal 19, no. 1, 1-19. 1965.
Discussion of trends, particularly those relating to the adoption of a new constitution in 1964.

961 Hasan, Zubeida. The Policy of Afghanistan. Pakistan Horizon 17, no. 1, 48-57. 1964.
A good, documented survey of the country's foreign policy goals.

962 Haywad [Homeland].
This weekly paper of the Pushtunistan movement began publication at Kabul about 1949. The contents are in Pushtu.

963 Indian News Chronicle. Afghanistan's Desire for Friendly Relation with Pakistan: Najib-Ullah Khan Explains Cause of Pukhtoonistan. Afghanistan 5, no. 1, 40-45. 1950.
Afghanistan's peaceable interest in a free Pushtunistan.

964 I'timadi, Muhammad Akbar Khan. Tasvib-i ruz-i Pushtunistan [Approval of Pushtunistan Day]. Kabul: Matba'eh-yi 'umumi, n.d. Pp. 101.
A work in Persian, probably printed between 1950 and 1954, reflecting a speech delivered in the National Assembly.

965 *Karimi. The Constitution of Afghanistan. Afghanistan 1, no. 1, 3-8. 1946.
An analysis of the provisions of the constitution adopted in 1931.

966 Khalid Khan. Afghan Minority in Pakistan. Afghanistan 5, no. 1, 48-49. 1950.
Khalid Khan's protest to the United Nations over Pakistan's imprisonment of thousands of Pushtun Nationals.

967 Khalil, Hakim Taj Mohamed. March of Pakhtoonistan. Bombay: Art

Litho and Printing Press, n.d. (1950?). Pp. 38.
Short articles by Afghans resident in India and excerpts from the
Afghan and Indian press on the subject in question.

968 Kohzad, Ahmad Ali. Frontier Discord between Afghanistan and Pakistan.
Kabul: Government Press Department, 1951. Pp. 25.
The Afghan government's views on Pushtunistan.

969 Kohzad, Ahmad Ali. Frontier Discord between Afghanistan and Pakistan.
Afghanistan 6, no. 1, 54-67. 1951.
A comment on Sir George Cunningham's article in the Manchester
Guardian. Mr. Kohzad objects to British support of Pakistan.

970 Kohzad, Ahmad Ali. Le différend afghano-pakistanais vu par Sir George
Cunningham [The Afghan-Pakistan Discord Seen by Sir George Cunning
ham]. Afghanistan 6, no. 2, 44-56. 1951.
An unfavorable--though temperate--comment on Sir George Cunningham's article in the Manchester Guardian.

971 Kohzad, Ahmad Ali. La politique extérieure afghane [The Afghan Foreign Policy]. Afghanistan 6, no. 3, 1-10. 1951.
In commenting on Sir Giles Frederick Squire's article in the Martin
Review, Mr. Kohzad complains of a century of English intervention
in Afghanistan, and of England's now considering Afghanistan as a
"buffer-state."

972 A(hmad) A(li) K(ohzad). L'Afghanistan au voisinage de l'Hindustan [Af-
ghanistan as a Neighbor of Hindustan]. Afghanistan 8, no. 3, 60-66.
1953.
The difficulties Afghanistan has suffered as a neighbor to Hindustan--
from conquerors eager for the riches of Hindustan and, especially in
the last century, from the colonizing English; ending inevitably with
an argument for the independence of Pushtunistan.

973 L'Abeille, Lucerne. Regards vers l'Afghanistan. L'Afghanistan dans la
presse mondiale [Glances toward Afghanistan. Afghanistan in the World
Press]. Afghanistan 9, no. 4, 60-62. 1954.
A general description of the country and the people, recommending
Afghanistan to those hardy enough to endure travel hardships.

974 Lerzezynski, G. L. "Die Landeseinteilung Afghanistans" [The Land-
Divisions of Afghanistan]. Neue Orient 9, no. 2/3, 46-57. 1929.
Contains the translation into German of the 1922 ordinance concern-
ing the administrative divisions of the country.

975 Levin, I. D., ed. Konstitutsii gosudarstvo blizhnego i srednego vostoka
[Constitutions of the States of the Near and Middle East]. Moscow:
Izdatel'stvo inostrannoy literaturī, 1956. Pp. 591.
Pages 9-28 contain the constitution of Afghanistan and notes on its
history.

976 Loyi Pushtun [Great Pushtun]. A monthly in Pushtu, which began publication at Kabul in 1953.

977 March of Pakhtoonistan. Bombay: Art Litho and Printing Press, n.d.
Pp. 38; sketch map of "Pakhtoonistan."
Short articles by various personalities and reprints of newspaper arti-
cles and radio broadcasts, all favoring Pushtunistan. Sponsor and
principal writer is Hakim Taj Mohamed Khalil, President of the
Pakhtoon Khudai Khidmatgar Jirga at Bombay.

978 Mayne, Peter. The Narrow Smile. London: John Murray, 1955. Pp. 264.
A former R.A.F. officer, with a background of four years of service
on the North-West Frontier and a knowledge of Pushtu, returned in
1953 to look up old friends. Part Two, pages 115-176, concerns his
visit to Kabul and a discussion concerning Pushtunistan. The American edition of the same year was entitled "Journey to the Pathans."

979 *Mir Munshi, Sultan Muhammad Khan. The Constitution and Laws of Afghanistan. London: John Murray, 1900. Pp. vii, 164.
A scholarly study by the former State Secretary of Amir Abdul Rahman.
Gives the constitution as promulgated by that ruler, together with his
reasons for that action. Other aspects of Afghan law are also presented, but the entire subject is too much based on European writings
on Moslem law.

980 Mu'ahadeh fima bayn Rus va-Afghanistan [Treaty between Russia and Af-
ghanistan]. Kabul [1921]. Pp. 6.
The Persian text of the Afghan-Russian treaty of 1921.

981 Najibullah Khan. Speech Delivered over the Radio. Afghanistan 3, no.
2, 1-38. 1948.
An introductory notice of the situation among the Pushtun tribes is followed by an account of a trip of the author--then Acting Minister of
Education--to Pakistan, where he discussed the need for the autonomy
of "Afghan" tribes within Pakistan and other subjects with the highest
officials of the neighboring country.

982 Najibullah Khan. Speech Delivered by His Excellency Najibullah Khan,
Afghanistan Representative to the Indonesian Conference Held in New

VI. POLITICAL STRUCTURE

Delhi. Afghanistan 4, no. 1, 37-40. 1949.
Supports the nationalistic aspirations of the Indonesian people.

983 Najib-ullah Khan. Pukhtoonistan Question: A Survey. Afghanistan 5,
no. 3, 52-57. 1950.
Another review of the Afghan-Pakistan dispute.

984 Najibullah Khan. Cultural Traditions of Afghanistan. Afghanistan 5,
no. 4, 40-45. 1950.
A brief cultural history--which becomes in the end political--with
emphasis on cultural relations with India and Persia.

985 Najib-Ullah Khan. Statement Given by His Excellency Dr. Najib-Ullah
Ambassador for Afghanistan in India on the Eleventh cf August, 1951.
Afghanistan 6, no. 3, 38-42. 1951.
A defense of Afghanistan against Pakistan's accusations.

986 Najib-Ullah. Dr. Najib-Ullah's Press Conference on the 19th June, 1952.
Afghanistan 7, no. 3, 45-50. 1952.
A denial of Pakistan's report that there is danger to foreigners flying
between Afghanistan and India, and protesting a ban on Afghan-
Indian air communication.

987 Najibullah. Dr. Najibullah's Statement in New Delhi. Afghanistan 8,
no. 2, 31-32. 1953.
A reaffirmation of Afghanistan's position with regard to Pushtunistan.

988 Najibullah. Dr. Najibullah Khan's Statement on Pashtoonistan Day. Afghanistan 8, no. 3, 45. 1953.
Afghanistan's duty to support Pushtunistan, meanwhile keeping peaceful relations with India.

989 National Assembly. Afghanistan 2, no. 2, 47-48. 1947.
Features an abstract of the speech from the throne delivered to the
Sixth Session of the National Assembly on May 22, 1947.

990 Nizamnameh-yi tashkilat-i asasiyeh Afghanistan [Constitution of the
Formation of the Fundamental Law of Afghanistan]. Kabul: Rafiq
zivar printing house, 1305 [1926]. Pp. 108 and 7.
The Persian text of the country's first constitution.

991 Odell, Ernest. Afghanistan. Contemporary Review 988, 240-244. London, 1948.

Discusses Afghanistan's concern for the future of tribal groups along
the North-West Frontier and the probable reasons for this concern.

992 On Sir Zaferullah Khan's Statement. Afghanistan 4, no. 2, 28-31. 1949.
The Afghan writer objects to the statement that there is no problem
to be solved between Afghanistan and Pakistan: the issue is said to be
the right of the frontier Afghans to liberty.

993 *The Pakhtun Question. Hove (Sussex), n.d. Pp. 60.
A publication, presumed to come from the Afghan Information Bureau
at London, which deals with the Pushtunistan question.

994 Pakhtunistan. Delhi: Coronation Press.
Fortnightly magazine published at Delhi in 1950, 1951, etc.

995 Pakhtunistan Day (9th of Sunbola 1328 A. H.). Hove (Sussex): Key
Press, n.d. Pp. 31.
Celebrates the hoisting of the flag of "Independent Pakhtunistan" on
September 2, 1949. A summary of the history and background of the
movement.

996 Le Pakistan et la Ligue Musulmane [Pakistan and the Musulman League].
Afghanistan 7, no. 1, 56-59. 1952.
On whether the Pakistan Prime Minister should also be the president
of the Musulman League.

997 *Pazhwak, Abdur Rahman. Pakhtunistan. The Khyber Pass as the Focus
of the New State of Pakhtunistan. Hove (Sussex): Key Press, Ltd.,
(1954?). Pp. 153; bibliography; sketch map.
This is a later version of a booklet issued in 1951 by the Afghan Information Bureau in London, entitled "The Pakhtun Question, " and is
sponsored by the same organization. A number of chapters describe
the area in question, the people and their language and literature, the
more recent history of the area, and the origin and growth of the dispute over the future of the region. The sketch map depicts the boundaries of "Pakhtunistan. "

998 Da Pushtunistan peh bab kay da Afghanistan nazariyat [The Ideas of Afghanistan on Pushtunistan]. (Kabul), 1333 [1954]. Pp. 35.
A pamphlet with statements in Persian and Pushtu. Much of the material reflects the opinions of Prime Minister Sardar Muhammad Daud.

999 *Rand, Christopher. Crisis in Afghanistan. Commonweal 03, no. 1, 7-
10. October 7, 1955.

An American writer, recently in Afghanistan, discusses the elements of crisis: the Pushtunistan issue, the current Soviet efforts at economic penetration, and the general isolation of the country from international interest and concern.

1000 Rathjens, Carl. Die Staats-und Wirtschaftsstruktur Afghanistans [The Structures of State and of the Economy of Afghanistan]. Geographisches Taschenbuch, pp. 382-392. 1956-57.

1001 Rishtin, Sadiqullah. Pushtun Yar [The Pushtun Yar]. Kabul: Matba'eh yi 'umumi, 1331 [1952]. Pp. 135.
   Articles and poems in Pushtu by leaders of the movement for Pushtunistan.

1002 Royal Afghan Embassy, New Delhi. Pakhtoons Determined to Achieve Independence. Afghanistan 5, no. 1, 46-47. 1950.
   A protest against Pakistan propaganda in the Pushtunistan trouble.

1003 Sablier, Edouard. Au coeur de l'Asie un nouvel état est né: le Pouchtounistan [At the Heart of Asia a New State Is Born: Pushtunistan]. Afghanistan 5, no. 4, 13-16. 1950.
   A recapitulation of the Pushtunistan problem.

1004 *Schwager, Joseph. Die Entwicklung Afghanistans als Staat und seine zwischenstaatlichen Beziehungen [The Development of Afghanistan as a State and her International Relations]. Leipzig: Noske, 1932. Pp. 110.
   Uniquely valuable study of the formation of Afghanistan's constitution, of the international relations of the country at this same period and of the position of Afghanistan in relation to international law. Gives the full text of the constitution promulgated by Amanullah in 1923.

1005 Shah, Aurang. Voice of the People of Pakhtunistan. Afghanistan 5, no. 4, 35. 1950.
   A reaffirmation, by the President of the Azad Pakhtunistan Association of America, of the right of Pushtuns to be free.

1006 Shah, Sayad Amir. Pakhtunistan. Afghanistan 5, no. 4, 36. 1950.
   The Pushtuns will "never become subjects of Pakistan."

1007 *Shah, Sirdar Ikbal Ali. The Tragedy of Amanullah. London: Alexander-Ousley, Ltd., 1933. Pp. xiv, 272; appendices.

The first third of this work by a very prolific Afghan writer, long
resident abroad, is the rather familiar background material common to a number of his works. The balance, which deals with the
reign and eventual downfall of King Amanullah, is of real importance. Appendices give the texts of an Anglo-Afghan Treaty of
November 22nd, 1921, of an Afghan-German Treaty of September
14th, 1926, and of an Afghan-Soviet Treaty of August 31st, 1926.

1008 Stephens, Ian. Horned Moon. London: Chatto and Windus, 1953.
Pp. x, 288; maps.
The former editor of a leading British-owned newspaper in India,
the Statesman, returned to familiar places in 1953 in his account
of a journey through Pakistan, Kashmir, and Afghanistan. Chapters
25 and 26 describe his trip to Kabul from Peshawar and include dis-
cussions of the Pushtunistan issue.

1009 Tchardi Wal. Les difficultés intérieures du Pakistan [Pakistan's Domestic Difficulties]. Afghanistan 5, no. 1, 50-54. 1950.
In reply to Pakistan's propaganda, an "exposé" of Pakistan's real internal situation--economic instability, undemocratic parliament,
lack of a free press, etc.

1010 Tchardi-Wal. La Ligne Durand et les relations afghano-pakistanaises
[The Durand Line and Afghan-Pakistan Relations]. Afghanistan 6,
no. 3, 58-61. 1951.
Tchardi-Wal cites Sir Thomas Holdich's statement that the legality
of the Durand Line depends on the Treaty of Gandomak and declares
that that Treaty is no longer valid.

1011 Tchardi-Wal. Les relations afghano-pakistanaises et le Pathanistan [Af-
ghan-Pakistan Relations and Pushtunistan]. Afghanistan 6, no. 4,
22-26. 1951.
A reply to propaganda circulated by the Pakistan Prime Minister.

1012 Tchardi-Wal. Le Cachemire et le Pachtounistan [Kashmir and Pushtun-
istan]. Afghanistan 7, no. 1, 33-38. 1952.
The Pushtunistan issue is of major importance, while the Kashmir
issue is merely a "local war."

1013 Toynbee, Arnold. Impressions of Afghanistan and Pakistan's North-West
Frontier in Relation to the Communist World. International Affairs
(London) 37, 161-169. 1961.
Communism is making headway in Afghanistan, and in time its
threat may lead Afghanistan, Pakistan, and India to settle their
common differences, according to this article.

1014 *Usul-i asasi-yi dawlet-i 'aliyeh-yi Afghanistan [Fundamental Principles of the Sublime Government of Afghanistan]. Kabul: Matba'eh-
yi 'umumi, n.d. Pp. 20.
Official text of the Constitution of Afghanistan, printed in Persian
and Pushtu in parallel columns. Separate sheets contain amend-
ments.

1015 Usul-i vaza'if-i dakhili-yi riyaset-i shura-yi milli-yi Afghanistan [Fun-
damentals of the Internal Duties of the Presidium of the National
Council of Afghanistan]. Kabul: Matba'eh-yi 'umumi, 1329 [1950].
Pp. 10.
Text printed in Persian.

1016 *Usul-nameh [Basic Regulations]. Kabul: Matba'eh-yi 'umumi.
A series of pamphlets, each of which contains the printed text of
one law together with its date of passage. The text is printed in
Persian and Pushtu in parallel columns.

1017 Usul-nameh. Da mahbusinu da mokafatu aw mojazatu peh Afghanistan
Keshi [Laws Governing the Penalties and Punishments for Prisoners
in Afghanistan]. Kabul: Matba'eh-yi doulati, 1339 [1960]. Pp. 30.
The title is in Pushtu; the laws are presented in Pushtu and Persian,
in parallel columns.

1018 Warner, Denis. Afghanistan: A House Without Doors. Reporter 26,
no. 2, 28-30. 1962.
A visit to Kabul by an Australian journalist, with emphasis on reflections of Afghan-Soviet relations and the Pushtunistan issue.

1019 Wilber, Donald N. Document. Constitution of Afghanistan. Middle
East Journal 19, no. 2, 215-29. 1965.
A commentary on the Constitution of 1964, pp. 215-16, is followed
by the text of the document.

1020 Wilson, Andrew. Inside Afghanistan--A Background to Recent Troubles.
Royal Central Asian Journal 47, 286-295. 1960.
According to this writer, current internal difficulties and the trouble
with Pakistan are not the result of Soviet influence or intervention,
since Soviet goals do not require direct control of the country.

1021 Yusufzai, Saidal. Regarding the Views of Sir George Cunningham. Afghanistan 6, no. 1, 68-74. 1951.
An uncomplimentary account of the career of Sir George Cunningham,
"giving the lie" to his article in the Manchester Guardian entitled
"Frontier Discord between Afghanistan and Pakistan."

VII. ECONOMIC STRUCTURE

Agriculture; industry; trade; finance;
taxation; handicrafts; labor force

Here is another vitally important subject on which contemporary materials are inadequate for a real understanding of what is going on in the country and of the goals and progress of economic development. Some of the difficulty stems from the lack of reliable official statistics, or the assumed unreliability of those statistics which are obtainable. Figures and studies having to do with finance and taxation are very hard to find. Articles relating to labor are almost nonexistent, due in large part to the absence of labor unions and other labor organizations.

It is indeed fortunate that it has been possible to include a fair number of unpublished reports and studies which shed a clear and detailed light into obscure aspects of the economic structure.

1022 *'Abd al-Majid Khan. Mushkilat-i iqtisadi va-mujadaleh ba anha [Economic Difficulties and Contending with Them]. Kabul: Matba'eh-yi 'umumi, 1328 [1949]. Pp. 67.
The then Minister of National Economy suggests solutions to pressing economic problems. The text is in Persian.

1023 Afghan Financial Statistics. Kabul: The Bank of Afghanistan, Research Department.
The first number of this monthly publication appeared in August 1964.

1024 Afghan Progress in the Third Year of the Plan. London: Information Bureau, Royal Afghan Embassy, n.d. (1960). Pp. 104.
A well-illustrated, comprehensive account of progress on the First Five Year Development Plan between September 1958 and September 1959.

1025 Afghan Progress in the Fifth Year of the Plan. London: Information Bureau, Royal Afghan Embassy, n.d. (1961). Pp. 92.
A well-illustrated, comprehensive account of progress on the First Five Year Development Plan for the year ending September 1961.

1026 L'Afghanistan [Afghanistan]. Bulletin du Chambre de Commerce France-Asiatique, numéro special, 1928. Pp. 48.
A publication commemorating the visit of Amanullah to Paris and including a number of brief articles on such subjects as Astrakan sheep, Kabul, and railroads in Afghanistan.

VII. ECONOMIC STRUCTURE

1027 Afghanistan as a Source for Crude Drugs and Essential Oils. Commerce
Department. (Industrial Reference Service, December 1946, Vol.
4, Pt. 2, no. 133.) Washington: U. S. Government Printing Office,
1946. Pp. 2.

1028 Da Afghanistan Bank. Kabul. Condensed Statement of the Accounts
for the Year 1328 (Ended March 20th, 1950).
Lacks date and place of publication. Contains 5 unnumbered pages
in English and the same number in Persian. Assumed to be an annual publication and of definite value for its presentation of hard-
to-find data.

1029 *Afghanistan; bihtar ast yak mamlaket-i san'ati bashad ya zira'ati?
[Afghanistan; Should it Be an Industrial or an Agricultural Country?].
Kabul: Matba'eh-yi 'umumi, 1318 [1939]. Pp. 178.
A publication in Persian issued by the Ministry of National Economy,
in which several local figures discuss the implications of the title.

1030 Afghanistan: The Country and its Resources. Bulletin of International
News 18, 1907-1921. London, 1941.

1031 Afghanistan. Structure Economique et Sociale. Commerce Extérieur
[Afghanistan: Economic and Social Structure. Foreign Trade].
Lausanne: Office Suisse d'Expansion Commerciale, 1965. Pp. 83;
bibliography; mimeographed.

1032 Afghanistan, Summary of Basic Economic Information. Commerce Department. (International Reference Service, July 1950, Vol. 7, no.
68.) Washington: U. S. Government Printing Office, 1950. Pp. 4.

1033 *Afghanistan's Economic Development Plan and Her Current Difficulties.
Unpublished report. Minister of National Economy. Washington, 1949
Pp. 236.
Reviews postwar economic changes and presents details of the Five
Year Plan (1949-1953) set up by the then Minister of National Econ-
omy (1932-1950), Abdul Madjid.

1034 Afghanistan's Foreign Trade (Revised) 1335 through 1340. Kabul: Statistical Department, Ministry of Commerce, 1963. Pp. 47.

1035 Afghanistan's Foreign Trade 1335 through 1342 (March 21, 1956, through

March 20, 1964). Kabul: Statistical Department, Ministry of Commerce, 1965. Pp. 154.

1036 Afghanistan's Reclamation Program. Reclamation Era 34, 55-56. Washington, 1948.

1037 Aitchison, James Edward T. Notes to Assist in a Farther Knowledge of the Products of Western Afghanistan and of North-Eastern Persia. Transactions of the Botanical Society of Edinburgh. 18, 1-228. 1891.

1038 Akram, Mohammad. L'Agriculture en Afghanistan [Agriculture in Afghanistan]. Afghanistan 3, no. 4, 50-52; 4, no. 1, 26-29. 1948, 1949.
A brief survey touching on climate, methods of irrigation, and local types of wheat, barley, and rice.

1039 Alekseenkov, P. Agrarnyi vopros v Afganskom Turkestane [Agricultural Question in Afghan Turkestan]. Moscow: Mezhdunarodnyi Agrarnyi Institut, 1933. Pp. 107; map.

1040 *Ali, Mohammad. Commercial Afghanistan. Delhi, 1946. Pp. ii, 70; appendices; sketch map.
Short sections deal with flora and fauna, minerals, commerce and industry, exports, imports, banking regulations and customs regulations. Given the scarcity of reliable information on most of these subjects, all are of value. Among the useful appendices is a list of 87 Afghan business firms, with their addresses, type of business, and capitalization, and also a list of newspapers and periodicals published in the country.

1041 Baker, Henry D. British India. With Notes on Ceylon, Afghanistan and Tibet. Washington: U.S. Government Printing Office, 1915. Pp. 638; map.
This work--Special Consul Report No. 72 of the Department of Commerce--contains scarce economic data for the period in question, including statistical tables. Pages 533-561 are devoted to Afghanistan.

1042 *Basic Data on the Economy of Afghanistan. Unpublished report. U.S. Department of Commerce. World Trade Information Service, Part 1, nos. 55-74. Washington: U.S. Government Printing Office, 1955. Pp. 11.

Up-to-date, detailed information on Afghan foreign trade. All values are given in dollars.

1043 Basic Statistics of Afghanistan. Kabul: Ministry of Planning, Statistics and Research Department, 1962. Pp. 36.

1044 Bogdanov, L. The Afghan Weights and Measures. Journal and Proceedings of the Asiatic Society of Bengal n.s. 24, 419-435. 1928.
Discusses and describes the systems of weights and measures in use in Afghanistan prior to 1925 (the date on which the country theoretically adopted the metric system).

1045 Bresse, L. Dans l'Asie que s'éveille. Découverte d'une mine de pétrole en Afghanistan et grands travaux d'irrigation dans la région de Caboul [In Awakening Asia. Discovery of an Oil Source in Afghanistan and Great Irrigation Works in the Region of Kabul]. Correspondance d'Orient, pp. 256-258. 1926.

1046 *Cervinka (also Cervin), Vladimir. Afghanistan: Structure économique et sociale. Commerce extérieure [Afghanistan. Economic and Social Structure. Foreign Commerce]. Lausanne: Office Suisse d'Expansion Commerciale, Zürich et Lausanne, 1950. Pp. 83; bibliography; sketch map.
The author, a social scientist, was resident in Afghanistan between 1938 and 1944. His article represents a particularly well-informed summary of the inadequately documented internal economic situation. Current economic and financial problems are analyzed and future developments outlined.

1047 Chernyakovskaya, Neonila Ivanovna. Razvitiye promyshlennosti i polozheniye rabochego klassa Afganistana [Development of Industry and Position of the Working Class of Afghanistan]. Moscow: "Nauka," Glav. red. Vostochnoy Literatury, 1965. Pp. 168.

1048 *Data Book--South Asia. Department of State. Office of Intelligence Research. IR-6310. September 1943.
Afghanistan is treated on pages 95-108, the material including a statistical summary covering vital facts and figures and a series of tables presenting financial and economic information.

1049 Davydov, Aleksandr D. Razvitiye Kapitalisticheskikh otnosheniy v

zemledelii Afganistana [Development of Capitalistic Relations in
Afghan Agriculture]. Moscow: Izdatel'stvo Vostochnoy Literatury,
1962. Pp. 160.

1050 Davydov, Aleksandr D. O sel'skoy obshchine i yeye Khozyaystvennom
znachenii v Afganistane [The Rural Commune and its Economic Sig-
nificance in Afghanistan]. In: Voprosy Ekonomiki Afganistana.
Moscow: Izdatel'stvo Vostochnoy Literatury, pp. 57-124. 1963.

1051 *Development Program. Unpublished report. Government of Afghanistan. San Francisco, July 1953. Pp. 90; maps; diagrams.
A report (with eleven separate appendices) intended for those concerned with finance, administration, engineering, and construction,
to present an over-all analysis of land and water resources of the
Helmand and Arghandab Valleys and to evaluate their economic
potential. Also includes a tentative long-range program for the
ultimate development of the area and a more specific plan for development within the next few years. Includes a history of the organizations established by the Afghan government to administer development programs.

1052 Economic Review of Afghanistan, 1949. Commerce Department. (International Reference Service, August 1950, vol. 7, no. 90.) Washington: U. S. Government Printing Office, 1950. Pp. 3.

1053 Economic Studies.
A periodical which first appeared in 1961, published by the Faculty
of Economics of Kabul University. The title is given in English on
the cover; the text is in Persian and Pushtu.

1054 *Economic Survey of Asia and the Far East, 1954. Economic Bulletin
for Asia and the Far East 5, no. 4. Bangkok: United Nations, 1955.
Pp. 223.
Chapter 6 (pages 57-64) reviews economic and financial progress in
Afghanistan during the postwar period. Contains hard-to-get official
data--partly unreliable.

1055 *Ekker, Martin H. Economic Aspects of Development of Afghanistan.
United Nations, 1952. Pp. 69.
Prepared by a Dutch economist under the auspices of the U. N.
Technical Assistance Administration at the end of one year of service

as economic advisor. Contains reliable financial data and a critical appraisal of major development projects and of government
economic policy and administration.

1056 Eltezam, Z.A. Afghanistan's Foreign Trade. Middle East Journal 20,
no. 1, 95-103. 1966.

1057 The Em-Kayan. Morrison-Knudsen Co., Inc., Boise, Idaho.
This monthly magazine contains occasional short articles, generously illustrated, of such projects of Morrison-Knudsen Afghanistan,
Inc., as the Kajakai Dam, the Arghandab Dam, and the Boghra
canal system.

1058 Eskilsson, Enar. Report on Coordinating the Development of Afghanistan's Energy Resources. No publisher, n.d. Pp. 85; 23 tables;
mimeographed.

1059 Ferdinand, Klaus. Ris. Traek af dens dyrkning og behandling i Østaf-
ghanistan [Rice. Aspects of Cultivation and Treatment in East
Afghanistan]. Kuml, pp. 195-232. (Aarhus, Denmark), 1959.

1060 Ferdinand, Klaus. The Horizontal Windmills of Western Afghanistan.
Folk 5, 71-89. 1963.

1061 *Field, Neil C. The Amu Darya: A Study in Resource Geography. Geographical Review 44, 528-542. 1954.
A study of proposed methods of developing the use of the water of
this great river dividing Afghanistan and the U.S.S.R. and an examination of the international problems which such development
would involve.

1062 *Franck, Dorothea Seelye and Peter G. Franck. Economic Review: The
Middle East Economy in 1949. Middle East Journal 4, no. 2, 228.
Washington, 1950.
A short factual paragraph, in a long article, on the drop in Afghan-
istan's imports and exports for 1949 and the reasons for this.

1063 *Franck, Peter G. Problems of Economic Development in Afghanistan.
Middle East Journal 3, no. 3, 293-314; 421-440. Washington, 1949.
Important study by an American economic consultant and teacher who
was advisor to the Afghan Minister of National Economy in 1948-1950.

Supported by reliable and difficult-to-obtain financial and economic data. The first installment deals with the impact on the
local situation of international conditions and the second with
planning and finance.

1064 Franck, Peter G. Afghanistan: A New Day Is Dawning. Middle East
Report 7, no. 6, 3 unnumbered pages. Washington, 1954.
Excellent, extremely condensed survey, with emphasis upon finan-
cial and economic problems and projected solutions.

1065 Franck, Peter G. Foreign Aid and Economic Development in Afghanistan.
Unpublished Ph.D. thesis. University of California at Berkeley, 1954.

1066 *Franck, Peter G. Obtaining Financial Aid for a Development Plan.
The Export-Import Bank of Washington Loan to Afghanistan. (Printed
for the Use of the Committee on Banking and Currency.) Washington: U.S. Government Printing Office, 1954. Pp. 55; list of documents consulted.
Exhaustive account, by the American economic advisor to the Afghan Minister of National Economy in 1948-1950, of the steps involved in obtaining a development loan of $21 million, and with an
interesting appraisal of the results of this expenditure.

1067 *Franck, Peter G. Technical Assistance through the United Nations--the
Mission in Afghanistan 1950-1953. In Howard M. Teaf and Peter G.
Franck, eds., Hands across Frontiers, pp. 13-61. Ithaca: Cornell
University Press, 1955.
Describes United Nations operations and evaluates results, based on
interviews and unpublished field reports.

1068 *Franck, Peter G. Economic Progress in an Encircled Land. Middle East
Journal 10, no. 1, 43-59; sketch map of the Helmand Valley; tables.
1956.
Evaluates changes in budget, trade, private and public investments,
economic organization, and international aid programs since 1947.

1069 *Franck, Peter G. Afghanistan Between East and West. Washington,
D.C.: National Planning Association, 1960. Pp. 86.
A report on the economics of competitive coexistence, including material on trade, economic development, and political relations with
the United States and the U.S.S.R.

1070 Fritz, Dale B. Simple Tools for Social Progress. The Asia Foundation.
      Program Bulletin 22, 4-6. 1962.
      Report by an American adviser on the introduction and local manu-
      facture of turning plows, seed drills, inertia pumps, and fly-shuttle
      looms.

1071 Furdoonjee, Nowrozjee. Report on the Weights, Measures, and Coins
      of Cabul, and Bukharie. Journal of the Asiatic Society of Bengal 7,
      392-900. 1838.
      Tables, with short remarks and explanations, of weights, measures
      and coins of Kabul, Bokhara (and Peshawar), with their correspond-
      ing values in English and Indian measures, weights, and coins.

1072 *Ghaussi, Aref. Afghan Carpet Industry. Afghanistan 8, no. 4, 42-45.
      1953.
      The chief characteristics of Afghan carpets, described so that the
      reader may be able to distinguish them from other oriental carpets.

1073 Ghaussi, Aref. Some Facts about Three Important Handicrafts of Af-
      ghanistan. Afghanistan 9, no. 2, 22-26. 1954.
      The process of cotton-weaving, and its cost; silk-weaving; and
      the long, painstaking method of carpet-weaving.

1074 Ghaussi, Muhammad Aref. Dictionary of Economics. English-Persian.
      Kabul, 1339 [1960]. Pp. 143 and 105. Mimeographed.

1075 Ginnever, O. R. Cotton in Afghanistan. Geographical Journal 104, 212-
      213. 1944.
      The tentative results obtained from planting American type cotton,
      obtained by the Afghan government from the U.S.S.R.

1076 Golovin, Y. M. Afganistan, ekonomika i vneshnyaya torgovlya [The
      Economy and External Trade of Afghanistan]. Moscow: Vneshtor-
      gizdat, 1962. Pp. 168.
      Chapters are devoted to industry, agriculture, transport, finance, and
      foreign trade, with emphasis on Afghan-Soviet relations.

1077 Golovin, Y. M. Sovetskiy soyuz i Afganistan. Opyt ekonomicheskogo
      sotrudichestva [The Soviet Union and Afghanistan. Economic Co-
      operation]. Mowcow: Izdatel'stvo Vostochnoy Literatury, 1962.
      Pp. 102; bibliography.

VII. ECONOMIC STRUCTURE

1078 Gurevich, Naum M. Vneshnyaya torgovlya Afganistana do Vtoroy
Mirovoy Voyny [Foreign Trade of Afghanistan before World War II].
Moscow: Izdatel'stvo Vostochnoy Literatury, 1959. Pp. 223; bib-
liography.
A survey from the early nineteenth century, with emphasis on the
years after 1919.

1079 Gurevich, Naum M. Gosudarstvennyy sektor v ekonomike Afganistana
[Government Business Enterprises in the Afghan Economy]. Moscow:
Izdatel'stvo Vostochnoy Literatury, 1962. Pp. 110.

1080 Gurevich, Naum M., ed. Voprosy ekonomiki Afganistana [The Problems of Afghanistan's Economy]. Moscow: Izdatel'stvo Vostochnoy
Literatury, 1963. Pp. 248.
Articles by the editor and four other specialists on the following subjects: The Question of Transit in Afghanistan's Economy and Policy,
On the Agricultural Common and its Economic Importance in Afghanistan, On the Question of Training National Technical Cadres
in Afghanistan, The Economic Position of the Imperialist States in
Present Day Afghanistan, and Export Articles of Afghanistan's Economy, 1939-1960.

1081 Hakimi, 'Abd al-Karim. Masa'l iqtisadi ma [Our Economic Problems].
Kabul: Matba'eh-yi doulati, 1337 [1958]. Pp. 54.
A number of essays in Persian.

1082 *Helmand Valley Industrial Survey--Phase I. Unpublished Report. International Engineering Company. San Francisco, 1955. Pp. 175;
maps.
First survey and appraisal of industrial activities in the Helmand
Valley, followed by an optimistic analysis of markets contributing
to potential expansion of industry in an area of 100,000 square miles
(2/5 of Afghanistan).

1083 Hinrichs, Harley H. Certainty as Criterion: Taxation of Foreign Invest-
ment in Afghanistan. National Tax Journal 15, no. 2, 139-154. 1962.

1084 Hoff, Hellmut. Die deutsch-afghanischen Wirtschaftsbeziehungen [Ger-
man-Afghan Economic Relations]. Orient 4, no. 3, 98-9. 1963.

1085 India. Trade Agency, Kabul. Report. 1st--1937/38. Delhi: Manager

of Publications, n.d. Pp. v.
Publication of the Department of Commercial Intelligence and
Statistics (India), Calcutta.

1086 Industrial Development in Afghanistan. A Forward Look. Robert R.
Nathan Associates, 1965. Pp. 77; mimeographed.

1087 *Iqtisad [Economics]. An illustrated monthly periodical which first
appeared in 1931.
Sponsored by the Ministry of National Economy, the articles are in
Persian, Pushtu, and English. The periodical has appeared irregularly, and its title has other forms.

1088 Janata, Alfred. Die landwirtschaftliche Struktur Afghanistans [The
Agricultural Structure of Afghanistan]. Bustan 3, 36-40. Vienna,
1963.

1089 Kajakai Report and its Relation to the Development of the Helmand Valley. Unpublished Report. International Engineering Company.
Washington, 1949. Pp. 50; map.
Appraises economic returns from harnessing the Helmand River and
irrigating 550,000 acres. Served to justify the 1950 dollar loan re-
quest from the U. S. Export-Import Bank.

1090 Kamal, Abdul Hadi. Das Agrarland Afghanistan und seine Zukunft
[The Farm Land of Afghanistan and its Future]. Zurich, 1954.

1091 Karhaneh [Agriculture].
The quarterly publication of the Department of Agriculture, which
first appeared at Kabul in 1952. The articles are in Pushtu and Persian.

1092 Kohzad, Ahmad Ali. Le lapis-lazuli et son rôle dans les relations de
l'Ariana avec les pays de l'Asie [Lapis-lazuli and its Role in the Relations of Aryana with the Countries of Asia]. Afghanistan 3, no. 4,
1-2. 1948.
Locates the mines in the country and tells of finds of worked lapis-
lazuli in ancient sites in Iran, Iraq, and Egypt.

1093 Kohzad, Ahmad Ali. Shah Shamiran et le raisin [Shah Shamiran and
the Grape]. Afghanistan 4, no. 3, 45-48. 1949.

VII. ECONOMIC STRUCTURE

Notes on ancient mentions of vineyards in Afghanistan are followed by a story of the legendary discovery of the grape vine in the reign of Shah Shamiran.

1094 K(ohzad, Ahmad Ali). "Nimrouz" ou le bassin inférieur de l'Hilmend ["Nimrouz" or the Lower Basin of the Helmand] . Afghanistan 8, no. 4, 46-50. 1953.
A summary account of numerous planned projects to utilize the Helmand was--before the invasion of Timur--fertile and well irrigated and that it may, under the government's efforts to recolonize and irrigate, be so again.

1095 *Labour Legislation in Afghanistan. International Labour Review 57, 83-85. 1948.
A summary of the labor regulations issued in the Royal Order of January 16, 1946. The regulations deal with wages, hours, accident compensation, social security, and health.

1096 The Law of Commerce (Commercial Law of Afghanistan). Kabul: Public Administration Service, USAID, n.d. Not paged, mimeographed.
A translation of the law of 1955.

1097 (Muhammad Kabir Khan Ludin). Afghan Government Views: The Kabul River Valley Development, by K. L. Afghanistan 3, no. 4, 44-49; map. 1948.
A summary account of numerous planned projects to utilize the water of the Kabul River for irrigation and power. Since the time of writing, the largest project, the Sarobi dam, has gone steadily forward.

1098 *Malik Abdurrahimzai, Abdul and associates. Economic Report of Afghanistan. Unpublished report. Istanbul, 1955. Pp. 41.
A brief review by the Minister of Finance of economic developments from 1919 on, with an optimistic description of new government-sponsored projects and new policy. Valuable as an official document.

1099 *Michel, Aloys A. The Kabul, Kunduz, and Helmand Valleys and the National Economy of Afghanistan. Washington, D.C.: National Academy of Sciences, 1959. Pp. 441; bibliography; maps.
A detailed account, based upon first-hand observations, of present and proposed irrigation and power projects in major river valleys.

VII. ECONOMIC STRUCTURE

1100 Michel, Aloys A. Foreign Trade and Foreign Policy in Afghanistan.
Middle Eastern Affairs 12, no. 1, 7-15. 1961.
An analysis of the country's foreign trade, reflecting an increasing
dependence on the U.S.S.R.

1101 Ministry of National Economy. The Economic Year Book. A Summary
of the Economic Activities in Afghanistan during the Year 1329 (1950)
Compiled by Yusuf "Aina." Kabul (1951?). Pp. 96 in Persian; 10
in English.
The English section is too short to give more than the briefest outline of financial and economic activities.

1102 Ministry of Planning. Survey of Progress. 1959. 4 vols., with vol. 1
in two parts. Kabul: Government Printing House, 1959.
Mimeographed report, each volume containing sections in Persian
and in English; the pages are not numbered consecutively.

1103 *Ministry of Planning. Survey of Progress. 1960. Kabul: Military
Printing Press, 1960. Pp. 215; 90 tables; map.
Comprises the third annual report on the First Five Year Development Plan. Part I is a progress report of the activities of the ministries, Part II an analytical review of significant economic and social developments, and Part III a series of statistic tables. The report was also published in Pushtu and in Persian.

1104 Ministry of Planning. Survey of Progress. 1961-62. Kabul: Government Printing House, 1963. Pp. 83; 51 pages of tables and charts.
A review of activity under the First Five Year Plan, 1956-1961.

1105 Mirzoyan, S. Uspekhi Khozyaystvennogo razvitiya Afganistana [Suc-
cesses of Economic Development in Afghanistan] . In: Mirovaya
Ekonomika i Mezhdunarodnyye Otnosheniya. Moscow, No. 11,
pp. 98-100, 1964.

1106 *Mohammed, Ali. Karakul as the Most Important Article of Afghan
Trade. Afghanistan 4, no. 4, 48-53. 1949.
Traces the early use of Karakul and its history as an item of commerce, lists sales of skins in recent years, and outlines steps which
should be taken to improve the marketing of this item.

1107 Moir, M. C. Afghanistan--Crossroads of Asia; Gateway to India. Foreign Commerce Weekly, September 4, 1943, pp. 10-15.

Itemizes the initial steps taken toward a modern economy through industrialization and the expansion of irrigation facilities.

1108 Nedeltcheff, Nicolaff. Le mouton "Kerekul" [The Karakul Sheep]. Lyon: Bosc et Rieu, 1929. Pp. 79.

1109 *Nikitine, Basile. La structure -économique de l'Afghanistan [The Economic Structure of Afghanistan]. Paris: Société d'Études et d'Informations Économiques. (Mémoires et Documents), 1932. Pp. 29.
A sound, rather thorough study, with a certain emphasis on a projection of the economic development of the country.

1110 Oksendahl, Wilma. Business Education for Afghan Women. The Asia Foundation. Program Bulletin 19, 5-7. 1961.
First-hand report by an American adviser at Kabul.

1111 Pangeh [Bank]. A monthly, largely in Persian, published at Kabul since 1941 by the Bank Melli Afghan.

1112 Pastidis, S.L. Summary of Literature on Food and Agricultural Marketing in Afghanistan. Kabul, no publisher, 1964. Pp. 14; mimeographed.
A descriptive listing of some 56 ephemeral reports by the author.

1113 Paul, Arthur. Role of Trade in Afghanistan's Development. Asia Foundation, Program Bulletin 29, 1-5. 1963.

1114 Peasant Life in Afghanistan. Moslem World 35, 259. 1945.
A short article on farms and farmers, presented anonymously.

1115 Pikulin, M. G. Razvitiye natsional'noy ekonomiki i kul'tury Afganistana 1955-1960 [The Development of National Economy and Culture in Afghanistan 1955-1960]. Tashkent: Izdatel'stvo Akademii Nauk Uzbekskoy S.S.R., 1961. Pp. 151; bibliography.
Largely concerned with the course of the First Five Year Plan. Material on cultural progress and on the need to eliminate feudalism in the society.

1116 Polyak, A. A. Ekonomicheskiy stroy Afganistana; ocherki [Economic System of Afghanistan; Essays]. Moscow: "Nauka, " 1964. Pp. 161.

1117 Preparing Shipments to Afghanistan. International Reference Service, Foreign and Domestic Commerce Bureau, U. S. Department of Commerce, vol. 7, no. 116, December 1950. Pp. 4.

1118 Project Progress Report. United States Operations Mission to Afghanistan. June 30, 1961. Kabul: Program Office, USOM, 1961. Pp. 157.
A mimeographed report which includes an historical analysis of the American aid program, a description of individual projects, and a list of contractors employed on the projects.

1119 *Reisner, Igor Mikhailovich. Afghanistan; ekonomiko-geograficheskaia kharakteristika [Afghanistan; Economic-Geographic Characteristics]. Moscow: Gosudarstvennoe izdatel'stvo geograficheskai literatury, 1953. Pp. 67; map.
A revision of a book entitled Afghanistan, published by the same author in 1939. More stress is placed on economic factors, and the material has been brought up-to-date.

1120 *Report of the Helmand River Delta Commission. Unpublished report. Washington: U. S. Department of State, 1951. Pp. 151; map of Sistan.
Describes agricultural and hydrological features of the Sistan basin as background for the dispute over division of the Helmand River water between Iran and Afghanistan. Contains data not available elsewhere. Prepared by a U. S. engineer, on behalf of an international arbitration commission after a 1950 field trip.

1121 Report on Development of the Arghandab Area. Unpublished report. International Engineering Company. Washington, 1949. Pp. 16; tables; maps.
Describes the agricultural potential of year-round irrigation of the fertile southwestern valley. Served to justify part of the 1950 loan from the U. S. Export-Import Bank.

1122 *Report on Development Program of Government of Afghanistan. Unpublished report. International Engineering Company. San Francisco, 1955. Pp. 48; map.
Introduced by a letter of transmittal from the Helmand Valley Authority, this report served as the formal loan application filed in November 1953 with the U. S. Export-Import Bank. It summarizes irrigation construction work since 1946 and appraises six new projects

in the Arghandab and Helmand valleys and a major road-building.
program.

1123 Report on Proposed Cement Factory near Kabul, Afghanistan. Unpublished report. International Engineering Company. San Francisco,
1948. Pp. 13; sketches.
Appraises the need for and the feasibility of a cement plant with
60,000 tons annual capacity.

1124 Report on Proposed Trunk Highways (Afghanistan). Unpublished report.
International Engineering Company. San Francisco, 1949. Pp. 23;
maps.
Describes the economic role of the existing Qandahar-Kabul-
Torkham route and the potential benefits of its reconstruction.

1125 *Report to the Government of Afghanistan on Handicrafts and Small-Scale
Industries. Unpublished report. International Labor Organization.
Geneva, 1954. Pp. 67.
Prepared by a technical expert serving under U. N. Technical Assistance Administration, from February 1953 to January 1954. Describes home weaving and the cotton, wool, silk and carpet industries, and appraises the economic potential of expanded handicraft
activities.

1126 Resai, Mohammed Ismail. Struktur und Entwick- lungsmöglichkeiten
der Wirtschaft von Afghanistan [The Structure and Development Potentials of the Economy of Afghanistan] . Bonn, 1958. Pp. 101;
bibliography.
A doctoral dissertation, privately printed by the author, based largely
upon European sources rather than research in Afghanistan.

1127 Rhein, Eberhard. Hilfe für Afghanistan aus Ost und West [Aid for Afghanistan from East and West] . Aussenpolitik 15, no. 8, 557-564.
1964.

1128 Rhein, Eberhard and A. Ghanie Ghaussy. Die Wirtschaftliche Entwick-
lungen Afghanistans. 1880-1965 [The Economic Development of Afghanistan. 1880-1965] . Köln/Opladen: C. W. Leske, 1966.
Pp. 208; bibliography.

1129 Rozhevits, R. IU. Novye Dannye po Flore zlakov Afganistana [New

Materials on the Cereal Family of Afghanistan] . (In Russian, with French Summary.) Bulletin of Applied Botany of Genetics and Plant Breeding 19, no. 1, 121-126. Leningrad, 1928.

The French summary, Nouveaux matériaux sur la flore des graminées de l'Afghanistan, begins on page 125--a list of 20 cereal specimens found in Afghanistan. An entirely new species, Oryzopsis Vavilovi Roshev, is described in Latin on page 123.

1130 Rosset, Louis-Felicien. Afghan Marble. Afghanistan 1, no. 2, 4-11. 1946.

Lists local sites and types and describes the Kabul marble works.

1131 Samini, A. Zustand und Entwicklungsmöglichkeiten der Wirtschaft Afghanistans unter besonderer Berücksichtigung der Landwirtschaft [The Condition and the Development Potential of Afghanistan's Economy under the Special Aspect of Farming] . Bonn, 1961.

1132 Schwarzenbach, Annemarie Clark. Afghanistan in Transition. Geographical Magazine 11, 326-341; map. London, 1940.

Condensed account of a trip taken throughout much of Afghanistan in 1939, with attention centered on the efforts at industrialization of the country.

1133 Schwob, Marcel. The Economic Challenge in Afghanistan. United Nations Review 2, 25-27. 1955.

An outline of plans for charting and developing mineral and economic resources with the assistance of various agencies of the United Nations.

1134 Second Five Year Plan. 1341-45 (March 1962-March 1967). Kabul, Government Printing House, 1963. Pp. 100.

Prepared by the Ministry of Planning.

1135 *Seifert, Bruno. Der Anteil Deutschlands an der wirtschaftlichen Entwicklung Afghanistans, von Bruno Seifert; hrsg. in Verbindung mit der Deutschen Akademie München und dem Institut für mittel-und südosteuropaische Wirtschaftsforschung an der Universität Leipzig [Germany's Participation in the Economic Development of Afghanistan, by Bruno Seifert; Published in Connection with the German Academy of Munich and the Institute for Middle-and-Southeast European Economic Research at the University of Leipzig] . Stuttgart: Ausland und Heimat Verlagsaktiengesellschaft, 1929. Pp. 66; map.

The author's dissertation.

1136 Semin, A. Sovetsko-afganskie ekonomicheskie otnosheniia [Soviet-
Afghan Economic Relations]. Vneshniaia Torgovlia 24, no. 5, 1-6.
Moscow, 1954.

1137 Sérignan, Claude. Le plan quinquennal afghan [The Afghan Five Year
Plan]. Orient 4, 77-96. 1960.
An analysis of the First Five Year Development Plan.

1138 *Shah, S. M. Trade with Afghanistan. Lahore: Ripon Printing Press,
n.d. (1946). Pp. vii, 103; appendices; folding map.
Some ten brief chapters deal with communications, education,
press, exports, imports, banks and currency, business concerns,
commerce, and related subjects. The author notes that "since the
Afghan Government do not publish any trade returns, the various
figures . . . cannot be calculated as unassailable. "

1139 *Shah, S. M. Afghan General and Commercial Directory 1327 (1948-
49). Karachi: Himaliya Press, n.d. (1948). Pp. iv, 170; folding
map.
The author, a Pakistani associated with the Ministry of Commerce
at Karachi, rightly claims that this is the first such publication on
Afghanistan. It does feature hard-to-find information on such subjects as names and positions of government officials, schools and
teachers, writers and publications, a street guide to Kabul, and a
considerable variety of miscellaneous information.

1140 Shalizi, Abdussattar. The Text of Mr. Shalizi('s) Speech in the Plenary
Session of the Asian Regional Conference at Nuwara Eliya, Ceylon.
Afghanistan 5, no. 1, 33-39. 1950.
The Afghan General Director of Labor sets forth Afghanistan's hopes
and work in the labor field and endorses the program of the Interna-
tional Labor Organization.

1141 Shalizi, Abdussattar. Problems and Characteristics of Afghanistan's Internal Development. Review of International Affairs 14, 6-10. 1963.

1142 Stewart, Ruth W. Caravan Trade in Asia With Special Reference to Af-
ghanistan. Kabul: Communications Media Division, USOM/A, 1961.
Not paged; mineographed; maps; bibliography.
Includes a Persian translation of the English text.

VII. ECONOMIC STRUCTURE

1143 Strany Vostoka. Ekonomicheskii spravochnik. 2. Srednyi Vostak. Afganistan pod redaktsiei I. M. Reisnera [Countries of the East. An Economic Bulletin. 2. The Middle East. Afghanistan. Edited by I. M. Reisner]. Moscow: Vsesoiuznaia torgovaia palata, pp. 207-325. 1936.

    A work that was superseded by the work on Afghanistan published by the editor in 1953 (see no. 1119).

1144 Survey of Progress 1962-64. Kabul: Education Press, 1964. Pp. 152; mimeographed.

    Prepared by the Department of Statistics and Research, Ministry of Planning.

1145 Survey of Progress 1964-65. Kabul: Government Printing Press, 1965. Pp. 58; 46 pages of tables.

1146 Survey of the Tourism Industry in Afghanistan. Chicago: Thomas H. Miner and Associates, n.d. [1965?]. Pp. 383; maps; bibliography.

1147 Swayze, Francis J. Foreign Private Enterprise and Afghanistan. No publisher, n.d. Pp. 33 and Appendix; mimeographed.

    The Appendix contains the text, in English translation, of the Law Encouraging the Investment of Private Foreign Capital in Afghanistan,which was enacted in 1958.

1148 Technical Cooperation Agreement between United States and Afghanistan Signed Kabul, February 7, 1951; Entered into Force February 7, 1951 U. S. State Department. (Treaties and Other International Acts Series 2210. State Publication 4166.) Washington: U. S. Government Printing Office, 1951. Pp. 3.

1149 Tromp, S. W. Report on the Oil Possibilities of North Afghanistan. Unpublished report. Kabul, 1951. Pp. 34; 5 appendices.

    Detailed technical analysis of geological structure and oil seepages found in the Northern Provinces during a field trip in October-December 1950. Prepared under the auspices of the U. N. Technical Assistance Administration for the guidance of the oil development program.

1150 United Nations, Economic Commission for Asia and the Far East. Multipurpose River Basin Development. Part 2D-Water Resources Development in Afghanistan, Iran, Republic of Korea and Nepal. Chapter I, Afghanistan. Bangkok, 1961.

1151 *Vavilov, N. I. and D. D. Bukinich. Zemledel'cheskiy Afganistan
[Agricultural Afghanistan]. Supplement 33 to the Bulletin of Applied Botany, of Genetics and Plant Breeding. Leningrad, 1929.
Pp. xxxii, 610; maps.
The full report of research in Afghanistan between 1924 and 1927
by experienced Soviet botanists. Several subjects were of major
interest: the collection of plant samples, study of the regularities
in crop distribution on the Hindu Kush, investigation of agricultural
technics, and a survey of agricultural resources. The work is uniquely valuable in its field, as is indicated by the important summary
in English given on pages 535-610.

1152 Volin, M. E. Chromite Deposits in Logar Valley, Kabul Province, Afghanistan. Washington: U. S. Department of Interior, Bureau of
Mines, 1950. Pp. 58.
Geological and economic appraisal (unfavorable) of 181,000 tons
of chrome ores.

1153 Zaman, Mohammed. L'Agriculture en Afghanistan et ses relations avec
l'économie nationale [Agriculture in Afghanistan and its Relations to
the National Economy]. Afghanistan 6, no. 3, 47-55. 1951.
In developing her resources, Afghanistan must concentrate on agriculture rather than on industry, according to the author. He examines several factors influencing agricultural productivity, such
as rainfall, climate, etc.

VIII. LANGUAGES AND LITERATURE

Languages and dialects; lexicons; grammars;
dictionaries; literature in prose and
poetry; manuscripts and editions of
manuscripts; folklore; songs
and ballads; inscriptions

In contrast with earlier chapters, the majority of the items in this chapter are in the Persian or Pushtu languages. Works of this nature have been listed in the bibliography by Akram (No. 11) and in the catalogues of printed books by Edwards (No. 47) and Arberry (No. 18); in fact Akram includes a number of elusive works printed in India in Pushtu during the nineteenth century which have not been included in this publication. However, many of the titles here given have not been listed elsewhere, since they represent works published in Afghanistan during the last 30 years. These titles reflect the efforts of an energetic group of modern Afghan scholars to promote the historical, literary, and sociological background of their country by means of original writings and by means of editions of neglected manuscripts. A royal decree of 1936 sparked the movement to bring Pushtu literature out of obscurity, and a great deal has been accomplished in this field under the sponsorship of the Pushtu Tolaneh, or Pushtu Society. In addition, the ancient and operative Code of the Pushtuns, or Pushtunwali, has been recorded and interpreted through the work of these scholars. It does seem amazing that in all the years when the British were engaged at close quarters with these tribal elements they did not collect the Pushtunwali; perhaps the omission was a deliberate one. In much the same way, the works of earlier writers who wrote in Persian but who remained almost unknown to the West have been recovered from oblivion. It may be some time before scholars in other countries take advantage of this source material.

Afghan scholars have written extensively in Pushtu for the periodical Kabul (No. 67), and in Persian for the periodical Aryana (No. 20). It has not been feasible to index these two periodicals, but a real effort has been made to illustrate the scope of local writing by including in this bibliography a complete listing of all the articles that have been published in the periodical Afghanistan (No. 1) through 1954--all either in French or English. Of somewhat uneven merit, the titles of these articles appear within the various chapters of this publication.

One extensive classification of works written and printed in Afghanistan has been omitted from this bibliography, although the items have been carefully examined. These are the school texts, lithographed or printed at Kabul by the government and distributed free of charge to the students by the Ministry of Education. Some 90 texts which were reviewed fell into the following categories: history; history of Afghan literature; history of Islam; religion (Islam); ethics; grammar; arithmetic and algebra; physics; biology; chemistry; geography; astronomy; and natural sciences. Most numerous were the grammars for teaching Persian and Pushtu, with second and third places taken by works on arithmetic and algebra and by works by foreign linguists concerned with Persian and Pushtu as spoken and written in Afghanistan.

It is of interest to note that local scholars, authors of textbooks, and figures in public life have contributed to the growing number of volumes of the Afghan Encyclopedia (No. 21). As this work progresses, the Afghans will have available for the first time an exhaustive knowledge of the modern world. They will have the facility of moving from a remote past into the urgent present. In quite another way, the scholarly works in Persian and Pushtu may supply firm contacts with traditional ethics, customs, and beliefs.

1154 Abayeva, T. Ob afganskom narodnom tvorchestve [On Afghan Folk Creativity]. Zvezda Vostoka 10, 78-83. 1958.
> Concerns the popular literature of the country, with examples of poetry.

1155 Da 'Abdul 'Ali Mestaghni diwan [The Collected Works of 'Abdul 'Ali Mestaghni]. Kabul: Pohani matba'eh, 1338 [1959]. Pp. 160.
> Poetry in Pushtu.

1156 'Abdullah Khan, Malik al-Shu'ara', ed. Kalid al-sarf [The Key of Accidence]. Kabul: Matba'eh-yi 'umumi. 1319 [1940]. Pp. 46.
> Poorly lithographed text in Persian of a work designed for classes in adult education.

1157 Abu Bakr, Ruqayyah. Golha-yi Khudrow [Wild Flowers]. Kabul, 1335 [1956]. Pp. 86.
> Poetry in Persian.

1158 Afghaninavis, 'Abdullah. Loghat-i 'amianeh farsi Afghanistan [A Dictionary of Colloquial Farsi in Afghanistan]. Kabul: Matba'eh-yi doulati, 1340 [1960]. Pp. 176.
> The initial effort at compiling a dictionary of the spoken Persian of Afghanistan.

1159 Afghanistan: Evergreen EVR 002.
> A recorded miscellany of Afghan music.

1160 Afganskiy sbornik [Afghan Collection] . Kratkiye Soobshcheniya Instituta Vostokovedeniya. Moscow. Vol. 33 (1959), pp. 137, and
Vol. 37 (1960), pp. 139.

1161 Afganskiye Skazki [A Collection of Afghan Tales] . Moscow: Goslitizdat, 1955. Pp. 155.
Afghan folklore, legends, and fables in Russian translation, not
identified as to sources.

1162 Archer, William Kay. The Music of Afghanistan and Iran. Society for
Asian Music. pp. 2-9. Summer, 1964.

1163 Asadabadi, mirza Lutfullah Khan. Sharh-i hal u athar-i Sayyid-i
Jamal al-Din-i Asadabadi [Life and Works of Sayyid Jamal al-Din
Asadabadi] . Berlin: Orientalistischer Zeitschriftenverlag Iranschahr,
1926. Pp. 128.
The nephew of Sayyid Jamal al-Din writes of his uncle's life and
gives a description of his literary works.

1164 Aslanov, M. G. O formirovanii afganskogo natsional'nogo yazyka [On
the formation of the Afghan national language] . In: Etnicheskiye
protsessy i sostav naseleniya v stranakh Peredney Azii. Moscow-
Leningrad: Izdatel'stvo Vostochnoy Literatury, 1963. Pp. 3-23.
Deals with the formation of Pushtu.

1165 'Ata', Muhammad Mirza. Nava-yi ma'arik [The Song of Battle-Fields]
Kabul: Matba'eh-yi 'umumi, 1331 [1952] . Pp. 229.
Edited by Ahmad 'Ali Kohzad, the Persian manuscript now in the
Kabul Museum was written in 1854 A.D.

1166 Athar, Qazi 'Abd al-Halim. Tir hir sho'aran [Forgotten Poets] . Peshawar: Peshawar University, 1963. Pp. 284; lithographed.
A collection of poetry in Pushtu.

1167 Ayazi, Muhammad A'zam. Qava'd-i pushtu [The Rules of Pushtu] .
Kabul: Matba'eh-yi 'umumi, 1318 [1939] . Pp. 224.
Pushtu grammar taught through the medium of a Persian text.

1168 Badakhshi, 'Abd Allah. Da Afghanistan da zino zhibo u lahjo qamus
[A Dictionary of some Languages and Dialects of Afghanistan] . Ka-
bul, 1339 [1960] . Pp. 225.
The text is in Pushtu.

VIII. LANGUAGES AND LITERATURE

1169 *Badakhshi, Shah Abdullah. Les langues du Pamir [The Languages of the Pamir]. Afghanistan 8, no. 3, 46-56. 1953.

A discussion of the similarity between European languages and Sanskrit, due to their Aryan origin, and an identification of the Pamirs as "Aryan Vadje," the birthplace of the race; finally, a laudatory note on the Minister of Education's Dictionary of Afghan Languages.

1170 Beardsley, Charles. The Naked Hills: Some Tales of Afghanistan. London: Peter Davies, 1959. Pp. 276.

Stories and true adventures as experienced by the author and his friends.

1171 Bedil, Mirza Abd al-Qader. Robay'at [Quatrains]. Kabul: Matba'eh-yi ma'ref, 1342 [1963]. Pp. 566.

A companion volume to the collected poetry of Bedil.

1172 *Bellew, Henry Walter. A Dictionary of the Pukkhtu or Pukshto Language, in which the Words Are Traced to their Sources in the Persian and Indian Languages. London: Thacker and Co., 1867. Pp. xi, 355.

The first part of this work gives Pushtu words in Arabic script and transliteration, their linguistic origins and their meaning in English. The second part gives English words with the Pushtu equivalent in transliteration only. Another edition was issued at Lahore in 1901.

1173 *Bellew, Henry Walter. A Grammar of the Pukkhto or Pukshto Language, on a New and Improved System . . . London: W. H. Allen and Co., 1867. Pp. xii, 155.

An important early work, long one of the chief sources of information about the language, and still of value.

1174 Belyayev, Viktor M. Afganskaya narodnaya muzyka [Afghan Folk Music]. Moscow: Sovetskaya Kompozitor, 1960. Pp. 27.

History and criticism of Afghan folk music. Included in text are Afghan folk dance music, folk songs, and dances.

1175 *Biddulph, C. E. Afghan Poetry of the Seventeenth Century--Being Selections from the Poems of Khush Hal Khan Khatak. With Translation and Grammatical Introductions. London: K. Paul, Trench, Trubner and Co., Ltd., 1890. Pp. xvii, 120 and 74.

The introduction sets the background of the second half of the seventeenth century, when the national poet in question was active. This is followed by a grammatical section dealing with Pushtu grammar and vocabulary, and then come the poems themselves-- presented in Pushtu and English translation.

1176 Benava, Abdul. Les poétesses de l'Aryana [The Poetesses of Aryana]. Afghanistan 9, no. 3, 49-55. 1954.
Some verses (translated into French) taken from the songs of Aryan poetesses which appear in the Vedic books.

1177 Benawa, Abdul Raouf. Fleurs de folk-lore afghan: hymnes nuptiaux de la littérature populaire [Flowers of Afghan Folk-Lore: Marriage Hymns of Folk Literature]. Afghanistan 1, no. 4, 44-48. 1946.
A number of quatrains in Pushtu are given in Arabic script and in translation.

1178 Binava, "Abd al-Ra'uf. Pushtani mirmani [Pushtun Ladies]. Kabul: Matba'eh-yi 'umumi, 1323 [1944]. Pp. 256.
Studies on a number of Afghan women in Pushtu.

1179 Binava, 'Abd al-Ra'uf. Da Ghanamu Wazhi [The Wheat Stalk]. Kabul: Matba'eh-yi 'umumi, 1325 [1946]. Pp. 31.
A poem in Pushtu describing the crowning of Ahmad Shah.

1180 *Binava, 'Abd al-Ra'uf, ed. Da Pir Muhammad Kakarr diwan [The Divan of Pir Muhammad Kakarr]. Kabul: Matba'eh-yi 'umumi, 1325 [1946]. Pp. 142.
The collected works in Pushtu of a scholar who was the first grammarian of that language and who died in 1781 A.D.

1181 Binava, 'Abd al-Ra'uf. Adabi funun [Literary Modes]. Kabul: Matba'eh-yi 'umumi, 1326 [1947]. Pp. 106.
An original work in Pushtu.

1182 *Binava, 'Abd al-Ra'uf, ed. Da Rahman Baba diwan [The Divan of Rahman Baba]. Kabul: Matba'eh-yi 'umumi, 1328 [1949]. Pp. 210.
The collected works in Pushtu of a member of the Mumand tribe who lived in 1632-1706 A.D. His verses are widely employed for taking auguries.

VIII. LANGUAGES AND LITERATURE

1183 *Binava, 'Abd al-Ra'uf. Khushhal Khattak tseh wayi [What Does
    Khushhal Khattak Say?]. Kabul: Matba'eh-yi 'umumi, 1329
    [1950]. Pp. 158.
       Selections from the national Pushtu poet, emphasizing his feelings
    of national independence and pride.

1184 Binava, 'Abd al-Ra'uf, ed. Da Kazem Khan Shayda diwan [The Divan
    of Kazem Khan Shayda]. Kabul: Matba'eh-yi 'umumi, 1331 [1952].
    The collected works of an eighteenth-century Pushtu poet.

1185 Binava, 'Abd al-Ra'uf. Da Hannan diwan [The Divan of Hannan].
    Kabul: Matba'eh-yi doulati, 1336 [1957]. Pp. 244.
    The collected works in Pushtu of the poet Hannan.

1186 *Binava, 'Abd al-Ra'uf. Landii [Landi]. Kabul: 'Askari matba'eh,
    1337 [1958]. Pp. 176.
       On each page a Pushtu couplet, with translations into Persian and
    English. Many full-page illustrations in color, related to the sub-
    ject matter of the verse.

1187 Binava, 'Abd al-Ra'uf, 'Abd al-Hayy Habibi, and Sayyid Qasem
    Rishtiya, trans. Da Darmesteter pushtu tsirrani [The Researches of
    Darmesteter in Pushtu]. Kabul: Matba'eh-yi 'umumi, 1326 [1947].
    Pp. 112.
    A translation into Pushtu of Darmesteter's grammar.

1188 Bivar, A. D. H. The Hephthalite Inscriptions of Uruzgan. Afghanistan
    8, no. 4, 1-4. 1953.
       On two inscriptions carved in Hephthalite Greek script on limestone
    blocks in an unknown language--their tentative translation and
    possible date (around 500 A.D.).

1189 Blumhardt, J. F. and D. N. MacKenzie. Catalogue of Pashto Manu-
    scripts in the Libraries of the British Isles. Bodleian Library, The
    British Museum, Cambridge University Library, India Office Library,
    John Rylands Library, School of Oriental and African Studies.
    Trinity College, Dublin. British Museum, 1965. Pp. xii, 147.

1190 Bogdanov, L. Stray Notes on Kabuli Persian. Journal and Proceedings
    of the Asiatic Society of Bengal n.s. 26, 1-25. 1930.
       A detailed and thoroughly informed study, which describes the dif-
    ferences between the Persian spoken in Iran and in Afghanistan.
    Includes a lengthy vocabulary.

1191 Bonelli, Luigi. Appunti fonetici sul volgare persiano di Kabul [Phonetic Features of the Persian Vernacular of Kabul]. Annali del Reale Instituto Orientale di Napoli 1, 5-14; 2, 24-26; 4, 20-33; 8, 43-53. 1928-29, 1930, 1931, 1936.
 Notes on the sounds and grammar, with a fairly extensive glossary of items that struck the author as dialectal peculiarities. Based on work with Afghan students in Italy.

1192 Buddruss, Georg. Die Sprache von Wotapur und Katarqala; linguistische Studien im Afghanischen Hindukusch [The Language of Wotapur and Katarqala; Linguistic Studies in the Afghan Hindukush]. Bonn: Universität Bonn, 1960. Pp. 144; map.

1193 Chand Kitab-i Khatti va chapi marbut bi-tarikh-i Afghanistan [Some Manuscripts and Printed Books Connected with the History of Afghanistan]. Aryana 12, no. 4, 181-186. 1954.
 An informed survey of primary and secondary sources.

1194 Charpentier, Joel. Some Remarks on Pashto Etymology. Acta Orientalia 7, 180-200. 1928.
 Notes on the derivation of 51 Pashto words. Georg Morgenstierne's comments follow the Charpentier article, beginning on page 198.

1195 Chavarria-Aguilar, Oscar L. Pashto Basic Course. Ann Arbor: University of Michigan, 1962. Pp. 36; 159.

1196 Chavarria-Aguilar, Oscar L. Pashto Instructor's Handbook. Ann Arbor: University of Michigan, 1962. Pp. 73.

1197 Chavarria-Aguilar, Oscar L. A Short Introduction to the Writing System of Pashto. Ann Arbor: University of Michigan, 1962. Pp. 22.

1198 Cook, Nilla C. La terre d'Ariana [The Land of Aryana]. Afghanistan 2, no. 1, 1-6. 1947.
 Unsubstantial reveries inspired by passage through Herat, Qandahar, and Ghazni.

1199 Cook, Nilla C. Songs of Kabul. Afghanistan 9, no. 2, 54-58. 1954.
 English verses on poetic aspects of Kabul life and Afghan history.

1200 Curiel, Raoul. Inscriptions de Surkh Kotal [Inscriptions of Surkh Kotal]. Journal Asiatique 242, pp. 189-205. 1954.

A detailed study of very fragmentary inscriptions cut in Greek characters into limestone and in an unidentified eastern middle-Iranian language.

1201 Darmesteter, James. Inscriptions de Caboul [Inscriptions at Kabul].
Journal Asiatique 8th ser., 11, 491-503. 1888.
Contains the texts of inscriptions and their translations, the inscriptions being on Babar's tomb and adjacent ones.

1202 *Darmesteter, James. Chants populaires des Afghans, recueillis par James Darmesteter [Folk-Songs of the Afghans, Collected by James Darmesteter]. 2 vols. Paris: Imprimerie nationale, 1888-1890.
Pp. (1) xii; (2) ccxviii, 228.
A discussion of the language, history, and origin of the Afghans, followed by a study of the popular literature of the country. Songs in the categories of history, religion, story, and love are given in text and in French translation.

1203 Darmesteter, James. La grande inscription de Qandahar [The Great Inscription at Qandahar]. Journal Asiatique, 8th ser., 15, 195-230.
1890.
Contains a detailed record and translation of carved inscriptions in the neighborhood of Qandahar, the inscriptions of historical importance. Persian texts are given in Arabic characters. Includes bibliographical notes relating to Qandahar.

1204 Davidson, John. Notes on the Bashgali (Kafir) Language. Calcutta, 1902.

1205 De Croze, J. Berjane. Aryana; Chanson libre [Aryana; Free Song].
Afghanistan 1, no. 4, 18-21. 1946.
Poetry and aphorisms from the cultivated pen of the Countess de Croze.

1206 Dianous, Hugues Jean de. La litterature afghane de langue persane [Afghan Literature in the Persian Language]. Orient 26 (1963), 47-63; and 31 (1964), 137-171.
A serious, valuable study. The first part deals with the earlier centuries of Islam and the second covers material of the present century. Translations into foreign languages are included.

1207   Diwan Ahmad Shah Abdali [Collected Works of Ahmad Shah Abdali].
         Peshawar: Peshawar University, 1963. Pp. 263; lithographed.
         Pushtu poetry ascribed to a ruler of Afghanistan.

1208   Dorn, Bernhard. A Chrestomathy of the Pushtu or Afghan Language to
         which Is Subjoined a Glossary in Afghan and English. St. Petersburg,
         1847. Pp. x, 260.
         Excerpts from a variety of written works with notes and glossary.

1209   Dorofeyeva, L. N. Yazyk Farsi-Kabuli [The Farsi-Kabuli Language].
         Moscow: Izdatel'stvo Vostochnoy Literatury, 1960. Pp. 83.

1210   Dvoryankov, N. A. O glavnykh chlenakh predlozheniya s ergativnoy
         konstruktsiyey v Pashto [On the Main Elements of a Sentence con-
         taining the Ergative Construction in Pushtu]. Sovetskoye Vostoko-
         vedeniye 5, 103-108. 1958.

1211   Dvoryankov, N. A. Yazyk Pushtu [The Pushtu Language]. Moscow:
         Izdatel'stvo Vostochnoy Literatury, 1960. Pp. 99; bibliography.

1212   Dzhafarova, A. A. Istoricheskaya tema v literature Afganistana, (na
         yazyke farsi) [The Historical Theme in the Literature of Afghanistan
         (in Persian)]. Kratkiye Soobshcheniya Instituta Narodov Azii. Mos-
         cow, 1964. Vol. 65, pp. 71-79.

1213   Elham, Muhammad Rahim, trans. Da Pushtu gramar [A Grammar of
         Pushtu]. Kabul, 1340 [1961]. Pp. 215.
         A translation into Pushtu of no. 1361.

1214   Ethe, Hermann. Die Tafelrunde Sultan Mahmuds und seiner unmittel-
         baren Nachfolger [The Round Table of Sultan Mahmud and his Im-
         mediate Successors]. Grundriss der Iranischen Philologie, Pt. 1,
         pp. 223-233. Strasbourg: Karl J. Trubner, 1897.
         An examination of the literary activity at the court of Mahmud of
         Ghazni, and his successors, by a noted cataloguer of Persian manu-
         scripts. See also no. 1222.

1215   Farhadi, Abd-ul-Ghafur. Le persan parlé en Afghanistan. Grammaire
         du Kaboli [The Spoken Persian of Afghanistan. A Grammar of
         Kabuli]. Paris: C. Klincksieck, 1955. Pp. 150; 44.
         A mimeographed publication by a young Afghan scholar who treats

the subject more intensively than in earlier works. The second section of the work illustrates quatrains of local poetry in transliteration and translation.

1216 Farhadi, Abd-ul-Ghafur Rawan, trans. Zendigi-yi Khwaja 'Abdullah Ansari [The Life of Khwaja 'Abdullah Ansari]. Kabul: Matba'eh-yi doulati, 1341 [1962]. Pp. 196.
A translation into Dari of a work by Père S. de Beaurecueil.

1217 Farhang, Mir Muhammad Sadiq. Saffarian [Saffarids]. Kabul: Matba'eh-yi 'umumi, 1334 [1955]. Pp. 40.
A short account in Persian of the Saffarid rulers.

1218 "Feraidoun," by D. A. A. Afghanistan 9, no. 2, 51-53. 1954.
Feraidoun, or Taritouna, was a great hero of the Avesta, who drove the Semitic conqueror from the Aryan kingdom of Peshadi and established himself as king.

1219 Freeman, Antonyi. The Music of Kabul. Asia Foundation, Program Bulletin 34, 1-3. 1965.

1220 Fufalza'i, Aziz al-Din Vakili. Honar Khat dar Afghanistan dar do qarn akhir [The Art of Calligraphy in Afghanistan in the last two Centuries]. Kabul: Doulati matba'eh, 1342 [1963]. Pp. 219.
A work in Persian, generously illustrated with specimens of calligraphy.

1221 Gablentz, H. C. von der. Ueber die Sprache der Hazaras und Aimaks [On the Speech of the Hazaras and Aimaks]. Zeitschrift der deutschen morgenländischen Gesellschaft 20, 326-335. 1866.
As evidence that the Aimaks and Hazaras are of Mongol origin, a short vocabulary, giving the Mongol word, its German translation, and variants in Central Asian dialects. A group of sentences is treated in the same way.

1222 Geiger, Wilhelm. Die Sprache der Afghanen [The Language of the Afghans]. In Wilhelm Geiger and Ernst Kuhn, Grundriss der Iranischen Philologie, 1, Pt. 2, 201-230. Strasbourg: Karl J. Trubner, 1898-1932.
Condensed description of the language, making full use of previously published books and articles.

1223 Geiger, Wilhelm. Etymologie und Lautlehre des Afghanischen [Ety-
mology and Phonology of the Afghan Language]. Munich: Verlag
der Akademie, 1893. Pp. 56.
Systematic exposition of the place of Pushtu phonology in the historical development of Iranian languages.

1224 Gerasimova, A. S. Obshchestvennyye motivy v sovremennoy literature
Afganistana [Social Trends in the Modern Literature of Afghanistan].
Moscow: Izdatel'stvo Vostochnoy Literatury, 1961. Pp. 159.

1225 Gerasimova, A. S. and G. F. Girs, eds. Literatura Afganistana [The
Literature of Afghanistan]. Moscow: Izdatel'stvo Vostochnoy Literatury, 1963. Pp. 194.

1226 Ghawareh ash'ar da Gol Pacha Olfat [Choice of the Poetry of Gol Pacha
Olfat]. Kabul, 1334 [1955]. Pp. 256.
Poetry in Pushtu.

1227 Ghulami, Muhammad Ghulam. Jangnameh [A Story of Combat]. Kabul: Matba'eh-yi doulati, 1336 [1957]. Pp. 210.
A long poem in Persian, dealing with the resistance to foreign invaders between 1839 and 1842.

1228 Gilbertson, George Waters. The Pakkhto Idiom: A Dictionary. 2 vols.
Hertford: Stephen Austin and Sons, Ltd., 1932. Pp. (1) xv, 496;
(2) 497-964; bibliography.
A most extensive English-Pushtu dictionary ("eastern dialect" only),
with the meaning and usage of each word illustrated by one or more
Pushtu sentences in Arabic script, transliteration, and translation.
The bibliography includes a list of works in and on the Pushtu lan-
guage.

1229 Girs, G. F. Stikhi poetov Afganistana [Verses from the Poets of Afghan-
istan]. Moscow: Izdatel'stvo Inostrannoy Literatury, 1963. Pp. 105.
Translations into Russian from poems in Dari and Pushtu.

1230 Gochenour, Theodore S. The Landdey, Mirror of the Pashtuns. Viewpoints 5, no. 6, 22-29. 1965.
Concerns a poetic form, two nonrhyming lines more frequently sung
than recited. Examples are given in Pushtu script, transliteration,
and translation.

VIII. LANGUAGES AND LITERATURE

1231 Grierson, George Abraham. The Languages of India: Being a Reprint
of the Chapter on Languages Contributed by George Abraham
Grierson to the Report on the Census of India, 1901, together with
the Census Statistics of Languages. Calcutta: Office of the Superintendent of Government Printing, India, 1903. Pp. 146; maps;
tables.
> A study of the languages and their families. Pages 43-93 deal with
> the Aryan subfamily of the Indo-European family. Pushtu is treated
> on pages 46-47. Tables show the number of persons speaking each
> language.

1232 *Grierson, George Abraham, ed. Linguistic Survey of India, Vol. 10.
Specimens of the Languages of the Eranian Family. Calcutta: Office
of the Superintendent of Government Printing, 1921. Maps.
> Grierson both edited the volume and wrote all the descriptive mate-
> rial. Includes brief but highly informative introductions to Iranian
> languages in general and for Pushtu. Specimens and comments for
> over a dozen varieties of Pushtu and for two out-of-the-way Persian
> dialects. Good map of the distribution of Pushtu. Also contains a
> description of the Pamir languages (called Ghalchah), with a map
> showing their distribution.

1233 Grierson, George Abraham. Part II. Dardic, or Pisacha Languages.
In Linguistic Survey of India, vol. 8. Calcutta: Superintendent of
Government Printing, 1921.

1234 Gordon, B. E. M., ed. Translation of the Ganj-i-Pukhto into the Khowar
Dialect. By Khan Sahib Abdul Hakim Khan. Calcutta: Office of the
Superintendent of Government Printing, India, 1902. Pp. 67.
> A collection of tales in colloquial Pushtu.

1235 Habibi, 'Abd al-Hayy. Paygham-i Shahid [The Message of the Martyr].
Kabul: Matba'eh-yi 'umumi, 1317 [1938]. Pp. 27.
> The work comprises poems written by the author and dedicated to the
> ruler; the poems deal with contemporary problems and subjects.

1236 Habibi, 'Abd al-Hayy. The Oldest Poems in Pashto, or The Oldest
Pashto Poet, Amir Krore Jahan Pahlawan. Afghanistan 1, no. 1, 9-
15. 1946.
> A brief account of the Sori tribes, followed by a description of the
> subject of the article, a ruler of the Sori dynasty of the eighth cen-
> tury. The article closes with a translation of a short passage from an
> epic.

1237 Habibi, 'Abd al-Hayy. Da pushtu adabiyatu tarikh [The History of Pushtu Literature]. Kabul: Matba'eh-yi 'umumi, 1325 [1946]. Pp. 137.
A study of the subject in Pushtu by the then Dean of the Faculty of Literature.

1238 Habibi, 'Abd al-Hayy. Pushtu wa loyikan-i Ghazneh; yek tahqiq jadid dar tarikh aw adabiyat Pushtu wa tarikh Ghazneh [Pushtu and the Loyaks of Ghazneh; a New Inquiry into the History and Literature of Pushtu and the History of Ghazneh]. Kabul: Matba'eh-yi doulati, 1341 [1962]. Pp. 154.

1239 Habibi, 'Abd al-Hayy. Zaban-i do hazar sal qabl Afghanistan ya mader-i zaban dari tahil Keh siyeh va sorkh Kutal baghlan [The Language of Afghanistan two thousand Years ago, or the Mother of the Dari language resolved at Sieh and Sorkh Kutal]. Kabul: Doulati matba'eh, 1342 [1963]. Pp. 140.

1240 Hamid, 'Abdul Razaq. Bahar-i Sa'adat [The Spring of Happiness]. Kabul: Matba'eh-yi doulati, 1338 [1959]. Pp. 138.
A collection of Pushtu poems.

1241 Hasan Khan, Ya'qub. Pushtu az nazar-i figh al-lugheh [Pushtu from the Grammatical View Point]. Kabul: Matba'eh-yi 'umumi, 1318 [1939]. Paged as 201-310.
A lithographed work in Persian.

1242 Henning, W. B. The Inscriptions of Tang-i Azao. Bulletin of the School of Oriental and African Studies 20, 335-342. 1957.
Rock-cut inscriptions in Persian, written in the Hebrew script and dated to 1351 A.D.

1243 Herati, Muhammad Hashim Omidvar. Diwan-i Khalilullah Khalili [The Divan of Khalilullah Khalili]. Tehran: Haidari, 1341 [1962]. Pp. 306.
A collection of the poet's work in Dari, with commentaries and appreciations by scholars in Iran.

1244 *Heravi, Ghulam Riza Mayil. Ma'refi: Ruznameh-ha; Jaraid; Majalat Afghanistan [Introduction: Newspapers; Periodicals; Magazines]. Kabul: Doulati matba'eh, 1341 [1962]. Pp. 144; index.

Uniquely valuable documentation in Persian; each item is described at some length.

1245 Heravi, Ghulam Riza Mayil. Sharh hal va athar-i Amir Husayn Ghuri
Heravi motavaffa 718 [An Account of the State and Remains of Amir
Husayn Ghuri Heravi, deceased in 718 [1318]]. Kabul: Vizarat-i
etala'at va Kultur, 1344 [1965]. Pp. 124.
A recent edition of a renowned book of learning.

1246 Heravi, Shaykh al-Islam Khwajeh 'Abdullah Ansari. Tabaqat al-
Sufiyeh [Compendium of Sufism]. Kabul: Matba'eh-yı doulatı,
1341 [1962]. Pp. 738.
An edition in Persian of a work written in 1088 A.D., compiled
from three manuscripts by 'Abd al-Hay Habibi.

1247 Hodge, C. T. Spoken Pashto. Unit 1. Pronunciation. Washington:
Foreign Service Institute, U. S. Department of State, 1954.
Excellent description, pedagogically oriented, of the phonemes of
Pushtu as spoken in the Wardak region.

1248 *Howell, Evelyn and Olaf Caroe, trans. The Poems of Khushal Khan
Khattak. Peshawar: University of Peshawar, 1963. Pp. xiv, 98.
The texts of the poems in Pushtu, accompanied by translations into
English.

1249 Hughes, Thomas P., ed. Ganj-i-Pukhto, or Pukhto Treasury. London:
W. H. Allen and Co., 1882. Pp. lv, 128.
A reader and glossary based on the conversational usage of unedu-
cated Pushtu speakers (eastern dialect), published as a government
textbook for examinations in Pushtu.

1250 Hughes, Thomas P., ed. The Kalid-i-afghani, Being Selections of
Pushtu Prose and Poetry for the Use of Students. Lahore: Munshi
Gulab Singh and Sons, 1893. Pp. iii, 418.
Includes prose material in Pushtu from the Ganj-i-Pushtu, the
Tarikh-i-Mahmud-i-Ghaznavi, and the Tarikh-i-Murassa; also
poetry from the Qissa Shahzada Bahram, Diwan-i-Abdur Rahman,
Diwan-i-Khushhal Khan, and the Chaman-i-Benazir; all in Pushtu.
There appears to have been an edition of this collection published
as early as 1872 at Peshawar and printed by the Panjab Educational
Press at Lahore: it is very rare.

1251 Imam al-Din, S. M., ed. Tarikh-i-Khan Jahani wa Makhzan-i-
Afghani, of Khwajah Ni'mat Allah ibn Khwajah Habib Allah of
Herat (Persian text). Dacca: Asiatic Society of Pakistan, 1960-1962.
Two vols., pp. (1) 93 and (2) 897.

1252 *Iqbal, Sir Mohammad. Khushhal Khan Khattack--the Afghan Warrior-
Poet. Islamic Culture 2, 485-494. Hyderabad, 1928.
The renowned poet and philosopher of modern Islam steps out of
his field and borrows the efforts of another scholar. Observations on
the seventeenth-century poet are followed by examples taken from
Raverty's translations (see no. 1380). Verses quoted include striking characterizations of the Afghans, Persians, Hazaras, etc.

1253 Iqbal, Muhammad. Musafir [The Traveller]. Lahore: Gilani, 1313
[1934]. Pp. 217.
A lithographed account in Persian verse by the noted poet and reformer of Islam. The work deals with a visit made to Kabul in 1933
and includes poetry written on that occasion.

1254 'Ismati, Ma'sumeh. Khushhal Khattak Kist [Who is Khushhal Khattak?].
Kabul: Matba'eh-yi 'umumi, 1334 [1955]. Pp. 158.
A biography in Persian of the national poet.

1255 Ivanow, W., trans. The Works of Khayr-Khwar of Herat. Bombay:
Ismaili Society (Series D., no. 16). 1964.
The Persian text of the Tasnifat-i-Khayr-Khwah-i Herat was pub-
lished by the Ismaili Society in 1961, as Series D., no. 13.

1256 Iz Afganskoy Poezii [From Afghan Poetry]. Moscow: Gosudarstvennoye
izdatel'stvo Khudozhestvennoy literaturi, 1955. Pp. 223.
The Pushtu and Persian poetry of Khushhal Khattak and others, in
Russian translation.

1257 Jami, Nur al-Din 'Abd al-Rahman. Tajlil-i panjsad va panjahomin
sal-i tavallod-i Nur al-Din 'Abd al-Rahman Jami [On the Occasion
of the 550th Year of the Birth of Nur al-Din 'Abd al-Rahman Jami].
Kabul: Matba'eh-yi doulati, 1344 [1965]. Pp. 108.

1258 Jan, Qazi Ahmad. How to Speak Pushtu. Lahore, 1917. Pp. 109.
Morgenstierne describes this work as "small, but very useful."

1259 Jarring, Gunnar. Studien zu einer osttürkischen Lautlehre [Studies toward an East Turkish Phonology]. Lund: Borelius, 1933. Pp. 1,
53; facsimile of manuscript fragment.
Part I is a technical phonological study of the East Turki dialect.
Part II contains texts in Turkish script, footnoted and explained in
German, and transliterated texts with translations in German on the
facing pages.

1260 Jarring, Gunnar. The Uzbek Dialect of Qilich (Russian Turkestan). With
Texts and Glossary. Lund: Lunds universitets arsskrift, N. F. Ard. 1,
33, no. 3, i, 56; list of works quoted. 1937.
The author (who spent four months in Kashmir collecting his material) discusses first the divisions and subdivisions of the Uzbek dialects, then, concentrating on that of Qilich, explains briefly some
points of phonetics and grammar. The texts--one folk-tale and
two poems (transliterated)--are translated into English. The glossary follows the translations.

1261 Jarring, Gunnar. Uzbek Texts from Afghan Turkestan with Glossary.
Lund: Lunds universitets arsskrift, N. F. Ard. 1. 34, no. 2, iii, 246;
list of works quoted. 1938.
This is a series of eighteen stories, three miscellaneous texts and
some proverbs, all given in transliteration and translated into Eng-
lish. There is a large glossary and an index of the supposed non-
Iranized equivalents to the Iranized words appearing in the glossary.
The dialect represented is the Uzbek speech of the town of Andkhui.

1262 Javid, Ahmad. Afsanahai qadim-i shahr-i Kabul [Old Legends of the
City of Kabul]. Kabul: 'Ameh, 1343 [1964]. Pp. 82.

1263 Khadem, Qiyam al-Din. Bayazid Rushan [Bayazid Rushan]. Kabul:
Matba'eh-yi 'umumi, 1324 [1945]. Pp. 164.
An account in Pushtu of an eighteenth-century Sufi who opposed the
Moghuls and whose sect was attacked by Akhund Darvizeh Ningarhari
(see no. 865).

1264 Khadem, Qiyam al-Din. Ruhi Goluneh [Wild Flower]. Kabul:
Matba'eh-yi 'umumi, 1326 [1947]. Pp. 152.
An original work in Pushtu.

1265 Khadem, Qiyam al-Din. Da pushtu keli [The Pushtu Key]. Kabul:

Matba'eh-yi 'umumi, 1327 [1948]. Pp. 62.
One of a series designed for the use of government officials engaged in learning Pushtu.

1266 Khadem, Qiyam al-Din, trans. Makarim al-Akhlaq [Noble Character].
Kabul: Matba'eh-yi 'umumi, 1333 [1954]. Pp. 317.
A translation from Arabic into Pushtu of a work on ethics by Shaykh 'Abd al-Qader al-Moghrabi.

1267 Khalili, az Ash'ar-i Ostad [From the Poems of Ostad Khalili]. Kabul:
Doulati matba'eh, 1340 [1961]. Pp. 502.

1268 Khalili, Khalilullah. Muntakhabat-i ash'ar [Selections of Poetry].
Kabul: Matba'eh-yi 'umumi, 1333 [1954]. Pp. 83.
Selections representing a number of contemporary Afghan poets who write in Persian.

1269 Khalili, Khalilullah. Fayz-i quds [Divine Grace]. Kabul: Matba'eh-
yi 'umumi, 1334 [1955]. Pp. 102.
The text, in Persian, is a study of Persian poetry by a contemporary Afghan scholar and former secretary of the Council of Ministers.

1270 Khalili, Khalilullah, ed. Kolliyat-i Hakim Sana'i [The Collected Works
of Hakim Sana'i]. Kabul: Matba'eh-yi doulati, 1338 [1959].
The Persian text of the poems of an author of the Ghaznavid period.

1271 Khan, Qazi Rahimullah. The Modern Pushto Instructor. Peshawar, 1938.

1272 Khasteh, ed. Mo'asiren sokhanvar [Contemporary Writers]. Kabul:
Doulati matba'eh, 1339 [1960]. Pp. 363.
An anthology of living Afghan poets writing in Dari, including biographical data and photographs of the authors.

1273 Kohzad, Ahmad Ali. Alexandre en Afghanistan. Pièce en quatre actes
[Alexander in Afghanistan. A Play in Four Acts]. Afghanistan 1, no. 3, 10-23; no. 4, 1-17. 1946.
Alexander meets local chieftains who tell him of their habits and customs.

1274 Kohzad, Ahmad Ali. Drama of Islam: A Comedy. Afghanistan 4,
no. 1, 45-67. 1949.

A turgid, involved description of a pageant in which colonization, the new nation of Pakistan, and the Afghan tribes are intermingled.

1275 Kohzad, Ahmad Ali. Parwati: jeune montagnarde de la région de Gomal [Parwati: A Young Mountain Woman of the Gomal Region]. Afghanistan 7, no. 1, 42-49. 1952.
The Aryan legend of a beautiful princess and her lover who had to seek his fortune.

1276 Kohzad, Ahmad 'Ali, ed. Guldasteh-yi 'ishq [Nosegay of Love]. Kabul: Matba'eh-yi 'umumi, 1331 [1953]. Pp. 14.
A commemorative souvenir in Persian to mark the 700th anniversary of Maulana Jalal al-Din Balkhi.

1277 Kohzad, Ahmad Ali. Mawlana Djallal-ud-Din Balkhi. [Maulana Jalal al-Din Balkhi]. Afghanistan 8, no. 1, 60-63. 1953.
Commemorating the 700th anniversary of his death, a biography of an Islamic mystic and philosopher of the thirteenth century A.D. (see no. 1276).

1278 Kohzad, Ahmad Ali. Zarir et Yatkazarizan [Zarir and Yatkazarizan]. Afghanistan 8, no. 1, 53-59. 1953.
On the Aryan hero Zarir, younger brother of the Bactrian ruler Aspah, and the epic of his deeds, Yatkazarizan.

1279 Kohzad, Mohammad Nabi. Afghanistan Crocevia dell'Asia [Afghanistan, Crossroads of Asia]. Afghanistan 6, no. 2, 40-43. 1951.
An appreciation of Caspani and Cagnacci's Afghanistan Crocevia dell'Asia (see no. 37), quoting the Preface, by the Italian Plenipotentiary in Afghanistan, in full.

1280 Kohzad, Mohammad Nabi. Akbar Nameh. Afghanistan 6, no. 4, 59-61. 1951.
The announcement of a book, a collection of poetry, concerned with the past 150 years of Afghan history.

1281 Kohzad, Mohammad Nabi. Un nouvel ouvrage "Légendes et coutumes afghanes" [A New Work "Afghan Legends and Customs"]. Afghanistan 9, no. 1, 55-57. 1954.
A note on the appearance of Legendes et coutumes afghanes (see no. 696), containing a mention of the Hackins' work in Afghanistan and a list of the book's contents.

1282 Koshan, Ghulam Hazrat, ed. Pazhwak, Abdur-Rahman. Gulhai
Andesha [Flowers of Meditation] . Kabul: Ministry of Education
Press, 1965. Pp. 159.
A collection of poems in Pushtu.

1283 Kovusov, Anna. Kozlovskiy, Yakovom, trans. Afganskiye Vstrechi
[Meetings in Afghanistan] . Sovetskiy Pisatel', 1964.
Verse by a Turkoman poetess, translated into Russian. Some poems
tell of the friendliness of the Afghan people, others are based on
Afghan folklore.

1284 Kratkii afgansko-russkii slovar'. Sostavil P. B. Zudin. Pod redaktsiei
chlena-korrespondenta AK. S. S. S. R. Prof. E. E. Bertel'sa [Short
Afghan-Russian Dictionary. Compiled by P. B. Zudin. Edited by
the Corresponding Member of the Academy of the U. S. S. R. Professor
E. E. Bertel's] . Moscow: Gosudarstvennoe izdatel'stvo inostrannykh
i natsional'nykh slovarei, 1950. Pp. 568.
A very useful work. The material is up-to-date, and there is a valuable grammatical sketch. Based in part on native Afghan dictionaries, with Pushtu entries given in Arabic script and in Cyrillic transliteration.

1285 Kratkii voennyi persidsko-russkii slovar'. S prilozheniem voennogo
slovaria Kabuli. Sostavili L. S. Peisikov, N. P. Savchenko, S. D.
Smirnov. Pod. red. N. P. Savchenko. Okolo 10,000 slov i terminov
[Short Persian-Russian Military Dictionary with a Supplementary Military Glossary in the Kabuli Language] . Moscow: Gosudarstvennoe
izdatel'stvo inostrannykh i natsional'nykh slovarei, 1954. Pp. 334.

1286 Kushkaki, Burhan al-Din. Peh pateh da pattu platenay [In Secrecy to
Search for Secrets] . Kabul: Matba'eh-yi 'umumi, 1318 [1939] .
Pp. 272.
An original work in Pushtu.

1287 Laugier de Beaurecueil, S. de. Manuscrits d'Afghanistan [Manuscripts
of Afghanistan] . Cairo: Imprimerie de l'Institut français d'archéologie Orientale, 1964. Pp. xiii, 420.

1288 Lazard, Gilbert. La Langue de plus ancient monuments de la prose
persane [The Language of the oldest examples of Persian prose] .
Paris: Klincksieck, 1963. Pp. 535; indices.

VIII. LANGUAGES AND LITERATURE

1289 Lebedev, Konstantin A. Grammatika yazyka pushtu [Grammar of the
Pushtu Language]. Moscow: IIMO, 1956. Pp. 223.

1290 Lebedev, Konstantin A. Karmannyy russko-Afganskiy slovar' [Russian-
Afghan Pocket Dictionary]. Moscow: GIS, 1961. Pp. 752.

1291 Lebedev, Konstantin A., Z. M. Kalinina, and L. S. Yatsevich.
Uchebnik afganskogo yazyka (Pushtu) [Textbook of the Afghan Language (Pushtu)]. Moscow: IIMO, 1963. Pp. 236.

1292 Leech, R. A Vocabulary of the Language of the Moghal Aimaks. Journal of the Royal Asiatic Society of Bengal 7, 785-787. 1838.
A short vocabulary, with a few sentences (all transliterated) translated into English.

1293 Leech, R. Grammar of the Pashto or Afghanee. Journal of the Asiatic
Society of Bengal 8, 1-16. 1839.

1294 Lentz, Wolfgang. Ein Lateinalphabet für das Paschto [A Latin Alphabet
for Pushtu]. Berlin: A. Eeine, 1937. Pp. 12.
A technical study of little apparent practical value.

1295 Literaturovedeniye. Indiya, Pakistan, Afganistan [History of Literature.
India, Pakistan, Afghanistan]. Kratkiye Soobshcheniya Instituta
Narodov Azii. Moscow: "Nauka," 1965. Vol. 80, pp. 188.

1296 Lorimer, David Lockhart Robertson. Pashtu Part I. Syntax of Colloquial
Pashtu, with Chapters on Persian and Indian Elements in the Modern
Languages, by Major D. L. R. Lorimer. Oxford: The Clarendon
Press, 1915.
In spite of the title, the book is a complete grammar (of "North-
eastern Pushtu"), not just a study of syntax. The alphabet is ex-
plained, but the bulk of the book uses only transliteration. Part II,
which was to deal with historical matters, never appeared.

1297 Lorimer, David Lockhart Robertson. The Phonology of the Bakhtiari,
Badakhshani, and Madaglashti Dialects of Modern Persian. With Vocabularies. London: Royal Asiatic Society, 1922. Pp. xi, 205.
Part II, on the Badakhshani and Madaglashti dialects, pages 127-
205, contains material on the phonology and morphology, brief
sample texts, and a vocabulary of the dialect of Persian spoken in

the northeastern corner of Afghanistan. The author, a member of
the Foreign and Political Department of the Government of India,
collected the material in the field.

1298 Lorimer, J. G. Grammar and Vocabulary of Waziri Pashto. Calcutta:
Office of the Superintendent of Government Printing, India, 1902.
Pp. x, 345.
The only extensive treatment of a dialect as such (other than Pesha-
war or Qandahar) without reference to the literary norm.

1299 *MacKenzie, D. N., trans. Poems from the Divan of Khushal Khan
Khattak. London: George Allen and Unwin Ltd., 1965. Pp. 258.

1300 Majmu'eh-yi ash'ar-i Vajid. Baksh-i chaharum [A Collection of Poems
by Vajid. Part Four]. (Fayzabad): Matba'eh-yi Badakhshahan,
1332 [1953]. Pp. 110.
A collection of modern Persian poetry in the dialect of the region.

1301 Majruh, Sayyid Shams al-Din. Montakhab sha'aruneh [Selected Poems].
Kabul: Matba'eh-yi doulati, 1337 [1958].
Poems in Pushtu.

1302 *Massé, Henri. L'Académie afghane et ses publications. Appendice:
La presse en Afghanistan [The Afghan Academy and its Publications.
Appendix: The Press in Afghanistan]. Revue des Études Islamiques
13, 180-199. 1939.
On the occasion of the opening of the ninth year of publication of
the periodical Kabul, a French scholar reviews the work of the sponsoring academy. Notices of publications issued by the Academy are
followed by summaries of articles on education, music, and folklore
from Kabul, and, finally, by a list of newspapers and periodicals
which have appeared in Afghanistan.

1303 Ma'sumi N. and M. Kholov, comps. Namuneh fol'klori Khalqhoi Afghanistan. Ruboiat va surudho [Samples of Afghan Popular Folklore.
Verses and Songs]. Dushanbe: Irfon, 1965. Pp. 320.
A publication in contemporary Tajik script containing 895 short
verses, 135 landay, and 22 songs--all in Dari. A second edition
was published in 1966.

1304 *Maylon, F. H. Some Current Pushtu Folk Stories. Memoirs of the

Asiatic Society of Bengal 3, 355-405. Calcutta, 1913.
Some ten Pushtu folk stories are given in translation by a British officer; the selection illustrates varieties of the dialects of the Orakzai, Afridi, and Yusufzai ethnic elements.

1305 Mel'nikova, G., ed. Skazki i stikhi Afganistana [Tales and Verse from Afghanistan]. Moscow: Gosudarstvennoe izdatel'stvo Khudozhestvennoy literaturī, 1958. Pp. 311.

1306 Montakhabat Khushhal Khan Khattak [Selections from Khushhal Khan Khattak]. Peshawar: Peshawar University, n.d. Pp. 320; index. Pushtu poetry, with translations into Urdu.

1307 *Morgenstierne, Georg. Report on a Linguistic Mission to Afghanistan. Oslo: H. Aschehoug and Co., 1926. Pp. 100.
This publication is Volume I-2 in Series C of the Instituttet for Sammenlignende Kulturforskning. Includes remarks on Pushtu and Persian spoken in Afghanistan and more detailed treatment of several languages of northeastern Afghanistan. The highly technical nature of the study is somewhat alleviated by the presence of an unusual and valuable bibliography, a linguistic sketch map of northeastern Afghanistan, and a sketch map of Pashai dialect boundaries. The author visited the area in 1924.

1308 Morgenstierne, Georg. An Etymological Vocabulary of Pashto. Oslo: I kom. hos Jacob Dybwad, 1927. Pp. 120.
Restricted chiefly to words for which cognates can be found in Indo-Iranian languages, and includes a few loanwords where they "present phonetic features of interest."

1309 Morgenstierne, Georg. Indo-Iranian Frontier Languages. I. Parachi and Ormuri. Oslo: H. Aschehoug and Co., 1929. Pp. 419.
The publication is Volume 11 in Series B of the Instituttet for Sammenlignende Kulturforskning. It includes a grammar and phonology for each language, with transliterated and translated texts of stories and poems, and vocabularies.

1310 Morgenstierne, Georg. The Language of the Ashkun Kafirs. Norsk Tidsskrift for Sprogvidenskap 2, 192-289. 1929.
The possible origins of the language, a grammar and texts, transliterated with interlinear translations. A lengthy vocabulary defines

words and gives corresponding words in other languages and dialects.

1311 Morgenstierne, Georg. The Wanetsi Dialect of Pashto. Norsk Tidsskrift
for Sprogvidenskap 4, 156-175. 1931.
This dialect of Pushtu is so divergent that it probably should be regarded as a separate language.

1312 Morgenstierne, Georg. Report on a Linguistic Mission to North-Western
India. Oslo: H. Aschehoug and Co., 1932. Pp. 76; maps.
The publication is Volume III-1 in Series C of the Instituttet for
Sammenlignende Kulturforskning. The work was carried on in 1929,
principally in Chitral but with the employment of cross-border in-
formants on such languages spoken within Afghanistan as Tirahi,
Ashkun, Pashai, Waigeli, and Prasun. One map of the region north
of the Kabul River indicates language localities on both sides of the
frontier.

1313 Morgenstierne, Georg. Additional Notes on Ashkun. Norsk Tidsskrift
for Sprogvidenskap 7, 56-115. 1934.
Additions to, and corrections of, The Language of the Ashkun Kafirs
(see no. 1310), with texts and vocabulary.

1314 Morgenstierne, Georg. Note on the Khetrani Dialect of Lahnda. Acta
Orientalia 13, 173-175. 1934.
A short list of words collected from a Khetran whom the author met
briefly.

1315 Morgenstierne, Georg. Notes on Tirahi. Acta Orientalia 12, 161-189.
1934.
A few additions and corrections to the knowledge of Tirahi, with vocabulary.

1316 Morgenstierne, Georg. Indo-Iranian Frontier Languages. II. Iranian
Pamir Languages (Yidgha-Munji, Sanglechi-Ishkashmi, and Wakhi).
Oslo: H. Aschehoug and Co., 1938. Pp. xxiv, 630; map.
The publication is Volume 35 of Series B of the Instituttet for
Sammenlignende Kulturforskning. The author covers phonology,
morphology texts, and a comparative vocabulary of these little-
known languages. Includes references to all previously published
studies.

VIII. LANGUAGES AND LITERATURE

1317 Morgenstierne, Georg. Archaisms and Innovations in Pashto Morphology. Norsk Tidsskrift for Sprogvidenskap 12, 88-114. 1940.

1318 Morgenstierne, Georg. Indo-Iranian Frontier Languages. III. The Pashai Language. 2. Texts and Translations. With Comparative Notes on Pashai Folktales by Reidar Th. Christiansen. Oslo: H. Aschehoug and Co., 1944. Pp. xxxviii, 304.
   The publication is Volume 40 of Series B of the Instituttet for Sammenlignende Kulturforskning. Pashai, belonging to the Dardic group of Indo-Aryan languages, is spoken in the hill country northeast of Kabul. Collected in 1924, the prose examples are of five dialects and stress fairy tales. Some fifteen dialects are represented in examples of poetry, in which poems of vendetta predominate over the epic and lyric.

1319 Morgenstierne, Georg. The Language of the Prasun Kafirs. Norsk Tidsskrift for Sprogvidenskap 15, 188-334. 1949.

1320 Morgenstierne, Georg. Indo-Iranian Frontier Languages. III. The Pashai Language. 3. Vocabulary. Oslo: H. Aschehoug and Co., 1956. Pp. xi, 232.
   The supplement to no. 1318.

1321 Morgenstierne, Georg and James A. Lloyd. Notes on the Pronunciation of Pashto (Dialect of the Hazara District). Bulletin of the Society of Oriental Studies, London Institute 5, 53-63. 1928.
   Careful, phonetic description of the speech of an informant in England, with IPA transcriptions of the examples.

1322 *Muhammad Hotak ibn Da'ud Khan. Puteh Khazaneh [The Secret Treasury]. 'Abd al-Hayy Habibi, ed. Kabul: Matba'eh-yi 'umumi, 1323 [1944]. Pp. 290.
   In this work written in Pushtu in 1729 A.D. the author gives biographies of some 51 contemporaries and traces the development of Pushtu poetry from earlier periods.

1323 *Mumand, Muhammad Gol. Pushtu sind ya'ni awwalin qamus afghani [Pushtu Stream, or The First Afghan Dictionary]. Kabul: Matba'eh-yi 'umumi, 1316 [1937]. Pp. (1) 399; (2) 366.
   Two volumes in Pushtu, bound as a single volume.

1324 Mumand, Muhammad Gol. Da pushtu da zhebay liyareh [The Path of
the Pushtu Language] . Balkh, 1317 [1938] . Pp. 239, 156.
A grammar of the language in Pushtu.

1325 Mumand, Muhammad Gol. Melli Hindara [National Mirror] . Kabul:
Matba'eh-yi 'umumi.
A collection of stories about the courage of the Afghans.

1326 Music of Afghanistan. Radio Kabul. Ethnic Folkways Library. Folkways FE-4361 (record).

1327 A Musical Anthology of the Orient (UNESCO Collection). Musurgia
BM30, Afghanistan, L2003 (record).

1328 Musique folklorique d'Afghanistan [Folklore Music of Afghanistan] .
BAM, Paris LD337 (record).

1329 Najaf 'Ali Khan. Tuhfeh-yi Amaniyeh [Gift to Aman(ullah)] . Lahore:
Karimi, 1924. Pp. 72.
A lithographed poem in Persian, celebrating the accession to the
throne of Amir Amanullah.

1330 Najib-ullah. Abouraihan Al-Beiruni and his Time. Afghanistan 6,
no. 1, 17-27. 1951.
About a phenomenal scholar at the court of Sultan Mahmud.

1331 Najib-Ullah Khan. Speech Delivered by Dr. Najib-Ullah Khan. Afghanistan 6, no. 4, 52-58. 1951.
On the importance of the Urdu language and the Khorasan school of
poetry in Afghan-Indian cultural relations.

1332 Najib Ullah. Islamic Literature, An Introductory History with Selections.
New York: Washington Square Press, 1963. Pp. 441.
A valuable and fascinating study by the late Afghan diplomat and
scholar. Includes material from Afghanistan.

1333 Nawis, 'Abd Allah Afghani. Afghan qamus. Farsi peh pushtu [Afghan
Dictionary. Persian into Pushtu] . Kabul, 1336 [1957] . Vol. 1,
pp. 133; 2, 128; 3, 124.

1334 Nawis, 'Abd Allah Afghani. Loghat 'amianeh-yi farsi Afghanistan [Dic-
tionary of the Popular Persian of Afghanistan] . Kabul: Matbu'atu

mostaqel riassat, 1340 [1961]. Pp. 592.
A work dealing with the "vulgar" dialect of the country.

1335 Ne'matulloev, H. and R. Hoshim, eds. Namunai ash'ori shoironi
afghan [Samples of the Poetry of Afghan Poets]. Stalinabad:
Nashriati daviatii Tojikiston, 1958. Pp. 184.
The poems, in Dari, are given in contemporary Tajik script.

1336 Ne'matulloev, H. and R. Hoshim, eds. Namuneh-yi ash'ar-i sha'iran-i
afghan [Samples of the Poetry of Afghan Poets]. Istalinabad:
Nashriyat-i doulati, 1959. Pp. 296.
The poems, in Dari, are given in Arabic script.

1337 Nohsadumin sal-i vafat-i Khwajeh 'Abdullah Ansari Heravi [The Nine
Hundred Year of the Death of Khwajeh 'Abdullah Ansari Heravi].
Kabul: Matba'eh-yi vizarat, 1341 [1962]. Pp. 216.
A commemorative volume, in Persian.

1338 Nuri, Muhammad Gol, ed. Da pushtu istilahat aw muhawari [The Colloquial Expressions Used in Conversation]. Kabul: Matba'eh-yi
'umumi, 1320 [1941]. Pp. 392.
Expressions in Pushtu, arranged under alphabetical headings.

1339 *Nuri, Muhammad Gol. Mataluneh [Proverbs]. Kabul: Matba'eh-yi
'umumi, 1327 [1948]. Pp. 156.
Arranged in alphabetical order are some 1900 popular proverbs and
sayings in Pushtu.

1340 Nuri, Nur Ahmad. Gulshan-i Emarat [Flowering of Court Life]. Kabul:
Doulati matba'eh, 1335 [1947]. Pp. 166.
Account of life in the courts of the nineteenth-century rulers of
Afghanistan, in Persian.

1341 Olfat, Gol Pacha. Loghawi tsiraneh [Philological Research]. Kabul:
Matba'eh-yi 'umumi, 1321 [1942]. Pp. 84.
A work in Pushtu, which traces the origin of root words of that lan-
guage to Sanskrit.

1342 Olfat, Gol Pacha. Ali afkar [The Great Thoughts]. Kabul: Matba'eh-
yi 'umumi, 1327 [1948]. Pp. 58.
A collection of Pushtu poetry.

1343 Olfat, Gol Pacha. Tseh likal ya lik puheh [Writing and the Art of Writing]. Kabul: Matba'eh-yi 'umumi, 1328 [1949]. Pp. 96.
A study in Pushtu.

1344 Olfat, Gol Pacha. Adabi bahsuneh [Literary Topics]. Kabul: Matba'eh yi 'umumi, 1332 [1953]. Pp. 132.
A contemporary work in Pushtu.

1345 Olfat, Gol Pacha. Ghoreh ash'ar [Selected Poems]. Kabul: Matba'eh-yi 'umumi, 1334 [1955]. Pp. 256.
A collection of poems in Pushtu.

1346 Olfat, Pacha. Lwer Khiyaluneh aw zhwer fikruneh [High Ideas and Deep Thoughts]. Kabul: Matba'eh-yi 'umumi, 1335 [1956]. Pp. 97.

1347 Olfat, Gol Pacha. Mantiq [Logic]. Kabul: Matba'eh-yi 'umuni, 1335 [1956]. Pp. 53.
A short introduction to logic, written in Pushtu.

1348 Olfat, Gol Pacha. Neshruneh [Prose]. Kabul: Matba'eh-yi 'umumi, 1336 [1957]. Pp. 118.
A collection of prose writings in Pushtu.

1349 Olfat, Gol Pacha. Da zrah waina [The Lament of the Heart]. Kabul: Pohani matba'eh, 1341 [1962]. Pp. 122.
A collection of poems in Pushtu.

1350 Paktiyani, N. M., ed. Palwashe. Da 'Abd al-Ghani Khan Ghani asha'ar [Radiance. The Poems of 'Abd al-Ghani Khan Ghani]. Kabul; 1339 [1960]. Pp. 236.
A collection of poems in Pushtu.

1351 Panj ganj [Five Treasures]. Kabul: Manzum 'amm-i barqi paris, 1353 [1934]. Pp. 72.
A lithographed edition of the very popular and frequently reproduced school text in Persian. Contains poetry and passages on religion and ethics from such sources as Sa'di, the Mahmud-nameh, the Pand-nameh of 'Attar, and the Nam-i haqq.

1352 Pasarlani mosha'areh [Poetry on Spring]. Kabul: Matba'eh-yi 'umumi, n.d. Pp. 32.
Short selections of Pushtu by more than a score of contemporaries.

VIII. LANGUAGES AND LITERATURE

1353 Pazhwak, Abdur-Rahman. The Lovers of Dilaram, Translated by
Abdusstar Shalizi. Afghanistan 1, no. 2, 35-45. 1946.
A romantic and tragic tale of young love: no indication of a lit-
erary source.

1354 Pazhwak, Abdur-Rahman. Afsaneh-ha-yi mardom [Fables of People].
Kabul, 1336 [1957]. Pp. 87.
A work in Persian.

1355 Pazhwak, Abdur-Rahman. Golha-yi andisheh [The Flowers of Reflec-
tion]. Kabul: Pohani Matba'eh, 1344 [1965]. Pp. 159.
Contemporary poetry in Dari.

1356 Pazhwak, Muhammad Din. Pushtu neshruneh [Pushtu Prose]. Kabul:
Matba'eh-yi 'umumi, 1335 [1956]. Pp. 122.

1357 Pazhwak, Muhammad Din, ed. Pushtuni sandarai [Pushtun Songs].
Kabul: Matba'eh-yi 'umumi, 1334 [1955]. Pp. 398.
The first volume of a two-volume collection.

1358 Penzl, Herbert. On the Cases of the Afghan (Pashto) Noun. Word 6,
70-73. 1950.
A study of the three Pushtu cases: direct, oblique, and vocative.

1359 Penzl, Herbert. Afghan Descriptions of the Afghan (Pashto) Verb.
Journal of the American Oriental Society 71, 97-110. 1951.
An analysis of the descriptions of the verb form as they appear in
native grammars of Pushtu.

1360 Penzl, Herbert. Orthography and Phonemes in Pashto (Afghan). Journal of the American Oriental Society 74, 74-81. 1954.
Study of the correlation between Pushtu orthography and phonemes,
with valuable comments on dialect differences and views of the native grammarians.

1361 *Penzl, Herbert. A Grammar of Pashto: A Descriptive Study of the
Dialect of Kandahar, Afghanistan. Washington: American Council
of Learned Societies, 1955. Pp. 169.
Material collected by the author, an American linguist, at Qandahar in 1948 forms the basis of a grammar in which structure is em-
phasized. Very useful introduction on the present status of the language.

VIII. LANGUAGES AND LITERATURE

1362 Penzl, Herbert. Western loanwords in modern Pashto. Journal of the
American Oriental Society 81, 43-52. 1961.
A list of these words, indicating that more of those in current usage
for scientific terms come from Arabic and Persian.

1363 Penzl, Herbert. A Reader of Pashto. Ann Arbor: University of Michigan,
1962. Pp. 274.
A reader prepared under contract between the University of Michigan
and the United States Office of Education. The text includes 31
selections in script, in transliteration, and in translation, with glos-
saries and exercises.

1364 Phillott, Lieut. Col. D. C. Higher Persian Grammar, showing differences between Afghan and modern Persian, with notes on rhetoric.
Calcutta: Baptist Mission Press, 1919. Pp. xii, 937.

1365 *Plowden, Trevor Chichele, trans. Translation of the Kalid-i-afghani,
the Text Book for the Pakkhto Examination, with Notes . . . . Lahore: Munshi Gulab Singh and Sons, 2d ed., 1893. Pp. 427;
genealogical tables.
A translation of the texts edited by Thomas P. Hughes (see no. 1250).

1366 Popay Ressena, by H. L. O. Afghanistan 9, no. 2, 48-50. 1954.
On a description in the Avesta of a mountain chain known to the
Aryans as Popai Ressena, and to the Greeks as Paropamisus.

1367 Pushtani arman [The Desire of the Pushtuns]. Kabul: Matba'eh-yi
'umumi, 1334 [1955]. Pp. 111.
An anthology of some 60 examples of patriotic and inspirational
poetry in Pushtu by both early and contemporary writers.

1368 Da pushtu munazareh peh Kabul radio kashay [The Prose Contest of
Pushtu over Radio Kabul]. Kabul: Matba'eh-yi 'umumi, n.d.
Pp. 46.
A collection of discourses delivered in Pushtu by some 16 officials,
writers, and members of the staff of Radio Kabul.

1369 *Pushtu qamus [Pushtu Dictionary]. 2 vols. Kabul: Matba'eh-yi
'umumi, 1331-1333 [1952-1954]. Pp. 995.
A very valuable Pushtu-Persian dictionary.

1370 *Qamus-i jughrafiya'i-yi Afghanistan [Dictionary of the Geography of

Afghanistan]. Kabul: Matba'eh-yi doulati, 1335-39 [1956-60].
A Pushtu edition of this four-volume work in Persian began to appear in 1962.

1371 Qandahari, Taleb, ed. Ash'ar-i Vasel [Poems of Vasel]. Kabul:
Doulati matba'eh, n.d. Pp. 130.
Vasel was a lyric poet, writing primarily between 1920 and 1930.
He was the secretary of 'Abd al-Rahman Khan.

1372 Qandahari, Taleb, ed. Azad Kabuli, Muntakhabat-i ash'ar [Azad Kabuli. Selections of Poetry]. Kabul: Doulati matba'eh, 1343 [1964].
Pp. 153.

1373 Rapp, E. L. Die Judisch-Persisch-Hebräischen Inschriften aus Afghanistan [The Jewish-Persian-Hebrew Inscriptions from Afghanistan].
Munich: J. Kitzinger, 1965. Pp. 77; bibliography.

1374 Rafiq, Muhammad. Dweh sareh mayen wrunneh [Two Loving Brothers].
Kabul: Matba'eh-yi 'umumi, 1318 [1939]. Pp. 140.
A work in Pushtu.

1375 Rahmani, Magdalene. Rabea-i-balkhi (Afghan Poetess). Afghanistan 2,
no. 3, 17-21. 1947.
An account of the tragic life of the tenth-century poetess, with one
sample of her verse.

1376 Rahmani, Mageh. Pardeh-nishinan-i sukhanguy [Concealed Eloquence].
Kabul: Matba'eh-yi 'umumi, 1331 [1952]. Pp. 94.
An anthology of Persian prose and poetry from various periods.

1377 Rahmany, Magdalina. Deux poétesses afghanes du XIIIe siècle [Two Afghan Poetesses of the Thirteenth Century]. Afghanistan 7, no. 1, 39-
41. 1952.
Short biographies of Aaicha, an Afghan court poetess, and Mahjoube,
a very gifted woman.

1378 Rashad, 'Abd al-Shakur. Lodi pushtaneh [Pushtun Lodis]. Kabul:
Matba'eh-yi doulati, 1336 [1957]. Pp. 425.
A work in Pushtu about the Lodi dynasty.

1379 *Raverty, Henry George, ed. The Gulshan-i-Roh: Being Selections,
Prose and Poetical, in the Pushto, or Afghan Language. Ed. by Captain

H. G. Raverty. London: Longman, Green, Longman and Roberts, 1860. Pp. viii, 408.

This "Mountain Bouquet" contains what the editor considered to be the most characteristic examples of the great writers of Pushtu poetry and prose.

1380 Raverty, Henry George, trans. Selections from the Poetry of the Afghans, from the XVIth to the XIXth-Century, Literally Translated from the Original Pushtoo; . . . London: William and Norgate, 1867.

The translation of the collection, Gulshan-i-Roh, made by the same author (see no.1379).

1381 Raverty, Henry George. A Grammar of the Puk'hto, Pus'hto, or Language of the Afghans. London: William and Norgate, 3d ed., 1867. Pp. x, 204.

Attempts to include all dialects, but is based chiefly on literary works. Contains a lengthy introduction. Now antiquated. The first edition appeared in 1855 and the second in 1860.

1382 Raverty, Henry George. A Dictionary of the Pukhto, Pushto, or Language of the Afghans; . . . London: William and Norgate, 2d ed., 1860. Pp. xxiv, columns 1166.

1383 Rishtin, Sadiqullah. Da pushtu da adab tarikh [The History of Pushtu Literature]. Kabul: Matba'eh-yi 'umumi, 1325 [1946]. Pp. 190.

A history of this literature written in Pushtu.

1384 Rishtin, Sadiqullah. Da pushtu ishtiqaquneh aw terkibuneh [The Derivatives and Compounds of Pushtu]. Kabul: Matba'eh-yi 'umumi, 1326 [1947]. Pp. 94.

An important work in Pushtu.

1385 Rishtin, Sadiqullah. Pushtu keli [The Pushtu Key]. Kabul: Matba'eh-yi 'umumi, 1326 [1947]. Pp. 59.

One of a series of Pushtu grammars designed for the use of government officials engaged in learning Pushtu.

1386 Rishtin, Sadiqullah, ed. Wish zalmayan [Enlightened Youth]. Kabul, 1326 [1947]. Pp. 191.

A collection of Persian and Pushtu poetry and prose by young Afghans.

VIII. LANGUAGES AND LITERATURE

1387 Rishtin, Sadiqullah. Pushtu gramar [Pushtu Grammar]. Kabul:
      Matba'eh-yi 'umumi, 1327 [1948]. Pp. 184.
      A grammar in Pushtu, with English headings for the subdivisions of
      the text.

1388 Rishtin, Sadiqullah. Naway Zhwand [The New Life]. Kabul: Matba'eh-
      yi 'umumi, 1330 [1951]. Pp. 181.
      A work dealing with Pushtunistan and written in Pushtu.

1389 Rishtin, Sadiqullah, ed. Da Abd al-Hamid Mumand diwan [The Divan
      of Abd al-Hamid Mumand]. Kabul: Matba'eh-yi 'umumi, 1331
      [1952]. Pp. 154.
      The work of a Pushtu poet who was active in 1725 A.D.: this Divan
      is known also as the Dur-o-Marjan.

1390 Rishtin, Sadiqullah, ed. Pushtaneh sho'ara [Pushtu poets]. Kabul:
      'Umumi matba'eh, 1331 [1952]. Pp. 283.
      A collection of Pushtu verse.

1391 *Rishtin, Sadiqullah, ed. Da Baha'i Jan Kolliyat [The Collected Works
      of Bahai Jan]. Kabul: Matba'eh-yi 'umumi, 1332 [1953]. Pp.
      134.
      The poetry in Pushtu of Bahai Jan Sahibzadeh, who was living at
      Qandahar.

1392 *Rishtin, Sadiqullah, ed. Baz nameh da Khushhal Khan Khattak [The
      Book of Falconry of Khushhal Khan Khattak]. Kabul: Matba'eh-yi
      'umumi, 1332 [1954]. Pp. 67.
      An edition of one of the major works of the Afghan national poet,
      a mathnawi in Pushtu.

1393 Rishtin, Sadiqullah. Da zhwand sandareh [The Life Story]. Kabul,
      1339 [1960]. Pp. 118.
      A work in Pushtu.

1394 Rishtin, Sadiqullah and Gholam Rahman Jarar, ed. Pushtu qesi [Pushtu
      Stories]. Kabul: Matba'eh-yi 'umumi, 1331 [1952]. Pp. 164.
      A collection of stories in Pushtu.

1395 *Roos-Keppel, George Olof, trans. Translation of the Ganj-e-Pakhtu.
      Lahore: Anglo-Sanskrit Press, 1905. Pp. 94.
      Rare English translation of the "Pakhtu Treasury," composed by
      Ahmad Maulavi.

1396 Roos-Keppel, George Olof. A Manual of Pushtu, by Major G. Roos-Keppel . . . and Qazi Abdul Ghani Khan. . . . London: Oxford University Press, 1943. Pp. xii, 310.
A contemporary reworking of a manual first published in 1901. Based on actual usage, written and spoken, of Peshawar. Includes a grammar, sections on composition and exercises, and a large collection of useful colloquial sentences. No transliteration.

1397 Saldjouqui, Fekri. Ostad Banay Heravi. Afghanistan 9, no. 3, 18-21. 1954.
On a famous poet, musician, mathematician, astrologer, and architect, a native of Herat.

1398 Saleh, Muhammad Khan. Khud amuz-i pushtu [Pushtu Self-Taught]. Qandahar, 1313 [1934].

1399 Saleh, Muhammad Khan. Pushtu zeba [Pushtu Language]. Kabul: 'Umumi matba'eh, 1316 [1937]. Pp. 100; lithographed.

1400 Saljuki, Fekri. Kolliyat-i Mirza Abd al-Qader Bedil [Collected Works of Mirza Abd al-Qader Bedil]. Kabul: Matba'eh-yi ma'ref. Vol. 1, 1340 [1961], pp. 1198; vol. 2, 1341 [1962]; vol. 3, 1342 [1963].
A definitive edition of the works of Bedil, widely regarded as the leading mystic poet of Afghanistan.

1401 Saljuqi, Salah al-Din. Áfkar sha'ar [Thoughts on Poetry]. Kabul: Matba'eh-yi 'umumi, 1334 [1955]. Pp. 137.
A commentary on selected poems in Persian.

1402 Saljuqi, Sahah al-Din. Naqd-i Bedil [The Wealth of Bedil]. Kabul: Pohani matba'eh, 1342 [1963]. Pp. 571.
A commentary and biography by the editor of Bedil's collected works, in Persian.

1403 Serraj, Dr. Mahbub. Maulana Balkhi va pedarash [Maulana Balkhi and his Father]. Kabul: Matba'eh-yi doulati, 1340 [1961]. Pp. 142.
A study of the effect on his poetry of paternal education.

1404 Shafeev, D. A. Kratkiy grammaticheskiy ocherk afganskogo yazyka [Short Essay on Afghan Language Grammar]. In: Zudin, P. B., Russko-afganskiy slovar'. Moscow: GIS, 1955. Pp. 1035-1174.
Excellent sketch of the phonology, morphology, and syntax of

Western Pushtu, with Arabic script and phonemic transcriptions. See also no. 1430.

1405 Shafeev, D. A. A Short Grammatical Outline of Pashto. Bloomington: University of Indiana, 1964. Pp. 89.
An edited translation by Herbert H. Paper of no. 1403.

1406 *Da Shams al-Din Kakarr diwan [The Divan of Shams al-Din Kakarr]. Kabul: Matba'eh-yi 'umumi, 1333 [1954]. Pp. 169.
The collected poems in Pushtu of a son of Pir Muhammad Kakarr.

1407 Shibli, Nu'mani. Da sirat al-nabi mustatab kitab [The Book of the Biography of the Prophet]. Kabul: Matba'eh-yi 'umumi, 1326 [1947]. Pp. 448.
A translation of the well-known Arabic work into Pushtu by Burhan al-Din Kushkaki.

1408 Shoironi Afgoniston; Obraztsy stikhov souremennykh poetov Afganistana [Shoironi Afghanistan; Verses of Contemporary Afghan Poets]. Stalinabad, 1958.
The text is in Tajik Persian.

1409 Sidqi, Muhammad 'Osman. Sorud-i hasti [Songs of Existence]. Kabul: Doulati matba'eh, 1343 [1964]. Pp. 127.
Short poems composed in Kabul, New York, and other places.

1410 Singh, Prabhjot-Kaur (Mrs. Narenderpal). Kandahari Hava. New Delhi: Vidya Prakashan Bhavan, 1963. Pp. 145.
A comparative study of Afghan Persian and Punjabi folk songs. In Punjabi, in Gurmukhi script, with translations of some quatrains (chahar-baiti) from Afghan Persian.

1411 Sokolova, V. S. Pamir jazyki [Pamir Languages]. In Ocherki po fonetike iranskikh jasykov 2, 81-240. Moscow: Izdatel'stvo Akademiia Nauk, 1953.

1412 Sourdel, Dominique. Un trésor de dinars Gaznawides et Salgulcides découvert en Afghanistan [A Treasure of Ghaznavid and Seljuk Dinars found in Afghanistan]. Bulletin d'Études Orientales de l'Institut Français de Damas 18, 197-208; plates. 1963-1964.
Description and analysis of a find of coins and jewelry discovered near Qunduz.

1413 Sovremennyye Literaturnyye Yazyki stran Azii [The Modern Literary
Languages of Asia]. Moscow, 1965.
Includes a chapter by N. A. Dvoryankov, "The Development of
Pushtu as the National and Literary Language of Afghanistan. "

1414 Stern, S. M. À propos de l'inscription juive de l'Afghanistan [Concern-
ing the Hebrew Inscription of Afghanistan]. Journal Asiatique 237,
47-49. 1949.
Concerns an inscription of 739 A. D. --its probable arrangement,
with a reproduction and translation.

1415 Tarzi, Mahmud, trans. Siyahet dar jaww-i hava [Trip in the Skies].
Kabul: 'Inayet, 1331 [1912]. Pp. 219.
A translation into Persian of Jules Verne's "Trip to the Moon. "

1416 Tarzi, Mahmud, trans. Jazireh-yi pinhan [The Mysterious Island].
Kabul: 'Inayet, 1332 [1913]. Pp. 479.
A translation into Persian of the work of the same title by Jules
Verne.

1417 Tarzi, Mahmud. Rauzeh-yi hikam [The Garden of Wise Sayings].
Kabul: 'Inayet, 1331 [1913]. Pp. 158.
A collection of political, moral, and literary essays in the Persian
language.

1418 Tarzi, Mahmud. Az har dahan sukhani va az har chaman samani
[From Every Mouth a Word and from Every Garden a Jasmine]. Kabul: 'Inayet, 1331 [1913]. Pp. 268.
A lithographed work containing a variety of noteworthy selections
in Persian prose and poetry.

1419 Trumpp, E. Die Verwandtschaftsverhältnisse des Pasto [The Relationships of Pushtu]. Zeitschrift der deutschen morgenländischen
Gesellschaft 21, 10-155; 23, 1-93. 1867, 1869.

1420 Trumpp, E. Grammar of the Pasto or Language of the Afghans. London
and Tübingen: Trubner and Co., 1873.
Sometimes regarded as the standard grammar, it is based exclusively
on literary sources, with no indication of current spoken usage. The
presentation is extremely scholarly, with a great parade of philologi-
cal learning, but the author's comparative and historical conclusions
are in large part erroneous.

1421 Vajid, Muhammad Qasim. Marg-i Farhad [Death of Farhad]. Fayza-
        bad: Matba'eh-yi Badakhshan, 1331 [1952]. Pp. 64.
        The familiar tale, in Persian, of Khosrow, Farhad, and Shirin.

1422 Vakil, Fazl Muhammad. Da Pushtu zhabe land gramar [The Short
        Grammar of the Pushtu Language]. Kabul, 1330 [1951]. Pp. 64;
        bibliography.

1423 Weesh, Raz Muhammad. Pushtu Kitabuneh [Pushtu Books]. Kabul:
        Matba'eh-yi doulati, 1337 [1958]. Pp. 236.
        A unique annotated bibliography of some 405 works in Pushtu.

1424 Wilson, J. Christy, Jr. An Introduction to Colloquial Kabul Persian.
        Presidio of Monterey, California: Army Language School, 1955.
        Pp. 58.
        A brief account of the vocabulary and constructions, most useful
        for foreigners wishing to speak Persian at Kabul, but complicated by
        the use of confusing symbols for many letters of the alphabet.

1425 Yaqubi, M. Din. Transliteration System for Geographical Names in
        Afghanistan. Kabul: Ministry of Mines and Industry, 1962. Pp. 9.
        Very useful pamphlet, with parallel columns in English and in
        Persian.

1426 Zachova, Eliska. Die Fee aus dem Granatapfel und andere afghanische
        Märchen [The Fairy from the Pomegranate and other Afghan Stories].
        Prague, n.d. Pp. 95.

1427 Zamir, Muhammad Hasan, ed. Pushtuni sandarai [Pushtun Songs].
        Kabul: Matba'eh-yi 'umumi, 1335 [1956]. Pp. 302.
        The second volume of a two-volume collection.

1428 Zawak, Muhammad Din. Khushhal Khan Khattak Kist? [Who is
        Khushhal Khan Khattak?]. Kabul: Matba'eh-yi doulati, 1334
        [1955]. Pp. 158.

1429 Zudin, P. B. Kratkiy Afgano-russkiy slovar' [Short Afghan-Russian
        dictionary]. Moscow: GIS, 1950. 568 pp.
        (See no. 1284 for a full description of this dictionary.)

1430 Zudin, P. B., ed. Iz afganskikh pesen i stikhov [From Afghan Songs

and Poetry] . Moscow: Goslitizdat, 1955. Pp. 224.
Translations into Russian.

1431 Zudin, P. B. Russko-afganskiy slovar' [Russian-Afghan dictionary] .
Moscow: GIS, 1955. Pp. 1176.
Defines about 12,000 words and includes a gazetteer. Pushtu words
are given in Arabic script and Cyrillic transliteration.

IX. ART AND ARCHAEOLOGY

Historical monuments and sites; excavation
reports and publications; history of art
and architecture; numismatics

In this section, the majority of the titles reflect the work of la Délégation archéologique française en Afghanistan. In 1921 the French government secured a virtual monopoly of archaeological excavation in the country,
and since then their work, which began the following year, has gone steadily
forward. Numerous volumes and many more articles reflect work at Buddhist
and Moslem sites: the listing of this material is not exhaustive. Within recent
years the ancient sites of the country have been opened to scholars from other
countries, and some indications of this fact appear in the articles listed here.
The steadily increasing concern of the Afghans with their own cultural and artistic heritage is finding expression in the numerous articles which have appeared in the periodical Afghanistan: many of them were initially written for
Kabul or Aryana.

Given the fact that material on Afghan numismatics is scattered and
relatively unknown, a special effort was made to collect pertinent references
on this subject.

1432 Alvad, Thomas and Lennart Edelberg. The Nuristani Harp. Afghanistan
8, no. 3, 34-44; map. 1953.
A description of the harp found among the Safid Push Kafirs and its
relation to other primitive harps, with a speculation that this may
be the forerunner of the Sumerian harp.

1433 Auboyer, Jeannine. Joseph Hackin (1886-1941): In Memoriam. Afghanistan 5, no. 3, 1-9; bibliography. 1950.
A biographical sketch, an appreciation of Hackin's archaeological
work, and a tribute to the man himself.

1434 Barger, Evert. Exploration of Ancient Sites in Northern Afghanistan.
Geographical Journal 93, 377-398; map. 1939.
Summary account of travels made in 1938 in the region of the Oxus
Valley in Northeastern Afghanistan, with descriptions of archaeologi-
cal sites studied by the French mission.

1435 Barger, Evert. Opening a Rich New Field of Archaeological Research in
Central Asia: The Pioneer Exploration of the Oxus Territories in
Northern Afghanistan by the First British Expedition in that Country.
Illustrated London News, pp. 682-683. April 22, 1939.
A brief account of an exploratory expedition to investigate mounds

that may contain Greek cities, with photographs of the mounds and artifacts. By the leader of the expedition, a lecturer in the University of Bristol.

1436 Barger, Evert. Some Problems of Central Asian Exploration. Geographical Journal 103, nos. 1/2, 1-18; map. 1944.

On the difficulties of dating and correlating archaeological evidence into an adequate history of early Afghanistan. The author sees promise in the finds in Bactria.

1437 Barthoux, J. Les institutions françaises en Afghanistan, écoles et travaux archéologiques [The French Institutions in Afghanistan, Schools and Archaeological Undertakings] . L'Europe Nouvelle 569, 16-17. 1929.

1438 *Barthoux, J. Les fouilles de Hadda. Figures et figurines [Excavations at Hadda. Figures and Figurines] . Paris and Brussels; Les Éditions G. Van Oest, 1930.

Part of the series: Mémoires de la Délégation archéologique française en Afghanistan (vol. 4, Pt. 3). The album of 112 plates illustrates nearly 500 pieces of sculpture excavated at Hadda.

1439 *Barthoux, J. Les fouilles de Hadda. Stupas et sites [Excavations at Hadda. Stupas and Sites] . Paris and Brussels: Les Éditions G. Van Oest, 1933. Pp. 213.

Also part of the series: Mémoires de la Délégation archéologique française en Afghanistan (vol. 4, Pts. 1 and 2). Descriptions of the stupas studied by the author, together with analysis and classification of types of these monuments.

1440 Berre, Marc Le and Daniel Schlumberger. Observations sur les Remparts de Bactres [Observations on the Ramparts of Balkh] . Paris: Libraire C. Klincksieck, 1964. Pp. 104; plates.

A separate publication of Pt. 3 of Volume 19, Mémoires de la Délégation archéologique française en Afghanistan.

1441 Biography of Some Members of the Danish Mission. Afghanistan 3, no. 3, 38-42. 1948.

Sketches, with photographs, of four of the members and brief lists of their publications.

1442 Bivar, A. D. H. Fire-Altars of the Sassanian Period at Balkh. Journal of the Warburg and Courtauld Institute 17, 182-183. London, 1954.

1443 Bivar, A. D. H. Seljuqid ziyarets of Sar-i-Pul (Afghanistan). Bulletin
of the School of Oriental and African Studies 29, no. 1, 57-63. 1966.

1444 Bombaci, Alessia. Summary Report on the Italian Archaeological Mission in Afghanistan. (I) Introduction to the Excavations at Ghazni.
East and West 10, nos. 1/2, 3-22. 1959.

1445 Bruno, Andrea. The Planned and Executed Restoration of Some Monuments of Archaeological and Artistic Interest in Afghanistan. East
and West 13, nos. 2-3, 99-185. 1962.

1446 Byron, Robert. The Shrine of Khwaja Abu Nasr Parsa at Balkh. Bulletin
of the American Institute for Persian Art and Archaeology 4, no. 1,
12-14. New York, 1935.
Summary description of the damaged, late fifteenth-century structure, and brief mention of the saintly figure there enshrined.

1447 *Byron, Robert. The Road to Oxiana. London: Macmillan and Co.,
Ltd., 1937. Pp. 341.
By the late British scholar of history and the arts. One third of the
book is a polished travelogue of northern and eastern Afghanistan
in 1934, with excellent accounts of important architectural monuments. A second edition appeared in 1950.

1448 Casal, Jean Marie. Mundigak: Une site de l'âge du bronze en Afghanistan [Mundigak: A Bronze Age Site in Afghanistan]. Afghanistan 7,
no. 4, 41-48. 1952.
The excavation of the mound, with an enumeration of the finds at
each level.

1449 Casal, Jean Marie. Fouilles de Mundigak [The excavations at Mundigak].
Paris: Mémoires de la Délégation archéologique française en Afghani-
stan, 1963. Volume 1, text, pp. 260; vol. 2, 188 plates.
Describes an early site near Qandahar.

1450 Caspani, P. E. "Lahore-Delhi." Afghanistan 1, no. 1, 39-40. 1946.
Locates the site of ancient Gorydale and points out its latter-day
derivation in local speech.

1451 Caspani, P. E. Les premiers contacts entre la Chine et l'Afghanistan et
les origines de la Route de la Soie [The First Contacts between China
and Afghanistan and the Origins of the Silk Route]. Afghanistan 1,
no. 3, 30-35. 1946.

Deals with the contacts established in the second century A. D. as reflected by Chinese writers.

1452 Caspani, P. E. "La promenade archéologique de Kaboul" ["The Archaeological Tour of Kabul"]. Afghanistan 1, no. 4, 35-43. 1946.
Describes ancient remains and monuments to be seen within a distance of 10 kilometers from Kabul and along the main highway toward Jalalabad.

1453 Caspani, P. E. The Walls of Kabul. Afghanistan 1, no. 2, 31-34. 1946.
A tour of these walls, supplemented by historical data.

1454 Caspani, P. E. "Le Nau-Bahur de Balkh" ["The Nau-Bahur of Balkh"]. Afghanistan 2, no. 1, 45-50. 1947.
Summary description of the most conspicuous ruins of ancient Balkh.

1455 Choukour, Simonne. Exposition de peinture de la Société "All India Fine Arts and Crafts" [Exhibition of Painting of the "All India Fine Arts and Crafts" Society]. Afghanistan 4, no. 2, 52-57. 1949.
Description, commentary, and illustrations give ample coverage to an exposition.

1456 *Combaz, Gisbert. L'Inde et l'Orient Classique. 2 vols. Paris: Libraire orientaliste Paul Geuthner, 1937. Pp. (1) 264; (2) 165 plates.
An exhaustive examination of the influences of Indian and late classical art upon each other, with many illustrations of art objects and monuments from within the limits of Afghanistan.

1457 Combe, E., J. Sauvaget, G. Wiet, et al., eds. Répertoire chronologique d'épigraphie arabe [Chronological Inventory of Arabic Epigraphy] 13 vols. Cairo: Imprimerie de l'Institut français d'archéologie orientale. 1931-1945. (1) Moslem years 1-243; (2) 243-285; (3) 285-320; (4) 320-354; (5) 354-386; (6) 386-425; (7) 425-485; (8) 485-550; (9) 550-601; (10) 601-626; (11:1) 627-636; (11:2) 637-653; (12) 653-680; (13) 680-705.
An invaluable work containing the texts of inscriptions in Arabic script and with translations into French.

1458 Curiel, R., and G. Fussman. Le Trésor Monetaire de Qunduz [The Monetary Treasure of Qunduz]. Paris: Mémoires de la Délégation archéologique française en Afghanistan, 1965.

1459 *Curiel, Raoul and Daniel Schlumberger. Trésors monétaires d'Afghanistan [Monetary Treasures of Afghanistan]. Paris: Imprimerie Nationale, 1953. Pp. 130.

The publication is Volume 14 of the Mémoires de la Délégation archéologique française en Afghanistan, and deals with three hoards of early coins found in that country. One was of Greek coins from the Achaemenid period; the second of Indian, Greek, and Indo-Greek coins of the fourth century B.C. to the third century A.D.; and the third of a collection of Sassanian and Kushano-Sassanian coins of utmost scholarly importance. The work concludes with a complete list of the Sassanian and Kushano-Sassanian coins found in Afghanistan and with a list of historical sources relating to the city of Kabul.

1460 Dagens, B., M. Le Berre, and Daniel Schlumberger. Monuments Préislamiques d'Afghanistan [Pre-Islamic Monuments of Afghanistan]. Paris: Mémoires de la Délégation archéologique française en Afghanistan, 1964. Pp. 104; 19 figures; 45 plates.

The three parts cover Buddhist sculpture, Buddhist monasteries in the Foladi Valley, and the walls of Balkh.

1461 Dames, M. Longworth. Coins of the Durranis. Numismatic Chronicle, 3d ser., 8, 325-363; plate. London, 1888.

A short account of the kings of the Durrani dynasty and their mints and coins. The paper includes a series of Persian couplets taken from the coins, a chronological table of the dynasty, a list of the kings, a genealogical table, a catalogue of coins, and an index of mints. Addenda and corrigenda to the article appear in the Numismatic Chronicle, 3d ser., Vol. 9, 1889.

1462 De Croze, Joel. Les empires afghans des Indes et leur style architecturel [The Afghan Empires of India and their Architectural Style]. Afghanistan 2, no. 1, 7-15; no. 2, 1-7. 1947.

A visitor to Afghanistan searches for architectural prototypes of structures erected in India. Interest then switches to the monuments erected in India under the Afghan kings.

1463 *Deydier, Henri. Contribution a l'étude oe l'art du Gandhara [Contribution to the Study of Gandharan Art]. Paris: Libraire d'Amérique et d'Orient, Adrien-Maisonneuve, 1950. Pp. xxviii, 325; 5 maps.

A detailed work, reflective of exhaustive labor by a young French scholar, the study is a critical and analytical bibliography of all material published on the so-called Gandharan art between 1922 and 1949. Most of the sites discussed are within the frontiers of Afghanistan.

1464 Dupree, Louis. Preliminary Field Report on Excavations at Shamshir Ghar, Koh-i-Duzd, and Deh Morasi Ghundai (Southwestern Afghanistan). Afghanistan 6, no. 2, 22-31; no. 3, 30-35; map; chart of excavation. 1951.
An explanation of the archaeological methods used and a description of the finds, with very tentative conclusions, in the cave called Shamshir Ghar. Part II deals with the excavation of Deh Morasi Ghundai, a prehistoric mound in southwestern Afghanistan.

1465 Dupree, Louis. Shamshir Ghar, a Historic Cave Site in Kandahar Province (Afghanistan). Arts asiatiques 3, no. 3, 195-206. 1956.
Excavations of a large cave near Kandahar, which yielded artifacts from the third through the twelfth centuries A.D.

1466 Dupree, Louis. Shamshir Ghar: Historic Cave Site in Kandahar Province, Afghanistan. Anthropological Papers of the American Museum of Natural History 46, no. 2, 137-312. 1958.
Detailed report of excavation conducted in 1951, including plates, diagrams, and tables.

1467 Dupree, Louis. Deh Morasi Ghundai: A Chalcolithic Site in South-Central Afghanistan. Anthropological Papers of the American Museum of Natural History 50, no. 2, 59-136. 1963.
Detailed report of the excavations in 1951, with plates, diagrams, maps, and contributions by specialists. Includes a bibliography.

1468 Edelberg, Lennart. Fragments d'un stupa dans la vallée du Kunar en Afghanistan [The Remains of a Stupa located in the Kunar Valley of Afghanistan]. Arts asiatiques 4, no. 3, 199-207. 1957.

1469 Ettinghausen, Richard. Muslim Art in Western Eyes. Afghanistan 6, no. 3, 43-46. 1951.
The adaptation of Moslem motifs in European art and the study of Moslem art by European and American scholars.

1470 Exhibition of Ancient Art of Afghanistan. Tokyo, 1936. Pp. 34; unnumbered plates.

Catalogue of an exhibition of treasures from the Kabul Museum. Text in Japanese and English.

1471 Fairservis, Walter A., Jr. Archaeological Research in Afghanistan. Transactions of the New York Academy of Sciences, ser., 2, 12, 172-174. 1950.

1472 Fairservis, Walter A., Jr. Archaeological Research in Afghanistan. Afghanistan 5, no. 4, 31-34. 1950.
Report of a survey expedition to investigate prehistoric sites in Afghanistan.

1473 Fairservis, Walter A., Jr. Exploring the "Desert of Death." Natural History 59, no. 6, 246-253; map. 1950.
The story of an expedition into Afghanistan to search for prehistoric sites. The article describes modern Afghanistan and the ghost city of Peshawarun. Mr. Fairservis served as a Special Field Assistant in the Department of Anthropology of the American Museum of Natural History.

1474 Fairservis, Walter A., Jr. Journey to 4000 B.C. Three parts. Collier's 128, no. 25, 22 f., no. 26, 23 f.; 129, no. 1, 32 f. December 22, December 29, 1951; January 5, 1952.
A popular account of the expedition in Afghanistan under the auspices of the American Museum of Natural History and headed by Mr. Fairservis. The article is the story of the expedition's troubles and adventures; the few reports of archaeological research are elementary.

1475 Fairservis, Walter A., Jr. Archaeological Studies in the Seistan Basin of Southwestern Afghanistan and Eastern Iran. Anthropological Papers of the American Museum of Natural History. New York: American Museum of Natural History, 1961. Pp. 128; 19 plates.

1476 *Flury, Samuel and Andre Godard. Ghazni (premiers résultats de la mission archéologique française en Afghanistan) [Ghazni (First Results of the French Archaeological Mission in Afghanistan)]. Paris, 1925. Pp. 33.
Includes a study of the Arabic inscriptions of the surviving monuments by Flury and a discussion of the topography of Ghazni by Godard.

1477 *Foucher, Alfred. L'Art greco-bouddhique du Gandhara. Étude sur les origines de l'influence classique dans l'art bouddhique de l'Inde et de

l'Extrême-Orient [The Greco-Buddhistic Art of Gandhara. A Study
of the Origins of the Classical Influence on the Buddhistic Art of India
and of the Far East]. 2 vols. Paris: Ernest Leroux, 1905-1922.
Pp. (1) 639; (2) 400.
Two volumes, published years apart, bring a meticulous method
and an analysis of the monuments to this problem.

1478 *Foucher, Alfred. La veille route de l'Inde, de Bactres à Taxila [The
Ancient Route from India, from Bactria to Taxila]. 2 vols. Paris,
1942-1947. Pp. (1) 1-173; (2) 174-426; maps; charts; reconstruc-
tions; plates; index-lexicon.
Volume 1 deals with the geography and archaeology, Volume 2 with
the history, of the Route. Lengthy, but informed and evocative.
Together, these two volumes form Volume 1 in the series: Mémoires
de la Délégation archéologique française en Afghanistan.

1479 Fouchet, Maurice. Notes sur l'Afghanistan. Oeuvre posthume. Preface
de J. Hackin [Notes on Afghanistan. Posthumous Work. Preface by
J. Hackin]. Paris: Éditions Maisonneuve, 1931. Pp. 228.
Posthumous work of the first French Minister to Afghanistan, who
served in 1923 and in 1924 until his early death. A general survey,
with emphasis on archaeological sites and still more on the program
and the efforts of King Amanullah. Kabul and its environs are also
described at some length.

1480 Frye, Richard N. Notes on the History of Architecture in Afghanistan.
Ars Islamica 11-12, 200-202. 1946.
Brief discussion of the earlier sites of Kabul and an account of a deco-
rative column and stupa near present-day Kabul.

1481 Frye, Richard N. Two Timurid Monuments in Herat. Artibus Asiae 11,
206-213. 1948.
Descriptions of the principal mosque (Masjid-i-Jami') and the extensive shrine of Khwaja 'Abdullah Ansari, accompanied by numerous
illustrations and a plan of the mosque.

1482 Frye, Richard N. An Epigraphical Journey in Afghanistan. Archaeology 7,
114-118. 1954.
The search for and discovery of a Parthian rock inscription at Tang-
i-Azao, west of Herat. More space is devoted to the trials of the trip
by car than to the inscription.

1483 Gardin, J. C. Céramiques de Bactres [Ceramics of Bactria (Balkh)] .
      Paris: Mémoires de la Délégation archéologique française en Af-
      ghanistan, Volume 15, 1957. Pp. 129; 38 figures; 24 plates.

1484 Gardin, J. C. Lashkari Bazar. Une Residence Royale Ghaznevide. II.
      Céramiques et Monnaies de Lashkari Bazar et Bost [Lashkari Bazar.
      A Royal Ghaznavid Residence. II. Ceramics and Coins of Lashkari
      Bazar and Bost] . Paris: Mémoires de la Délégation archéologique
      française en Afghanistan, Volume 18. 1963. Pp. 220; 30 plates;
      56 illustrations.

1485 Gardner, Percy. The Coins of the Greek and Scythic Kings of Bactria
      and India in the British Museum. London: Stuart Poole, 1886.
      Pp. lxxvi, 193, xxxii; plates.

1486 Gardner, Percy. New Greek Coins of Bactria and India. Numismatic
      Chronicle, 3d ser., 7, 177-181; plate. 1887.
      A description of a coin found in Bokhara, and of the evidence through
      which the author ascribes it to a Greek king of the second century
      B.C.

1487 Gettens, Rutherford J. The Materials in the Wall Paintings of Bamiyan,
      Afghanistan. Technical Studies in the Field of the Fine Arts 6, no.
      3, 186-193. 1937.
      Discusses the technique which was tempera with an animal glue
      binder and not true fresco. The earths employed to produce seven
      colors are identified.

1488 Ghirshman, Roman. Fouilles de Nad-Ali, dans le Seistan afghan [Exca-
      vations at Nad-Ali in Afghan Sistan] . Revue des Arts Asiatiques 13,
      10-12. 1939.
      First account of the preliminary explorations of a remotely situated
      prehistoric site.

1489 *Ghirshman, Roman. Begram, recherches archéologiques et historiques
      sur les Kouchans [Begram, Archaeological and Historical Research on
      the Kushans] . Cairo: Institut français d'archéologie orientale, 1946.
      Pp. xiv, 277.
      The publication is Volume 12 in the Mémoires de la Délégation
      archéologique française en Afghanistan. The author describes the
      site and the excavations, and then displays solid erudition in a nu-
      mismatic study, a new chronology of the Kushan kings, and a
      reconstruction of the history of the Kushans.

IX. ART AND ARCHAEOLOGY

1490 Ghirshman, R., and T. Ghirshman. Les Chionites-Hephtalites. Cairo:
      Mémoires de la Délégation archéologique française en Afghanistan,
      Volume 13, 1948. Pp. 156.

1491 Gnoli, Gherardo. Le Iscrizioni Giudeo-Persiane del Gur (Afghanistan)
      [The Jewish-Persian Inscription of Gur (Afghanistan)]. Rome:
      Istituto Italiano per il Medio ed Estremo Oriente, 1964. Pp. 70;
      8 plates; bibliography.
         An inscription, cut on a rock, dating from the late twelfth or early
      thirteenth century.

1492 *Godard, Andre and Joseph Hackin. Les antiquités bouddhiques de
      Bamiyan [The Buddhistic Antiquities of Bamiyan]. Paris and Brus-
      sels: Les Éditions G. Van Oest, 1928. Pp. 113; 98 plates; short
      bibliography.
         This excellent documentary work by two French archaeologists is
      the second volume of the series: Mémoires de la Délégation arch-
      éologique française en Afghanistan. Later study at the site by Hacki
      served to augment this initial research.

1493 Goetz, Hermann. Late Gupta Sculpture in Afghanistan: The "Scorretti
      Marble" and Cognate Sculptures. Arts asiatiques 4, no. 1, 13-19.
      1957.

1494 Goya, Sarwar. The Green Dome, or The Mausoleum of the Timurid
      Princes. Afghanistan 1, no. 1, 16-19. 1946.
         Concerns the mausoleum which the wife of Shah Rokh, Gowhar Shad
      erected at Herat between 1417 and 1437 A.D.

1495 Grousset, Rene. Un savant français; Joseph Hackin [A French Scholar;
      Joseph Hackin]. Afghanistan 5, no. 4, 1-12. 1950.
         In the form of a biography, high praise of the man and his work.

1496 Gullini, Giorgio. Attività archeologica italiana in Asia. Mostra dei
      risultati delle missioni in Pakistan e in Afghanistan, 1956-1959.
      Torino, Galleria Civica d'arte moderna, 1960. Pp. 8, 70; 35 plates.
         The catalogue of an exhibition at Turin, which describes the exca-
      vations at Ghazni and illustrates thirteen of the objects found.

1497 Gullini, Giorgio. L'Afghanistan dalla Preistoria all'Islam. Capolavori
      de Museo di Kabul [Afghanistan from Prehistory until Islam. Master-
      pieces of the Kabul Museum]. Turin: Galleria Civica d'arte modern
      1961. Pp. 171; 67 plates; bibliography.

1498 Hackin, Joseph. Répartitions des monnaies anciennes en Afghanistan [The Distribution of Ancient Coins in Afghanistan]. Journal Asiatique 226, 287-292; map. 1935.
On the sites of major coin discoveries, with a map showing the places where coins (and what kind of coins) are plentiful.

1499 Hackin, Joseph. Asar-i 'atiqeh-yi Kotal Khayr Khaneh-yi Kabul [Ancient Remains of Kotal Khair Khaneh at Kabul]. Kabul: Matba'eh-yi 'umumi, 1316 [1937]. Pp. 51.
A translation into Persian by Qasim Khan Rishtiya of a publication in French.

1500 Hackin, Joseph. L'Art bouddhique de la Bactriane et les origines de l'art greco-bouddhique [Buddhistic Art of Bactria and the Origins of Greco-Buddhistic Art]. Afghanistan 5, no. 1, 1-9. 1950.
Examination of masks taken from excavations in Bactria to show that Greco-Buddhistic art rose in Bactria toward the end of the Greek domination.

1501 Hackin, Joseph. The Buddhist Monastery of Fonduqistan. Afghanistan 5, no. 2, 19-35. 1950.
Detailed descriptions of painting and statuary found in the Buddhist sanctuary at Fonduqistan.

1502 Hackin, Joseph. Les fouilles de Begram [The Excavations of Begram]. Afghanistan 6, no. 4, 1-10. 1951.
Examples of Hellenistic, Greco-Roman, Indian, and Chinese art excavated at Begram, with a note on the historical circumstances (first and second centuries A.D.) which made such a collection possible.

1503 *Hackin, Joseph and Joseph Carl. Nouvelles recherches archéologiques à Bamiyan [New Archaeological Research at Bamiyan]. Paris and Brussels: Les Éditions G. Van Oest, 1933. Pp. 90; 84 plates.
This volume, the third of the series: Mémoires de la Délégation archéologique française en Afghanistan, continues the study presented in the second work of this series (see no. 1492).

1504 *Hackin, Joseph and Joseph Carl. Recherches archéologiques au Col de Khair Khaneh près de Kabul [Archaeological Research at the Pass of Khair Khaneh near Kabul]. Paris: Les Éditions d'Art et d'Histoire, 1936. Pp. 34; plates.
Volume 7 in the Mémoires de la Délégation archéologique française

en Afghanistan. It is concerned with the excavation of three sanc-
tuaries, built on the roof of still another, and dated in the fifth century A. D. There is much attention given to the principal piece of
sculpture, a white marble representation of a solar god.

1505 Hackin (Joseph) and Godard (André and Yedda). Asar-i 'atiqeh-yi
Buda'i Bamiyan [Antiquities of Ancient Buddhistic Bamiyan]. Kabul:
Matba'eh-yi 'umumi, 1315 [1936]. Pp. 87, 3.
A translation into Persian by Admad 'Ali Khan, of the original work
in French. The original illustrations are reprinted.

1506 *Hackin, Joseph and J. R. Hackin. Recherches archéologiques à Begram
[Archaeological Research at Begram]. 2 vols. Paris: Les Éditions
d'Art et d'Histoire, 1939. Pp. (1) 137; (2) 88 plates; maps.
Volume 9 in the Mémoires de la Délégation archéologique française
en Afghanistan. Volume 1 is largely a catalogue of the objects
found in the ancient city identified as Alexander's Nicea. An introductory chapter discusses the excavation and the finds, particularly
the carved ivories.

1507 Herzfeld, Ernst. Kushano-Sasanian Coins. In Memoirs of the Archaeological Survey of India, No. 38. Calcutta: Government of India,
Central Publication Branch, 1930. Pp. 51; plates.
A discussion of the evidence for a new chronological arrangement
and dating of known coins of the Sassanian-Kushan period. Includes
a list of coins, with a description of each.

1508 Itemadi, Guya. The General Mosque of Herat. Afghanistan 8, no. 2,
40-50. 1953.
A history of the mosque, with the various traditions of its building,
and accounts of its reconstruction and redecoration.

1509 *Jacquet, E. Notice et mémoires sur les découvertes faites par le Dr.
Honigberger en Afghanistan [A Notice and Records of the Discoveries
Made by Dr. Honigberger in Afghanistan]. Journal Asiatique, 3d ser.,
2, 234-277; 4, 401-440; 7, 385-404. 1836, 1837, 1839.
The beginning of archaeological research in Afghanistan. A German
doctor found his way into the country sometime after 1815 and--under
the protection of the Afghan government--excavated and looted stupas
and other sites. This material stems from his own account of these
adventures and is often lively reading.

1510 Khalili, Khalilullah. Aramgah-i Babar [The Resting Place of Babar].
      Kabul: Matba'eh-yi 'umumi, n.d. Pp. 70.
      A description in Persian of the site on the outskirts of Kabul.

1511 King, L. White. History and Coinage of the Barakzai Dynasty of Af-
      ghanistan. Numismatic Chronicle, 3d ser., 16, 277-344; plates.
      1896.
      The article is intended as a continuation of M. Longworth Dames'
      Coins of the Durranis (see no. 1461). It is a fairly comprehensive
      account of the decline of the Durrani dynasty and the rise of the
      Barakzai, with biographical sketches of the most prominent mem-
      bers of the family; some generalizations about their coinage and
      descriptions of the coins, quotations from the coins and a catalogue
      of coins. The author spent "a long residence on the northwest fron-
      tier of India . . . [and] had opportunities of meeting many mem-
      bers of both the Royal Families (Durrani and Barakzai). "

1512 Kohzad, Ahmad 'Ali. Begram [Begram]. Kabul: Matba'eh-yi 'umumi,
      1317 [1938]. Pp. 108.
      An account in Persian of the site, the excavations conducted by the
      French archaeological mission, and a description of the important
      finds.

1513 *Kohzad, Ahmad 'Ali. Maskukat-i qadim-i Afghanistan [Ancient Coins
      of Afghanistan]. Kabul: Matba'eh-yi 'umumi, 1317 [1938]. Pp.
      40; plates of coins.
      Valuable study in Persian of coins issued by the pre-Islamic rulers of
      the area, with emphasis upon the Greco-Bactrian coinage.

1514 Kohzad, Ahmad Ali. La statuaire au Nouristan et le travail sur bois
      [Nuristan Statuary and Woodwork]. Afghanistan 3, no. 3, 1-4. 1948.
      A brief discussion of the types of carving, illustrated with several
      examples.

1515 Kohzad, Ahmad Ali. Les travaux sur métal de l'époque ghaznevide
      [The Metal Work of the Ghaznavid Period]. Afghanistan 3, no. 3,
      24-32. 1948.
      The director of the Kabul Museum discusses some of the earliest
      dated pieces of Islamic metalwork, attributes a number to Afghan
      soil, and describes pieces from Ghazni which are now in the Kabul
      Museum.

1516 Kohzad, Ahmad Ali. Lashkargah (camp militaire) [Lashkargah (Military Camp)]. Afghanistan 4, no. 1, 30-35. 1949.

Describes the Ghaznavid site, adjacent to Bust at the confluence of the Helmand and Arghandab rivers, and announces forthcoming excavations by the French mission.

1517 Kohzad, Ahmad Ali. Marenjan Hill. Afghanistan 4, no. 4, 24-26. 1949.

A mound on the eastern outskirts of Kabul yielded a collection of very early Greek coins, a horde of Sassanian coins, and statuary from two Buddhist temples.

1518 Kohzad, Ahmad Ali. Premiers échantillons de la peinture ghaznevide [First Examples of Ghaznavid Painting]. Afghanistan 4, no. 2, 48-51. 1949.

Enthusiastic comment on discoveries made in the excavations at Lashkari Bazaar.

1519 Kohzad, Ahmad Ali. The Tour of the Archaeological Mission of the American Museum of Natural History in Afghan Seistan. Afghanistan 5, no. 1, 29-32. 1950.

An indignant refutation of "reports of a lost Afghan city" that were circulated by "American romance-hunting periodicals" (see no. 1473).

1520 Kohzad, Ahmad Ali. Uniformes et armes des gardes des Sultans de Ghazna [Uniforms and Arms of the Sultans' Guard at Ghazni]. Afghanistan 6, no. 1, 48-53. 1951.

On the eleventh-century murals found in the Audience Chamber of the Palace at Bashkari Bazaar--a discussion of the costume worn by the pictured guardsmen and an attempt to place them within the framework of Central Asiatic painting.

1521 Kohzad, Ahmad Ali. Four Months' Visit to Museums in the United States. Afghanistan 7, no. 2, 1-8. 1952.

Mr. Kohzad's impressions of the leading museums of the United State in relation to collections of objects from the Afghan-Iranian plateau region.

1522 Kohzad, Ahmad Ali. L'Influence artistique de l'art de l'Afghanistan ancien en Chine et en Asie centrale [The Artistic Influence of Ancient Afghan Art on China and Central Asia]. Afghanistan 7, no. 2, 42-53. 1952.

IX. ART AND ARCHAEOLOGY

On early Afghan art, particularly Greco-Buddhistic, and its spread
into China.

1523 Kohzad, Ahmad Ali. Arms of the Arian(s) Heroes in Avesta Period. Afghanistan 8, no. 3, 27-33. 1953.
The weapons of ancient heroes as described in the Avesta, the
names of which, with slight variations, have survived into current
use.

1524 A(hmad) A(li) K(ohzad). Gardien de la ville de Capici et ses armoires
[The Guardian of the City of Kapici and his Symbols]. Afghanistan
8, no. 2, 18-21. 1953.
On the patron god of the old city of Kapici, who appeared on coins
as an elephant's head.

1525 *Kohzad, Ahmad 'Ali. Lashkargah [Lashkargah]. Kabul: Matba'eh-yi
'umumi, 1332 [1953]. Pp. 152.
An account, in Persian, of the site currently under excavation by
the French archaeological mission.

1526 A(hmad Ali) K(ohzad). Le plus ancien temple de Bamyan [The Most
Ancient Temple of Bamiyan]. Afghanistan 8, no. 2, 58-64. 1953.
The oldest temple yet found at Bamiyan, dated in the third century
A.D., and its sculpture and paintings. A poor English translation
appears in the same number, on pages 12-17.

1527 *Kohzad, Ahmad Ali. Recherches archéologiques en Afghanistan [Ar-
chaeological Research in Afghanistan]. Afghanistan 8, no. 2, 1-11.
1953.
A report on 30 years of archaeological research, with notes on the
major excavations at Hadda, Kapici, Bamiyan, Balkh, and Lashkari
Bazaar.

1528 A(hmad) A(li) K(ohzad). Recherches archéologiques à Sorkh Kotal situé
dans le district de Chori [Archaeological Research at Surkh Kotal in
the District of Chor]. Afghanistan 8, no. 2, 51-57. 1953.
On the inscriptions and remains discovered by M. Daniel Schlumberger, and thought to be Kushanid. The inscriptions, though in Greek
letters, were in a language not Greek, and have not yet been identified.

1529 Kohzad, Ahmad Ali. Le Temple de Sakawand [The Temple of Sakawand].
Afghanistan 8, no. 1, 34-42. 1953.

On the prosperous cult of the sun god practiced in the once-
flourishing city of Sakawand, in the district of Logar.

1530 *Kohzad, Ahmad Ali. Recherches archéologiques et monuments anciens
en Afghanistan--le musée de Kaboul [Archaeological Research and
Ancient Monuments in Afghanistan--the Museum of Kabul]. Afghanistan 9, no. 4, 1-18. 1954.
A survey of archaeological research done in Afghanistan, with descriptions of the important excavations and of the finds that are in
the Kabul Museum.

1531 Kohzad, Ahmad Ali. Rahnuma-yi Bamiyan [Guide to Bamiyan]. Kabul: Matba'eh-yi 'umumi, 1334 [1955]. Pp. 50.

1532 Kohzad, Mohamad Nabi. L'Inauguration du Salon d'Automne à Kaboul
[The Inauguration of the Autumn Salon at Kabul]. Afghanistan 1,
no. 4, 30-34. 1946.
An exposition of works by local painters, nearly all of which illustrated an episode of Afghan history.

1533 Kohzad, Mohamad Nabi. Trois jours à Lashkari-Bazar [Three Days at
Lashkari-Bazaar]. Afghanistan 4, no. 3, 60-62. 1949.
A local observer describes finds made in the second period of the
first season's excavations at the site--notably decorated and inscribed
brickwork.

1534 Kohzad, Mohamed Nabi. Un ouvrage afghan sur Lashkargah [An Afghan
Work on Lashkargah]. Afghanistan 8, no. 3, 57-59. 1953.
A congratulatory review of Ahmad Ali Kohzad's book on Lashkari-
Bazaar.

1535 Lezine, A. Trois Stupa de la Région de Caboul [Three Stupas in the
Kabul area]. Artibus Asiae 27, nos. 1/2, 24. (1964.)

1536 Manchester Guardian. On the Fringe of the Indus. Afghanistan 8, no. 1,
pp. 43-46. 1953.
A note reprinted from the Manchester Guardian on Jean Marie Casal's
excavations in the mound called Mundigak--describing briefly the
finds at successive levels.

1537 Mandel'shtam, A. M. O nekotorykh rezul'tatakh raboty Frantsuzskoi
arkheologicheskoi missii v Afganistane [Some Results of the Work of

the French Archaeological Mission in Afghanistan]. Sovetskaia
Arkheologiia 21, 415-429. Moscow, 1954.

1538 Maricq, André et Gaston Wiet. Le Minaret de Djam [The Minaret at
Jam]. Paris: C. Klincksieck, 1959. Pp. 90; xvi plates, index.
Volume 16 of the Mémoires de la Délégation archéologique française
en Afghanistan is concerned with the discovery of the capital of the
Ghorid rulers, with special emphasis on its lofty minaret.

1539 Martin, D. R. Postal History of the First Afghan War, 1838-42. Bath:
Postal History Society [n. d.]

1540 Martin, D. R. Further Postal History of the Second Afghan War, 1878-
81, with Kandahar and Baluchistan, 1881-87. Bath: Postal History
Society, 1961. Pp. 41.

1541 Matheson, Sylvia. Time Off to Dig; Archaeology and Adventure in Re-
mote Afghanistan. London: Olhams Press Ltd., 1961. Pp. 286; index.
A chatty, pleasantly informative account of excavations in 1955 at
Mundigak, near Qandahar, and of impressions of the country.

1542 *Meunie, Jacques. Shotorak. Paris: Les Éditions d'Art et d'Histoire,
1942. Pp. 74; plates; sketch map.
Volume 10 in the Mémoires de la Délégation archéologique française
en Afghanistan. The excavation of a Buddhist monastery--its stupas,
sculpture and decorative motifs--with a discussion of the cultural elements found there and their influence.

1543 Mizuno, Seiichi, ed. Haibak and Kashmir-Smast Buddhist cave-temples
in Afghanistan and Pakistan surveys in 1960. Kyoto: Kyoto University,
1962. Pp. 107.

1544 Momal, C. Exposition Simonne Choukour sur le haut patronage de S. E.
l'Ambassadeur de France en Afghanistan [Simonne Choukour Exhibition,
under the Patronage of His Excellency the French Ambassador to Afghan-
istan]. Afghanistan 4, no. 2, 45-47. 1949.
Describes a number of paintings in an exhibition of the work of a
French-trained artist.

1545 Morgan, J. de. Manuel de numismatique orientale de l'antiquité et du
moyen âge. Publication achevée sous la direction de K. J. Basmadjian.
Vol. 1 [Handbook of Oriental Numismatics of Antiquity and the Middle Ages. Published under the Direction of K. J. Basmadjian. Vol. 1] .

Paris: Paul Geuthner, 1923-1936. Pp. 480; maps; bibliographies. Chapters IX, X, XI, and XV deal in a general way with the history and coinage of ancient and medieval Afghanistan.

1546 Musée Guimet. Exposition d'art asiatique: Chine, Asie centrale, Afghanistan [Guimet Museum. Exhibition of Asiatic Art: China, Central Asia, Afghanistan]. Afghanistan 6, no. 1, 28-40. 1951.
A description of the contents of the exhibit.

1547 Musée National d'Afghanistan, Kaboul. Guide du Visiteur [National Museum of Afghanistan, Kabul. Visitor's Guide]. Kabul, 1961. Pp. 31; mimeographed.

1548 Naimi, Ali Ahmad. Afghan Calligraphy, Illumination and Miniature-Work in the 9th Century A. H. Afghanistan 1, no. 1, 33-38. 1946.
Deals with the artists of the so-called "Herat" school, who were active under the Timurid rulers.

1549 Naimi, Ali Ahmad. Behzad. Afghanistan 3, no. 2, 63-66. 1948.
Sketchy account of the life and work of the greatest miniaturist: with bibliographical notes.

1550 Naimi, Ali Ahmad. Une famille d'artistes [A Family of Artists]. Afghanistan 3, no. 3, 43-46. 1948.
A brief resumé of the life and works of two younger relatives of the noted miniaturist, Behzad.

1551 Naimi, Ali Ahmad. Boste. [Bust.] Afghanistan 3, no. 4, 14-16. 1948.
An historical account of the site at the confluence of the Helmand and Arghandab rivers, with citations from local, early historians.

1552 Naimi, Ali Ahmad. Ostad Mohammadi. Afghanistan 4, no. 1, 1-3. 1949
Discusses a contemporary of the miniaturist Behzad, and gives a brief checklist of his surviving works.

1553 *Naimi, Ali Ahmad. Les monuments historiques et les mausolées de Ghazni [The Historic Monuments and Tombs of Ghazni]. Afghanistan 7, no. 2, 9-12. 1952.
A short history of Ghazni and descriptions of the principal tombs and monuments.

1554 Omar, Gholam. Commentaire sur les résultats des derniers fouilles archéologiques françaises en Afghanistan [Comment on the Results of the Latest French Archaeological Excavations in Afghanistan] . Afghanistan 4, no. 1, 19-29. 1949.

A review of the results of the excavations at Begram.

1555 Paruck, Furdoonjee D. Sassanian Coins. Bombay: The Times Press, 1924. Pp. xx, 536; tables; map; bibliography.

A learned and exhaustive study of the history and coinage of the Sassanian kings. It contains a history of each reign and a note on its coinage; extensive tables, with explanations, of mint-monograms; a glossary of the words used in inscriptions, with a discussion of each word; a catalogue of coins arranged under kings and a Sassanian bibliography.

1556 Patterson, Frank E. Afghanistan, its Twentieth Century Postal Issues. New York, Collectors Club, 1964. Pp. 208.

An example of arduous research conducted at Kabul from 1946 through 1949.

1557 *Poole, Reginald Stuart. The Coins of the Shahs of Persia, Safavis, Afghans, Efsharis, Zands, and Kajars. London and Paris, 1887. Pp. xcvi, 336; chronological and genealogical tables; plates; indices.

A catalogue of the coins of the Shahs of Persia in the British Museum; including those of the Afghans Mahmud and Ashraf (pages 64-68) and Azad Khan (page 130). An introductory chapter explains the chronology of the rulers and their use of inscriptions, with some distichs reproduced in Persian and translated into English couplets.

1558 Pope, Arthur Upham. The Mosque at Qal'a-i-Bist. Bulletin of the American Institute for Persian Art and Archaeology 4, 7-11. 1935.

A brief description and the first good photographs to be published of the remains of this early Moslem structure, probably the arch of the entrance portal of a monumental structure of about 1000 A. D.

1559 Prinsep, James. Additions to Bactrian Numismatics and Discovery of the Bactrian Alphabet. Journal of the Asiatic Society of Bengal 7, 636-655. 1838.

A description of some new coins and a theory of the Bactrian alphabet, giving the letters with English equivalents and explanations. A table shows the names of the kings in Bactrian, Greek, and English.

1560 Pugachenkova, G. A. Iskusstvo Afganistana [Culture of Afghanistan] .

Moscow: "Iskusstvo," 1963. Pp. 248.
A well-illustrated survey of the arts and architecture of the country
from pre-Islamic times.

1561 Rainey, Froelich. Afghanistan; Reconnaissance Summer, 1953. University Museum Bulletin 17, 40-56. Philadelphia, 1953.

1562 Rodgers, Charles J. The Coins of Ahmad Shah Abdalli or Ahmad Shah
Durrani. Journal of the Asiatic Society of Bengal 54, 67-76. 1885.
The use of coins to illustrate the ruler's invasions of India.

1563 Rogers, Millard. An Ivory Sardula from Begram. Artibus Asiae 15, 5-9.
1942.
This sardula, an animal with the body of a lion and the beak of a
parrot, is in the Kabul Museum. The author ascribes it to the middle of the first century A. D.

1564 Rosenfield, John M. The Dynastic Arts of the Kushans. Berkeley: University of California, 1966. Pp. 544; bibliography; index; over 200
illustrations.
Traces the political history of the Kushans, using numismatic and
epigraphic sources. Analyzes the arts, relating them to western Asia
and the Roman empire.

1565 Rowland, Benjamin, Jr. The Dating of the Sassanian Paintings at Bamiyan
and Dukhtar-i-Nushirvan. Bulletin of the Iranian Institute 6-7, 35-
42. New York, 1946.
Assigns the paintings to the period of Khrusraw II--early seventh cen-
tury--and to nominal Buddhists still retaining the Sassanian artistic
heritage.

1566 *Rowland, Benjamin, Jr. The Hellenistic Tradition in Northwestern India.
Art Bulletin 31, 1-10. 1949.
A leading American art historian discusses the survival of first-century
Hellenistic forms in fifth-century sculpture at Hadda and other sites.
He is critical of certain of the opinions of members of the French
archaeological mission in Afghanistan.

1567 Rowland, Benjamin, Jr. A Cycle of Gandhara. Bulletin of the Boston Museum of Fine Arts 62, 114-129. 1965.
Excellent account of the Gandhara schools of art and their monuments
in Afghanistan and Pakistan.

1568 *Rowland, Benjamin, Jr. Ancient Art from Afghanistan. Treasures of
the Kabul Museum. New York: Asia Society, 1966. Pp. 144; map;
111 illustrations; 5 color plates.
The catalogue of a traveling exhibition.

1569 Scerrato, Umberto. Summary Report on the Italian Archaeological Mission in Afghanistan. (II) The First Two Excavation Campaigns at
Ghazni, 1957-1958. East and West 10, nos. 1-2, 23-55. 1959.

1570 Schlumberger, Daniel. Surkh Kotal and the Ancient History of Afghanistan. London: The Afghan Information Bureau, n.d. Pp. 24.

1571 *Schlumberger, Daniel. L'Exploration archéologique de l'Afghanistan:
Résultats acquis et perspectives d'avenir [Archaeological Exploration
of Afghanistan: Results Achieved and Prospects for the Future] . Afghanistan 2, no. 4, 1-23. 1947.
A sketch of the geography and early history of the country is followed
by a very informative account of major archaeological sites and by
a summary of excavations already carried out.

1572 Schlumberger, Daniel. Archaeology in Afghanistan. Work of the
French Archaeological Delegation. Archaeology 2, no. 1, 11-16.
1949.
Mr. Schlumberger, Director of the French Archaeological Delegation
in Afghanistan since 1946, gives a very brief but clear and abundant-
ly illustrated summary of more than a score of years of digging by
French scholars.

1573 Schlumberger, Daniel. Les fouilles de Lashkari Bazar: Recherches archéologiques sur l'époque ghaznevide [The Excavations at Lashkari Bazaar:
Archaeological Research on the Ghaznavid Era] . Afghanistan 4, no.
2, 34-44. 1949.
Discusses the history of the site and its present topography and describes the first season of excavation.

1574 *Schlumberger, Daniel. Les fouilles de Lashkari Bazar [The Excavations
of Lashkari Bazaar] . Afghanistan 5, no. 4, 40-50. 1950.
The excavation of the Great Palace and the Audience Chamber, with
a description of the mural paintings of the Sultan's Guard; and of the
Central Palace and the Bazaar, with a note on what remained to be
done.

1575 Schlumberger, Daniel. The Ghaznavid Palace of Lashkari-Bazar. Illustrated London News 216, 458-462. March 25, 1950.
    The initial account of the highly successful excavations of an
    eleventh-century Moslem palace, situated on the banks of the Hel-
    mand in southwestern Afghanistan.

1576 *Schlumberger, Daniel. La grand mosquée de Lashkari Bazar [The Great
    Mosque of Lashkari Bazaar]. Afghanistan 7, no. 1, 1-4. 1952.
    The finding and dating of the twice-built mosque.

1577 *Schlumberger, Daniel. Le temple de Surkh Kotal en Bactriane [The
    Temple of Surkh Kotal in Bactria]. Journal Asiatique 240, 433-453.
    1952.
    Initial scholarly report of the excavation of the first Hellenistic type
    of structure to be discovered within the boundaries of Afghanistan.

1578 *Schlumberger, Daniel. Surkh Kotal: A Late Hellenistic Temple in
    Bactria. Afghanistan 9, no. 2, 41-47. 1954.
    A further report on the Greco-Iranian temple which contains the
    fire-altar of an unknown Iranian cult.

1579 Schlumberger, Daniel. Surkh Kotal: Un site archéologique d'époque
    kouchane en Bactriane [Surkh Kotal: An Archaeological Site of the
    Kushan Epoch in Bactria]. Afghanistan 9, no. 1, 44-54. 1954.
    The discovery and excavation of a Fire-Sanctuary evidently belong-
    ing to the Great Kushan epoch. It is the first of its kind to be found,
    and appears to be the seat of an Iranian cult, not yet identified.

1580 *Schlumberger, Daniel. Le temple de Surkh Kotal en Bactriane (II) [The
    Temple of Surkh Kotal in Bactria (II)]. Journal Asiatique 242, 161-
    187. 1954.
    Continues the account given in an earlier number of this periodical
    (see no. 1576) of the uncovering of the temple site.

1581 Schlumberger, Daniel and P. Bernard. Ai Khanum. Bulletin de Corre-
    spondence Hellenique 89, 590-657. 1965.
    A preliminary report on a first season of excavation at Ai Khanum, a
    Bactrian site on the Amu Darya River.

1582 Sedqi, Osman. Un aperçu d'histoire de l'art afghan [A Glance at the His-
    tory of Afghan Art]. Afghanistan 3, no. 4, 53-56. 1948.
    A sketch which covers too many centuries in too few pages to be of
    real value or interest.

IX. ART AND ARCHAEOLOGY

1583 Shakur, M. A. A Dash through the Heart of Afghanistan. Being Personal
Narrative of an Archaeological Tour with the Indian Cultural Mission.
Peshawar: Imperial Press, 1947. Pp. 126; folding sketch map;
sketch plans of Balkh and Qandahar.
The mission, of which the author, Curator of the Peshawar Museum,
was a member, traveled extensively by car and visited such notable
sites as Bamiyan, Balkh, Begram, Mazar-i Sharif, Ghazni, and
Qandahar.

1584 *Le site archéologique de Bamiyan. Guide du visiteur [The Archaeological Site of Bamiyan. Visitor's Guide]. Paris: Les Éditions d'Art et
d'Histoire, 1934. Pp. 60.
Succinct, reliable description of the Buddhas and the painted grottoes
at Bamiyan, published by la Délégation archéologique française en
Afghanistan.

1585 Sourdel, Dominique. Inventaire de Monnaies Musulmanes Anciennes du
Musée de Caboul [Catalogue of the Old Muslim Coins of the Kabul
Museum]. Cairo: Institut Français de Damas, 1953. Pp. 145; 6
plates.

1586 Strzygowski, Joseph. The Afghan Stuccos of the N. R. F. Collection.
New York: Stora Art Gallery (1932). Pp. 30.
A discussion of some 46 Greco-Buddhistic statues found near Tashqur-
ghan and displayed at the Nouvelle Revue Française gallery at Paris.

1587 Trousdale, William. Rock Engravings from the Tang-i Tizao in Central
Afghanistan. East and West n.s. 15, nos. 3/4. 1965.

1588 Wheeler, Mortimer. Trois semaines en Afghanistan [Three Weeks in Af-
ghanistan]. Afghanistan 1, no. 4, 49-50. 1946.
Very brief report by the head of an archaeological mission which
came from India to travel through Afghanistan.

1589 Wheeler, R. E. Mortimer. Archaeology in Afghanistan. Antiquity 21,
57-65. 1947.
An account of the Indian mission sent to visit archaeological sites in
Afghanistan. Mr. Wheeler, then Director-General of Archaeology
in India, was a member of the Mission.

1590 Whitehead, Richard Bertram. Notes on Indo-Greek Numismatics. Numismatic Chronicle, 5th ser., 3, 294-343. 1923.

IX. ART AND ARCHAEOLOGY

The author, an amateur coin collector in India for many years, was inspired by a find of Indo-Bactrian tetradrachms at Kabul in 1917 to undertake this first extensive survey of the subject.

1591 Whitehead, Richard Bertram. The Coins of Nadir Shah and the Durrani Dynasty. Journal of the Royal Asiatic Society of Bengal. Letters. Numismatic Supplement No. 46, 2, no. 3, 107-110. 1936.
A note on some Durrani coins not listed in the author's Catalogue of the Coins of Nadir Shah and the Durrani Dynasty.

1592 Wilson, Horace Hayman. Ariana Antiqua. A Descriptive Account of the Antiquities and Coins of Afghanistan: With a Memoir on the Buildings Called Topes, by C. Masson, Esq. London: Published under the Authority of the Honorable the Court of Directors of the East India Company, 1841. Pp. xvi, 452.
Important as a pioneering effort into the ever-broadening field of the archaeology of Afghanistan. For "topes," read "stupas."

1593 Wolfe, Nancy Hatch. The Valley of Bamiyan. Kabul, Defense Ministry Printing Department, 1963. Pp. 79; bibliography.

1594 Wolfe, Nancy Hatch. An Historical Guide to Kabul. Kabul: Education Press, 1965. Pp. 171; maps.
An historical introduction, followed by five detailed tours of the city.

1595 Wolfe, Nancy Hatch. Herat, A Pictorial Guide. Kabul: Education Press, 1966. Pp. 66.
An illustrated history and guide, with a map of the city.

1596 Young, Rodney S. Afghanistan Reconnaissance. Archaeology 7, Pt. 1, 51-52. 1954.
Describes field work carried on in the summer of 1953 by a group from the University Museum of the University of Pennsylvania. Records surface observations, digging at Qunduz, and putting down trial trenches at Balkh.

1597 Young, Rodney S. The South Wall of Balkh-Bactra. American Journal of Archaeology 59, 267-76. 1955.

1598 Zestovski, P. Esquisses architecturales de l'Afghanistan [Architectural Sketches of Afghanistan]. Afghanistan 3, no. 2, 38-62. 1948.
A topographical description of the site of Bamiyan, accompanied by

reproductions of surveys, of plans, and of sketches of monuments
and ruins.

1599 *Zestovsky, P. I. Esquisses d'architecture afghane: Herat, Kaboul-
Herat [Sketches of Afghan Architecture: Herat, Kabul-Herat]. Afghanistan 4, no. 3, 1-25; bibliography. 1949.
An interesting and valuable article on Herat and its vicinity by a
European engineer. A description of the town is followed by an ex-
tended historical notice. Eighteen pen drawings--including a plan
of Herat and a plan of the Masjid -i Jami'--are included.

1600 Zestovsky, Paul. L'Oasis de Sultan Bakva [The Oasis of Sultan Bakva].
Afghanistan 5, no. 3, 41-51. 1950.
A description of the oasis, its crumbled mosque and nomad ceme-
tery; of the town and cemetery of Farah; and of a nomad caravan.

A

INDEX

INDEX

INDEX

Gettens, Rutherford J., 1487
Ghani, A. R., 59
Da Gharbi Pakistan Yunitt, 955
Gharzi, General Muhammad Safar Vakil, 694
Ghaussi, Aref, 1072, 1073
Ghaussi, Muhammad Aref, 1074
Ghawareh ash'ar da Gol Pacha Olfat, 1226
Ghirshman, Roman, 449, 1488, 1489
Ghirshman, R. and T. Ghirshman, 1490
Ghose, Dilip K., 450
Ghosh, K. P., 956, 957
Ghubar, M., 810, 958
Ghubar, mir Ghulam Muhammad, 451, 452
Ghulami, Muhammad Ghulam, 1227
Gilbertson, George Waters, 1228
Gillett, Sir Michael, 959
Ginnever, O. R., 1075
Girs, G. F., 1229
Gnoli, Gherardo, 1491
Gobj, Robert, 453
Gochenour, Theodore S., 960, 1230
Godard, Andre and Joseph Hackin, 1492
Goetz, Hermann, 1493
Golovin, Y. M., 1076, 1077
Gordon, B. E. M., 1234
Gosti iz Afganista, 811
Goya, Sarwar, 1494
Gray, John Alfred, 812
Grenard, Fernand, 454
Grierson, George Abraham, 1231, 1232, 1233
Griesinger, W., 455
Grodekov, N. I. (Grodekoff, N.), 164
Grousset, Rene, 1495
Gul Muhammad, 456
Gullini, Giorgio, 1496, 1497
Gupta, Harl Ram, 457
Gurevich, Aleksandr Mikhailovich, 165
Gurevich, Naum M., 1078, 1079, 1080

INDEX

H

Habberton, William, 458
Habib, Mohammad, 459
Habibi, 'Abd al-Hayy, 460, 461, 1235, 1236, 1237, 1238, 1239
Habibiyeh 1282-1322, 813
Habibullah, Amir, 462
Habibullah, Sardar, 463
Hackin, Joseph, 166, 695, 1498, 1499, 1500, 1501, 1502
Hackin, Joseph and Joseph Carl, 1503, 1504
Hackin (Joseph) and Godard (André and Yedda), 1505
Hackin, Joseph and J. R. Hackin, 1506
Hackin, Ria and Ahmad Ali Kohzad, 696
Haddad, Nikulay, 814
Hadiyeh bi-dustan, 815
Haekel, Ingeborg, 167
Hahn, Helmut, 168
Hakim, Abdul, 816
Hakimi, 'Abd al-Karim, 1081
Hameed-ud Din, 464
Hamid, 'Abdul Razaq, 1240
Hamid Kashmiri, Hamid Allah, 465
Hamilton, Angus, 169
Hanna, Henry B., 466
Hannah, Norman B., 817
Hanstein, Otfrid von, 170
Harat, 818
al-Haravi, Sayf ibn Muhammad ibn Ya'qub, 467
Harlan, Josiah, 468
Harris, Fred, et al., 819
Hasan, K., 469
Hasan Khan, Ya'qub, 1241
Hasan, Zubeida, 961
Hashim Khan, mir, 470
Hashmat, A., 171
Hasrat, Aman Allah, 471
Hauser, Ernest O., 472
Havelka, Jan, 172
Havelock, Henry, 473
Hawa, 820
Hay, William R., 173, 174
Hayden, H. H., 175

INDEX

INDEX

N

INDEX

R

Rafiq, Muhammad, 1374

Rahim, M. A., 575

Rahmani, Magdalene, 1375

Rahmani, Magdeline, 877

Rahmani, Mageh, 1376

Rahmany, Magdalina, 576, 1377

Rahmany, Magdaline, 577

Rahnuma-yi Qattaghan va Badakhshan ya'ni mulakhkhas-i safar-
nameh-yi 1301 sipahsalar-i sardar-i Muhammad Nadir Khan
vazir-i harbiyeh murattabeh-yi janab Mawlawi Burhan al-Din
Khan Kushkaki, 263

Rahnuma-yi tadavi va-viqayeh az maraz-i trakhom, 878

Rainey, Froelich, 1561

Ramazani, R. K., 578

Rand, Christopher, 730, 999

Rao, J. Sambashiva, 579

Rapp, E. L., 1373

Rashad 'Abd al-Shakur, 1378

Rashad, Shah Muhammad, 879, 880

Rasmi Jarideh, 83

Rastogi, Ram S., 580

Rathjens, Carl, 264, 1000

Rattray, James, 265

Raverty, Henry George, 266, 1379, 1380, 1381, 1382

Rebuff, 581

Redard, Georges, 84

Reinaud, M., 267

Reisner, Igor Mikhailovich, 268, 269, 582, 1119

Reisner, Igor Mikhailovich and R. T. Akhramovich, 85

Reissner, Larissa, 583

Report of the Helmand River Delta Commission, 1120

Report on Development of the Arghandab Area, 1121

Report on Development Program of Government of
Afghanistan, 1122

Report on Proposed Cement Factory near Kabul,
Afghanistan, 1123

Report on Proposed Trunk Highways (Afghanistan), 1124

Report to the Government of Afghanistan on Handicrafts and
Small-Scale Industries, 1125

INDEX

INDEX

Weesh, Raz Muhammad, 1423
Weston, Christine, 649
Wheeler, Mortimer, 1588
Wheeler, R. E. Mortimer, 1589
Wheeler, Stephen, 650
Whistler, Hugh, 333
Whitehead, Richard Bertram, 1590, 1591
Wilber, Donald N., 108, 109, 651, 923, 924, 1019
Wild, Roland, 652
Williams, Maynard Owen, 334, 335, 336
Wilson, Andrew, 337, 1020
Wilson, Horace Hayman, 1592
Wilson, J. Christy, Jr., 1424
Wolanga, 925
Wolfe, Nancy Hatch, 1593, 1594, 1595
Wood, John, 338

Y

Yapp, M. E., 653
Yaqubi, M. Din, 1425
Yate, Arthur Campbell, 339
Yate, Charles Edward, 340, 341
Young, Rodney S., 1596, 1597
Yuldashbayeva, Fatima K., 654
Yule, H., 342
Yusufi, Muhammad Akbar, 110
Yusufzai, Saidal, 1021

Z

Zachova, Eliska, 343, 1426
Zahir, Payendeh Muhammad and Sayyid Muhammad
   Yusuf 'Elmi, 927
Zahir Shah, 926
Zahma, 'Ali Muhammad, 928
Zaidi, Manzur, 655
Zaman, Mohammad, 344, 1153
Zambaur, Eduard Karl Marx von, 111
Zamir, Muhammad Hasan, 1427
Zarubin, I. I., 750
Zawak, Muhammad Din, 1428

INDEX